Grace Livingston Hill is one of the most popular authors of all time because of her unique style of combining elements of the Christian faith with tasteful and exciting romance.

Find out why generations of readers of all ages have been entertained and inspired by the fiction of Grace Livingston Hill.

Grace Livingston Hill ... fiction that fills the heart as well as the spirit!

GRACE LIVINGSTON HILL

Because of Stephen
Lone Point

Two complete and unabridged novels in one volume

Barbour Books
164 Mill Street
P.O. Box 1219
Westwood, New Jersey 07675

Because of Stephen

Chapter 1

The room was full of blue smoke from bacon sizzling on the stove when Philip Earle came in.

Philip was hungry, but there was a weirdly monotonous reminder of preceding meals in the odor of the bacon that took the edge from his appetite.

The lamp was doing its best to help both the smoke and the odor that filled the room; any other function it might have had being held in abeyance by the smoke.

The lamp was on a little shelf on the wall, and under it, half hidden by the smoke, stood another young man bending over the stove.

There was nothing attractive about the room. It was made of rough boards: walls, floor, and ceiling. The furniture was an old extension table, several chairs, a cheap cot covered with a gray army blanket, and a desk which showed hard usage, piled high with papers and a few books. A wooden bench over by the stove held a tin wash-basin and cooking-utensils in harmonious proximity.

Several coats and hats and a horse-blanket hung on nails driven into the walls. A line of boots and shoes stood against the base-board. There was nothing else but a barrel and several boxes.

The table was set for super: that is, it held a loaf of bread, two cups and knives and spoons, a bag of crackers, a paper of cheese, a pitcher of water, and a can of baked beans newly opened.

Philip added to the confusion already on the table by throwing his bundles down at one end. Then he stood his whip in one corner, and tossed his felt hat across the room to the cot, where it lay as if accustomed to staying where it landed.

"A letter for you, Steve!" he said as he sat down at the table and ran his hands wearily through his thick black hair.

Stephen Halstead emerged from the cloud of smoke by the stove, and examined the postmark on the letter.

"Well, I guess it can wait till we've had supper," he said carelessly. "It's not likely to be important. I'm hungry!" and he landed a large plate of smoking bacon and shrivelled, blackened fried eggs on the table beside the coffee-pot, and sat down.

They began to eat, silent for the most part, with keen appetites, for both had been in the open air all day. Stephen knew that his partner would presently report about the sale of cattle he had made, and tell of his weary search for several stray animals that had wandered off. But that could wait.

Philip, however, was thinking of something else. Perhaps it was the texture of the envelope he had just laid down, or the whiff of violet scent that had breathed from it as he took it from his pocket, that reminded him of old days; or perhaps it was just that he was hungry and dissatisfied.

"Say, Steve," said he, setting down his empty cup, "do you remember the banquet in '95?"

A cloud came over Stephen's face. He had reasons to remember it of which his friend knew not.

"What of it?" he growled.

"Nothing; only I was thinking I would like to have the squabs and a few other little things I didn't eat that night. They wouldn't taste bad after a day such as we've had."

He helped himself to another piece of cheese, and took another supply of baked beans.

Stephen laughed harshly. He did not like to be reminded of that banquet night. To create a diversion, he reached out for the letter.

"This is from that precious sister of mine, I suppose," he said, "who isn't my sister at all, and yet persists every once in a while in keeping up the appearance. I don't know what she ever expects to make out of it. I haven't anything to leave her in my will. Besides, I don't answer her letters once in an age."

"You're a most ungrateful dog," said Philip. "You ought to be glad to have some one in the world to write to you. I've often thought of advertising for somebody who'd be a sister to me, at least enough of one to write to me. It would give a little zest to life. I don't see why you have such a prejudice against her. She never did anything. She couldn't help it that her mother was your father's second wife. It wasn't her affair, at all, nor yours either, as I see. When did you see her last?"

"Never saw her but once in my life, and then she was a little, bawling, red thing with long clothes, and everybody waiting on her."

"How old were you?"

"About ten," said Stephen doggedly, not joining in the hilarious laughter that Philip raised at his expense. "I was old enough to resent her being there at all, in my home, where I ought to have been, and her mother managing things and having me sent off to boarding-school to get rid of me. I could remember my own mother, Phil. She hadn't been dead a year when father married again."

"Well, it wasn't her fault anyway, that I can see," said Philip amusedly; "and, after all, she's your sister. She's as much your father's child as you are."

"She's nothing but a half-sister," said Stephen decidedly, "and of no interest in the world to me. What on earth she's taken to writing me long letters for I can't make out. It's only since father died she's done it. I suppose her mother thought it would be well to appease me, lest I make trouble about the will; but I knew well enough there wouldn't be much of anything father had for me. His precious second wife did me out completely from the first minute she set eyes on me. And she's dead now, too. If it hadn't been for what my mother left, I wouldn't have had a cent."

"Who's the girl living with?" asked Philip.

"O, with an aunt,—her mother's sister,—an old maid up in New England."

Then Stephen tore open the letter, and shoved his chair back nearer to the lamp. There was silence in the room while Stephen read his letter; and Philip, emptying the coffee-pot, mused over the life of an orphan girl in the home of a New England maiden aunt.

Suddenly Stephen's chair jerked about with a sharp thud on the bare floor, and Stephen stood up and uttered some strong language.

He had a lot of light hair, originally a golden brown, but burnt by exposure to sun and rain to a tawny shade. He was a slender fellow, well knit, with a complexion tanned to nature's own pleasant brown, out of which looked deep, unhappy eyes of blue. He would have been handsome but for a restless weakness about the almost girlish mouth.

He was angry now, and perplexed. His yellow brows were knit together in a frown, his head up, and his eyes darker than usual. Philip watched him in languid amusement, and waited for an explanation.

"Well, is she too sisterly this time?" he asked.

"Altogether!" said Stephen. "She's coming to see us."

The amusement passed rapidly from Philip's face. He sprang to his feet, while the color rolled up under his dark skin.

"Coming to see us?" he ejaculated, looking round and suddenly seeing all the short-comings of the room.

"Coming to see us?" he repeated as if not quite sure of the sound of his own words. *"Here?"*

"Here!" asseverated Stephen tragically with outspread hands, and the two looked about in sudden knowledge of the desolation of the place they had called "home" for three years.

"When?" Philip managed to murmur weakly, looking about in his mind for a way of escape for himself without deserting his partner.

Stephen stooped to pick up the letter he had thrown on the floor in his excitement.

"I don't know," he said dejectedly. "Here, read the thing, and see if you can find out." He handed the letter to Philip, who received it with alacrity, and settled into the chair under the light, suddenly realizing that he was tired.

"She'll have to be stopped," said Stephen meditatively, sitting down on the cot to study it out, "or sent back if it's too late for stopping. She can't come here, of course."

"Of course!" agreed Philip decidedly. Then he read:

"My dear Brother Stephen: — "

Philip suddenly felt strong jealousy of his friend. It would be nice to get a letter like that.

"It is a long time since I have been able to write to you, but you have never been out of my thoughts for long at a time. Aunt Priscilla was taken ill the day after I wrote you the last time. She was confined to her room all winter, and some of the time a little flighty. She took queer notions. One of them was that I was going to run away and marry a Spaniard. She could not bear me out of her sight. This tied me down very much, even though we had a nurse who relieved me of the entire care of her. I could not even write when I was in her sight, because she imagined I was getting up some secret plot to send her away to an old ladies' home of which she had a great horror.

"I don't like to think of those long, dreary months; but they are all over now, and I will not weary you with talking of them. Aunt Priscilla died a month ago, and now I am all alone in the world save for you. Stephen, I wonder if you have any idea how dear you have grown to me. Sometimes it has seemed as if I just could not wait any longer to see you. It has kept me up wonderfully to know that I have a lovely, big, grown-up brother to turn to."

Philip's eyes grew moist, and he stopped to clear his throat as he turned the page and glanced surreptitiously toward the unloving brother, who sat in a brown and angry study, his elbows on his knees, his chin in his hands.

"So now, Stephen, I am going to do just what I have wanted to do ever since mother died and I left college and came home to Aunt Priscilla. I am coming to you! There is nothing to hinder. I have sold the old house. There was a good opportunity, and I cannot bear the place. It has been desolate, desolate here." Philip wondered what she would think of her brother's home. "I cannot bear the thought of staying here alone, and I know I could not coax you away from your beloved West. So I am all packed up now, except the things that have been sold, and I am starting at once. Perhaps you may not like it, may not want me; and in that case of course I can come back. But anyway I shall see you first. I could not stand it without seeing you. I keep thinking of what father said to me just before he died. I never told you. I have always thought I would rather wait till I could say it to you, but now I will send it on to you as my plea for a welcome. It was the last afternoon we had together. Mother was lying down, and I was alone with him. He had been asleep, and he suddenly opened his eyes and called me to him. 'Don't forget you have a brother, when I am gone,' he said: 'Tell him I'm afraid I wasn't wise in my treatment of him always. Tell him I loved him, and I love you, and I want you two to love each other.'

"I began to love you then, Stephen, and the longing to know you and see you has grown with the years, five years, since father died. I never told mother about it. She was not well enough to talk much, you know; and she did not live long after that. Of course, I never told Aunt Priscilla. She was not the kind of woman to whom one told things. But I have never had opportunity to claim that love, or to seek it except in just writing you letters occasionally; and sometimes I've been afraid you didn't care to get them. But now I'm coming to see for myself; and, if I'm not welcome, why, I can go back again. I shall not be a burden to you, brother; for I have enough, you know, to take care of myself. And, if you don't want me, all you have to do is to tell me so, and I can go away again. But I hope you'll be able to love me a little for father's sake."

"Have you read the whole of this, Steve?" asked Philip, suddenly looking up as he reached the end of one sheet of paper and was starting on another.

"No," said Stephen gruffly; "I read enough."

"Read the rest," commanded Philip, handing over the first sheet while he went on with the second.

"Now I have burned my bridges behind me, Stephen; and I have not let you know until just the last thing. This letter will reach you only a few days before I do; so it will not be of any use to telegraph me not to come if you don't want me, for I shall be well on my way, and it will be too late. Please forgive me; I did this purposely because I felt I must at least see you before I gave up my plan, or I should never be able to give it up. And I am hoping that you will be glad to see me, and that perhaps I can be of some use to you, and put a little comfort into your life. You have never told me whether you are boarding or housekeeping or what. It is strange not to know more about one's brother than I do about mine, but I shall soon know now. I am bringing all the little things I care about with me; so, if you let me stay, I shall have nothing to send for; and if I have to go back, they can go back, too, of course.

"I shall reach your queer-sounding station at eight o'clock Friday evening, and I hope you will be able to meet me at the train, for of course I shall be very lonely in a strange place. Forgive me for surprising you this way. I know Aunt Priscilla would think I was doing a dreadful thing; but I can't feel that way about it myself, and anyway I have myself to look out for now. So good-by until Friday evening of next week, and please make up your mind to be a little glad to see your sister,

"MARGARET HALSTEAD."

Philip handed over the last sheet to Stephen, and sat up, looking blankly at the wall for a minute. He could not deny to himself that he was wholly won over to the enemy's cause. There was something so fresh and appealing about that letter written from a lonely girlish heart, and something so altogether brave and daring in her actually starting out to hunt up a renegade brother who had shown no wish to brotherly, that he could but admire her. But what could they do with her there? Of course she must go back. A pity, too, when she seemed to have her heart so set. But, if she stayed, she would be disappointed. Philip looked at Stephen sadly. It was a good thing she must go back, and would not need to know how little worthy of her love and admiration this unknown brother of hers was. He was a good-hearted fellow, too. A pity for the girl she had not some one to care for her.

Suddenly a new thought came to him as he looked idly down at the envelope of the letter Stephen had carelessly flung aside. The date on it was a week old.

He picked it up excitedly.

"Steve, what day was that letter written?"

"The twenty-eighth," said Stephen, looking up to see what caused the unusual note in Philip's tone.

"Man alive!" exclaimed Philip, "that letter's lain in the office for more than a week now, or else it's been off up to Humstead's ranch, lying around till some one had time to bring it back to the office. Such a postmaster as they have out here anyway! Get up, Steve, and do something! This is Friday night! Don't you realize that your sister's almost here? If it wasn't that the Northern Central is always an hour or more behind time, she would be standing alone down there on the platform, in the dark, this minute, with all that howling mob of loungers that congregate near by. What are you going to do?"

"I don't know," said Stephen in a dazed way.

Philip towered over him fiercely. "Well, you better know. Get up. It's five miles away, and the express due now if it's on time."

Chapter 2

Margaret Halstead stood alone on the narrow board platform that seemed to float like tiny raft in a sea of plains and darkness.

The train on which she had come her long and interesting journey had discharged her trunks, and taken up some freight, and wound its snakelike way out into the darkness, until now even the last glimmer of its red lights had faded from the mist that lay around.

The night winds swept about her, touching hair and cheek and gown, and peering solicitously into her face as if to inquire who this strange, sweet thing might be that had dropped, alien, among them, and then, deciding in her favor, softly kissed her on the cheek and ran away to tell the river of her coming.

A few lights dotted here and there the murk and gloom about her, and loud, uncultured voices sounded from the little shanty that served, she supposed, as a station. She dreaded to move a step toward it, for a strange new terror had seized upon her in the darkness since the friendly train had disappeared from view.

She remembered that the porter had been solicitous about leaving until her brother arrived to claim her, and had paused beside her until the last car swept slowly up and began to travel by; then, eying dubiously first the silver piece she had put in her hand, and then the fast-gliding train, he had finally touched his cap and swung himself onto the last car, calling back to her that he hoped she would be all right. She had not realized till then what it was going to be to be left alone at night in this strange place, with no assurance whatever, save her own undaunted faith, that her brother had even received her letter, much less, would meet her.

Apprehension and alarm suddenly rose and began to clamor for attention, while she suddenly realized how rash she had been to follow a fancy half across a continent, only to bring up in this wild way.

What should she do? She supposed she ought to go over to that dreadful group of rough men and ask some questions. What if, after all, she had been put off at the wrong station? She half turned to walk in that direction; but just then a wild shriek followed by a pistol-shot rang out in the air, and she stopped, frightened, a whispered prayer on her lips for help. Had she come all this way on what her heart had told her was a mission, to be forsaken now?

The clamor was heard by Philip as he rode through the night.

Stephen heard it also, and hastened his horse's footsteps.

Then from out the gloom and horror there came to the young girl's ears the soft regular thud, thud, thud, of horses' hoofs, and almost at once there loomed before her out of the mist two dark shapes which flung themselves apart, and appeared to be two men and two horses.

She started back once more, her heart beating wildly, and wondered which way to flee; but almost at once she heard a strong, pleasant voice say:

"Don't be afraid. We are coming!" and what seemed a giant landed before her. With a little gasp in her voice that sounded like a half-sob she said,

"O Stephen, you have come!" and put her hands in those of Philip Earle, hiding her face against his shoulder with a shudder.

Philip felt a sudden gladness in his strength, and it was revealed to him in a flash that there were sweeter things in life than those he had counted upon.

Instinctively his arm supported her for just an instant, and a great wave of jealousy toward her brother went over him. His impulse was to stoop and give her the welcoming kiss that she was evidently expecting; but he held himself with a firm grasp, though the blood went in hot waves over his face in the darkness.

To have the unexpected and most unwelcome guest of his partner thus suddenly precipitated upon him, and to find that she was not altogether undesirable, after all, was a circumstance most embarrassing, as well as extremely delicate to handle. He blessed the darkness for its hiding. It was but an instant and Stephen was beside them, and he managed in some way—he never could describe it to himself afterward—to get the young women faced about toward the real brother and her attention turned in that direction, and then stood watching while Stephen, the impressible, welcomed the new sister with open arms.

It was like Stephen, though he had grumbled all the way to the railroad about what a nuisance it was going to be to have her come, that he should succumb at once to a sweet voice and a confiding way.

Philip's lips were dry, and his throat throbbed hot and chokingly. He felt the pressure of little, soft, gloved hands in his hard ones. He turned away angry with himself that he should be so easily affected and by some one whom he had never met except in the pitch dark. Yet even as he said this to himself he knew the face would fit the voice and the hands when he should see them.

So, after all, though Philip, because he rode the fleeter horse, had been the first to greet her, and though his was the cool head, and he had expected to have to explain why they had been so late to meet her, it was Stephen's eager voice that made the explanations.

"You see I never got your letter until an hour ago. It was miscarried or something, and then we don't get to the office often when we're busy. So, when I took it in that you were really coming and looked at the time, your train was already overdue; and, if it had not been for their habit of being always two hours behind time, you might have stood here alone all this time."

Stephen said it gayly. He was beginning to think it a nice thing to have a sister. He had forgotten utterly how Philip had to insist on his coming at once to meet her, and that he had been most reluctant and ungracious.

It occurred to him at this juncture to introduce his partner.

Philip came to himself as he heard his name mentioned, and was glad again for the darkness. Margaret Halstead blushed, and wondered whether this giant knew how extremely near she had come to greeting him with a kiss, and hoped that he had not noticed how her head had rested against his shoulder for an instant when she was frightened. What would he think of her?

Her voice trembled just a little as she acknowledged the introduction; but her words were few and frigid, and made Philip feel as if she had suddenly held him off at arm's length and bade him come no nearer. She said:

"I did not know you had a partner, Stephen. You never said anything about it in your letters. I am afraid I have been wrong in coming without waiting to hear from you before I started."

But Philip had noticed the tremble in her voice, and he hastened to make her most welcome as far as he was concerned.

Nevertheless, a stiffness hung about the trio which made it hard for them to be natural; and, had it not been for another pistol-shot from the shanty down the road and another clamor of voices, they might have stood still some time longer.

Margaret started in spite of herself, and asked nervously:

"Oh! what can be the matter? What a dreadful place this must be!" And Philip found in himself a new instinct of protection.

"We must get your sister out of this, Steve," he said. "We must take her home."

And somehow the word "home" sounded a haven as he pronounced it. The thoughts of the two young men galloping furiously on their way to the station had been but of how they should reach there as soon as the train. They had made no plans. It was impossible for them to realize the importance of the charge that was about to be put upon them.

But now the manners of the world from which they had come some years before, and from which this young woman had but just come, suddenly dropped down upon them as a forgotten garment, and they knew at once the wretchedness of their limitations.

"It isn't much of a place to call home," said the brother, apologetically, "but I guess it's better than this. If we had only known before, we'd have had something fine fixed up someway."

He made the statement airily, and perhaps he thought it was true. Philip found himself wondering what it would have been. There was not a house where she might have been lodged comfortably within fifty miles.

"How do you think we'd better arrange the journey?" said Stephen, suddenly brought face to face with a problem.

"You see," said he in explanation to his sister, "we had no time to hitch up, if we had thought of it, though I'm blamed if it occurred to me but that we could carry you in our pockets. Say, Phil, guess I'll go over and see if I can get Foxy's buckboard."

"Foxy's gone over to Butte in his buckboard with his mother. I saw him go this afternoon," answered Philip.

Stephen whistled.

"I'll ask Dunn for his wagon," said Stephen starting off.

"Hold on!" said Philip shortly. "I'll go myself. You stay here."

"Couldn't we go down to the station and see after my trunk, Mr. Earle?" said Margaret timidly. And to his ears the name never had so sweet a sound.

"Give me your checks, and stay here, please," he said in quite a different tone from that in which he had addressed Stephen; and, turning, he left them standing in the dark, while the mist closed in behind him and shut him from their sight as if he had left the world.

Alone with her brother, Margaret suddenly put out her hands appealingly to him.

"You are a little bit glad I've come, aren't you, Stephen?" she said.

"I'm no end of glad," he answered, rousing out of his sulkiness that Philip would not let him go. He knew that Philip had good reason for making him stay. "But we're a rough lot out here. I don't know how you'll stand it."

His voice had lost a shade of the gayety, and she thought it was touched with anxiety. She hastened to assure him.

"O, I shall not mind a bit. And I shall try to make things a little pleasanter for you. You think I can, don't you?" This in an anxious voice.

"I'm sure you can," said Stephen heartily. There was something in her voice that appealed to his better self, and reminded him strangely of his childhood. It could not be his father; for his father had always been silent and grave, and this voice was sweet and enthusiastic, and flowed out as if it loved to speak. And yet it must be the likeness to the father's voice he noticed.

"I am so anxious to get you in the light and see how you look," she said ardently, and then added softly, " My dear brother."

Stephen slid his arm about her awkwardly, and kissed her on the forehead. He felt embarrassed in doing this; yet it was by no means the first time he had kissed a girl. Perhaps it was the memory of those other kisses hovering near that shamed him now. He half felt this, and it made him awkward. He was glad to hear Philip's step coming toward them.

"Dunn's wagon has broken down, and both the front wheels are off for repairs. There isn't a thing we can get in town to-night," said Philip anxiously. "Miss Halstead, can you ride? Horseback, I mean."

"Why, I can try," said Margaret a little tremulously. This was a rather startling proposition to even her dauntless courage. Involuntarily she glanced down at her city-made gown in the darkness. She felt hampered by it.

"It's too bad, Miss Halstead," he said apologetically, while Stephen in the dark wondered at his new tone and manner. "But there's no other way, and I think you'll enjoy getting out of this, anyway. There's going to be a big row over there," he added in a low tone to Stephen. "Jim Peters is on his high horse. Hurry!"

Then in a cheery tone he said:

"It won't be so bad. You can rest your foot in the stirrup, and Steve and I'll take turns walking beside the horse. She'd better ride your horse, Steve. He's the gentler of the two."

Margaret Halstead felt herself suddenly lifted in the dark by strong arms and seated on a horse. She clung to the saddle, and left her foot obediently in the stirrup where it was placed by a firm hand; but she was not certain whether her brother or his friend had put her there. It was bewildering, all in the dark that way, and neither of them spoke till both were standing by her side. She was glad the horse stood quite still. She expected him to start nervously. She felt timid about Western horses. They had a reputation for wildness. But it was Stephen who after a moment of low talk came and stood by her side and placed his arm about her as they started.

"My suit-case and my bag," she murmured.

"Phil has them all safe," said her brother.

"And the trunks?"

"They are locked safe in the station, Miss Halstead, and we will get them early in the morning," said a voice out of the mist before her.

Then there was silence as she looked anxiously into the darkness, and could not see a spot of road for the horse to place his foot.

The road was rough and her seat unsteady. A man's saddle is not the surest thing to ride sideways upon. She put her hand timidly on her brother's shoulder, and the touch seemed to give her courage. It gave Stephen a strange new sense of his power of protection.

They went slowly, for the night was dark and the mist lay thick about them. The road was so rough that horse and leader could keep together only by moving slowly. The sounds of disturbance behind them grew fainter as they went on, but now and then a shriek or a fragment of an oath would reach them as if it had been flung out wildly in the night and lost its way.

Margaret shuddered when this happened, and said in a half-frightened tone:

"What awful people they must be, Stephen! Isn't it unpleasant to live in their neighborhood?"

And Stephen somewhat uneasily answered:

"O, they never bother us. They've got a little too much to-night, that's all; and, when they get like that, they can't stand a difference of opinion."

"How dreadful!" said Margaret in low, awestruck tones. Then after a minute she added:

"O Stephen, I'm so glad my brother is not like that. Of course it wouldn't be likely, but they must be somebody's brothers, and how their sisters must feel—and their mothers!"

Stephen felt his face grow hot. He said nothing for a long time. He could not think of anything to say. There was a strange feeling about his throat, and he tried to clear it. The mist kept getting in his eyes. He was glad when his sister began to tell of her aunt's illness and the long, weary months when she had been chained to the sick-room at the beck and call of a whimsical, wandering mind.

She did not say much about herself, but he felt touched by her sweet self-sacrifice and her loneliness. It reminded him of his own lonely boyhood, and his heart went out in sympathy. He decided that it was a nice thing, after all, to have a sister. It was like Stephen to forget all about the end of their journey and the poor accommodations he had to offer her, utterly unfit for a woman, much less fit for one who had been brought up in luxury. He grew gay as they went on, and talked more freely with her. When Philip suddenly appeared out of the silent darkness ahead of them, and said it was time to change guides, he was almost loath to leave his sister.

Margaret, too, would rather not have had the change; but she could scarcely ask her brother to walk the whole of the five miles. There was something about him that reminded her, even in the dark, of their father, and so he did not seem strange; but this other tall man, who had taken control of the entire expedition, frightened her a little. She wished she could get a glimpse of his face and know what kind of a man he was. It was hard to know what to say to him, and still more embarrassing to keep entirely still.

But the road was growing rougher. The new guide had to give a good deal of attention to the horse, and she to keeping her unsteady seat. The road was steadily rising before them now. She could feel that by the inclination of the saddle. It seemed to be stony also.

Once she slipped, and would have fallen from the saddle if Philip had not caught her. After that he placed his arm about her and steadied her. She could not object, for there was nothing intimate or personal in the touch. She concluded that Philip was a gentleman, whatever else he might not be.

She gripped the saddle in front of her a little tighter, and looked into the darkness, wondering whether this journey would ever end. She essayed one or two sentences of conversation, but the young man beside her was distraught, and seemed to be more interested in looking ahead and guiding the horse.

The road was even steeper now. Margaret wondered whether they were going up the Rocky Mountains. It seemed as if they had come far enough to have almost reached them, according to her vague notion of the geography of that land.

"Wouldn't it be better if I were to get off and walk?" she asked timidly, after the horse had almost stumbled to his knees.

"No," answered Philip shortly; "we'll soon be over this. Put your arm around my neck and hold on now. Don't be afraid! Steady, there, steady, Jack!"

The horse scrambled, and seemed to Margaret to be walking on his hind legs up into the air. She gave a little scream, and threw her arm convulsively about her companion's neck. But she was held firmly, and seemed to be riding upon Philip's shoulder with the horse struggling under her for a moment. Then like a miracle they reached upper ground, and she was sitting firmly on the horse's back, Philip walking composedly beside her, his arm no more about her.

It was lighter too, here; and all the mist seemed to have dropped away and to be melting at their feet.

"It's all over now," said Philip, and there was a joyous ring in his voice quite different from the silent, abstracted man who had walked beside her for so long. "I hope you weren't much frightened. I've been afraid how Jack would act there. That is an ugly place. It must be fixed before you come this way again. You see the bridge was broken down the way we usually go, and we had to come around another way. You were perfectly safe, you know; only it was bad to frighten you when you have just come, and you are tired, too. But we are almost there now. And look! Look ahead!"

Margaret looked, and saw before her a blaze of light flare up till it made a great half-circle on the edge of the horizon. Not until it rose still higher — like a human thing, she thought — did the girl recognize the moon.

"O, it is the moon!" she said awestruck. "Is it always so great out here?"

Philip watched her as she looked. He felt that for the first time in his life he had companionship in this great sight of which he never tired.

"It is always different," he said musingly, "and yet always the same," and he felt as he was saying it that she would understand. He had never talked to Stephen about the moon. Stephen did not care for such things except as they were for his personal convenience or pleasure. Moonlight might be interesting if one had a long ride to take, in Stephen's economics, but not for purposes of sentiment.

"I see," said Margaret. "Yes, I recognize my old friend now. It seems as if it wore a smile of welcome."

"Do you mean the man in the moon, or the lady? Which do you claim?"

"O, both!" laughed Margaret, turning toward him for the first time since there had been any light. And now she could see his fine profile outlined against the moon, the firm chin, the well-moulded forehead and nose, and the curve of the expressive lips.

"Now, look down there, back where we have come!" said Philip, as she looked.

The mist was glorified like an expectant one waiting to be redeemed from the state where it was put till its work was done.

"O!" breathed the girl in wonder. "You can fairly see the darkness flee away!"

"So you can," said Philip, looking off. "I never noticed that before."

And they started forward round the turn in the road where Stephen was waiting impatiently for them to come up with him, and almost at once they saw before them the outlines of the rude building the two young men called home, lying bathed in the new-risen moonlight.

Chapter 3

The moonlight was doing its best to gild the place with something like beauty to welcome the stranger, but it was effective only out-of-doors, and the two young men were painfully conscious of the state in which they had left the inside of their house, as they helped their guest from the horse and prepared to take her in. All the impossibility of the situation suddenly came upon them both, and made them silent and embarrassed.

Stephen took on his sulky look, which ill became him, while he stumbled over the moonbeams that followed him when he opened the door, and lighted the wicked little oil lamp. He had no mind to welcome his sister there. What did he want of a sister anyway? His foot caused the crisp rattle of paper as he threw the match down, and he knew it was her letter lying on the floor. The same mood that had seized him when he read it was upon him again; and he turned, scowling, determined to show her that she had made a serious mistake in rushing out here unbidden.

Margaret Halstead turned from the brilliant moonlight to the blinking lamplight bravely, and faced the scene of her self-chosen mission.

There may have been something in the half-defiant attitude of her brother that turned her from her purpose of having a good long look at him and making sure of her welcome. She may have seen that she had yet to win her way into the citadel of his heart, and wisdom or intuition taught her to break the embarrassment of this first moment in the light by a commonplace remark.

Her eyes roved anxiously about the dreary room in search of something to bring cheer. They fell upon the old desk in the corner.

"O Stephen! There is the desk from your old room!" she cried eagerly, going over to it and touching it tenderly. "I used to go up into your room and sit by it to study my lessons. And sometimes I would put your picture on the top, — the one you sent father when you were in the military school, — and sit, and admire you, and think how nice it was to have a straight, strong brother dressed in a military suit."

Stephen turned toward her with a look of mingled astonishment and admiration. His ugly mood was already exorcised. The soft rustle of hidden silk, made by her garments as she moved, created a new world in the rough place. She stood by the old desk, loosening the hat-pin and taking off her hat: he could see the grace of every movement. And this beautiful girl had cared for him enough to look at his picture once in a while when he was just a boy! He half wished he had know it then; it might have made some things in his life different. His voice was husky as he said, "You don't mean you ever thought of me then, and called me your brother!"

"Yes, surely," she said, looking at him with a bright smile as she ran her fingers through the soft hair over her forehead, and settled it as if by magic into a fitting frame for her sweet face. "O, you don't know how I idealized you! I used to put myself asleep at night with stories about you, of how brave and good and true you were, and how you did all sorts of great things for me—I'll tell you them all some day. But now, do you know you haven't welcomed me home yet? You're sure you're going to be glad I came?"

She looked up anxiously, a sweet pleading in her lovely eyes as she came over to him, and held up her face. Stephen bent over her awkwardly, and kissed her forehead, and then turned away in embarrassment, knocking down the tin basin from the bench as he moved; but Margaret felt she had her welcome, and set herself to win this brother.

Philip would fain have escaped to the barn from the confusion of the first few minutes, but had been drawn back to the door for very shame at deserting his partner in time of embarrassment, and had heard the little dialogue.

He turned silently away from the door, and slipped back to the horses thoughtfully. He had never seen that look on Stephen's face before, nor heard his voice so huskily tender. Perhaps, after all, there was something in a sister.

Margaret Halstead folded her wisp of a veil as carefully and precisely as if she had just come home from a concert in the East, instead of being dropped down in this land that knew her not; but all the while she was taking mental note of the place, its desolation, its need of her, its paucity of material with which to work, and wondering how these two men had lived and been comfortable.

"And now you are hungry," she said in a matter-of-fact tone, just as if her brother were the guest and she the hostess, "and what can we get for supper?"

Stephen had returned from a chase after the tin wash-basin, which had chosen, after the manner of inanimate articles, to take a rattling excursion under the stove. He was looking helplessly about the room. He did not know what he ought to do next.

"There isn't much but bacon and beans, the same old stuff. We have it morning, noon, and night."

Margaret came over to the table and began to gather the dishes together. It was a strange assortment, and she felt like laughing as she extracted the hammer from under the paper of cheese and looked about for a place to lay it; but she kept her face as sober as if that were the proper place for hammers and cheese, and said thoughtfully:

"Haven't you any eggs? I think you mentioned poultry in one of your letters."

"O yes, there are eggs. There are always eggs and bacon. They would be good if they weren't always the same."

"How would you like an omelet? Do you ever make them?"

"Yes, we've tried, but they lie around in little weary heaps, and won't 'om' for us," said Stephen, laughing at last. "I'll go out and get some eggs if you think you could make one."

"Yes, indeed!" said Margaret with alacrity. "Just show me how this stove works first, and fill the tea-kettle. I always use boiling water for my omelets; it makes them fluffier than milk. Where is your egg-beater kept?"

"Egg-beater!" said Stephen with a shrug of his shoulders. "Don't ask me. I wouldn't know one if I met him on the street. Can't you make an omelet without an egg-beater?" he added anxiously.

"O yes," said Margaret, laughing; "a fork is slower, but it will do. Bring me the eggs now. I will have them ready by the time the kettle boils and the frying-pan is hot."

Margaret worked rapidly while he was gone, and managed to clear the table and wash three plates and cups before he returned. Then she went to her bag that Philip had put just inside the door, and after a little search brought forth four large clean handkerchiefs, a supply of which she usually took with her on a journey. These she spread, one under each plate and one in the centre. At least, it would not seem quite so uncivilized as did that bare table.

An examination into her lunch-box showed a glass of jelly still untouched and half a dozen sugary doughnuts, the farewell contribution of an old neighbor of her aunt's. These she arranged on the table with a plate of bread cut in thin slices, and was just searching for possible coffee when she heard the voices of the two young men.

Stephen went whistling out to the barn for the eggs. "Christopher Columbus, Phil! She knows how to make omelet ! Hustle there, and help me get a lot of eggs. We'll have something worth eating again if it takes every egg on the place."

Philip had been wondering whether he might not be excused from going back to the house that night at all. But at the appetizing sound he went to work with a will.

They stopped in astonishment at the door, and gazed at the table as if it had been enchanted, and then gazed anew at the cook. They had left her there a fashionably attired young woman of a world that was theirs now no longer. They found her now a busy woman, with frock daintily tucked up and a white towel pinned about her waist apron-fashion, her sleeves rolled up, revealing white, rounded arms, and her cheeks pink with interest over her work.

"That lamp smokes horribly," she remarked, looking up at it vindictively; and there was something so true and human about her voice and words that both young men laughed.

The stiffness was broken, and did not return; but the relations were established and the guest was commander-in-chief. She told her hosts what to do, and they did it. She took the eggs, and deftly broke them, the whites into one dish, the yolks into another; and giving Stephen one dish with a fork to beat them, she took the other herself, meanwhile commanding Philip to find the coffee and make it.

They enjoyed it as much as three children at play, and their appetites were keen, when a few minutes later, having watched the puffy omelet swell and billow and take on a lovely brown coat, they drew up to the table to supper.

Margaret told little incidents of her journey, and described the people who had been her fellow travellers, showing a rare talent for mimicry, which entertained her audience exceedingly.

It was late when the meal was finally concluded and the room put into what Margaret thought was a poor apology for order. The problem of the night was now to be faced, and Margaret wondered what was to become of her. She suddenly realized how very weary she was, and that her nerves, long over-strained by new experiences, were ready to give way in tears.

Stephen knew that something must be done about sleeping now; but he had no idea what they were going to do with the new sister, any more than if she had been an orphan baby left upon his door-step. He turned helplessly to Philip. Philip always knew what to do in emergencies, though Stephen did not like to admit that he depended upon him.

Philip had done some thinking while he stood by the horses in the moonlight. There was little log lean-to opening off this large one-roomed cottage of theirs. It was divided by a board partition into two fair-sized rooms. One of these had been Philip's room and the other Stephen's. There was little furniture in them besides a bunk with heavy blankets. Blankets were the only bedclothing the house possessed, and with them beds were easily made. Philip turned toward the door of his room now, and in the dark went about the walls, hastily gathering an armful of clothing from the nails driven into the logs, which he threw out the window. Then he struck a match, and picked up a few things thrown here and there in confusion, and decided that was the best he could do toward clearing up.

He explained to Stephen in a low tone that he was to give his sister that room, and he himself would sleep in the hay. Then, saying good-night, he went out.

Margaret almost laughed aloud when she looked about her primitive bedroom a few minutes later, and by the light of the blinking lamp took an inventory of her surroundings. Then her eye caught a photograph pinned to the wall, and she went over to study it. It was Philip's one possession that he prized, and he had forgotten it in his haste. It was a sweet-faced woman with white hair and eyes like Philip's that followed one about the room sadly.

She had been shocked, even prepared as she was for the primitive, to find her brother living among surroundings so rough. Nevertheless, her determination was firm. She had come to help her brother, and now that she had seen him she would not turn back. There might be some hardships; but in the end, with the help of God, she would win. She felt shy of Philip, and inclined to wish him away. Perhaps he did not have a good influence over Stephen. He seemed to be very dictatorial, and the strange part about it was that Stephen yielded to him. It might be that she would have to help Philip in order to help her brother. That would complicate matters.

She knelt down beside the hard gray cot, and put the work she had come to do at the foot of the cross, asking help and guidance. And she wondered as she prayed whether she had been rash and taken her own way, instead of waiting for heavenly guidance, in coming to this strange land where evidently, to say the least, her presence had not been desired. Then she added, "O Jesus Christ, if this work is of Thee, bless me in it; and, if it was merely a wild impulse of my own, send me back where Thou wouldst have me."

Then with a feeling of contentment she lay down wrapped in the gray blankets, and was almost immediately asleep.

"Is she there?" asked the wind, whispering softly.

"Yes, asleep," said a moonbeam peeping through a crack between the logs, and then stealing in across the window-ledge.

"And will she stay?" sighed the night wind again.

"Yes, she has come to stay," affirmed the moonbeams; "and she will be a blessing."

Out in the sweet-scented hay lay Philip, but he was not asleep. There was planning to be done for tomorrow. Would the guest choose to stay, or would she fly from them at the morning light? Could she stand it there, so rough and devoid of all that had made her life what it was? Of course not. She had come only on a tour or curiosity. She would probably give it up and go back reasonably in a few days. But in the meantime, unless she came to her senses by morning and knew enough to go back to civilization at once, what was to be done?

In the first place, there must be a woman of some sort found, a servant, if you please. A chaperone she would be called back in the East. Here perhaps such things were not necessary, especially as she was really Stephen's sister; but it would be better to have a woman around. She must not be allowed to do the cooking, and surely they could not cook for her. It had been bad enough for them, men as they were, to eat what they cooked. How good that supper had tasted! The omelet reminded him of his mother, and he drew his hand quickly across his eyes. What would his mother think of his staying out here in the wilds so long? And all because a pretty girl had chosen to flirt with him for a while and then throw him aside. But was it all that? Did he not stay for Stephen's sake? What would become of Stephen without him?

But perhaps, now, Stephen's sister had brought him a release. He might just pretend to have business calling him away and leave them together. Then a vision of the frightened hands that came through the mist to greet him at the station recalled him sharply. No! He could not leave her alone with her brother! It would not do. And at once he knew that his mother, if she were able to know of what went on in this life, would approve of his staying here.

But where was a woman to be found who would be a fit servant for Miss Halstead?

He searched the country in his mind all round and about, and at last came to a conclusion.

The hay settled and crackled about him, and the hens near by clucked anxiously in their sleep; the horses moved against the stall now and then, and away in the distance came the sharp, vigilant bark of a dog. Philip dropped asleep for a little while, and dreamed of a small hand clinging to his neck and a wisp of soft, sweet hair blowing across his face, and awoke to find the hay hanging over and touching his cheek and a warm ray of morning lighting the sky.

The morning was all cool and fresh with sleep yet, when he rose and rode away, hurrying his horse onward through the dewy way. He found himself wondering what Stephen's sister would say to this or that view or bit of woodland that he passed, and then checked his thoughts angrily. She was nothing to him, even if she had understood his thoughts about the moon. Women were all alike, heartless—unless it might be mothers. With these thoughts he flung his horse's bridle over the saddle-horn, and sprang down at the door of a rude dwelling, where after much ado he brought to the door a dark-faced woman with straggling black hair and a skin that told at once of Mexican and Indian blood.

What arguments he used or what inducements he offered to bring the curious creature to promise she would come, he never told. But when a half-hour later, with the additional burden of a large, greasy-looking bundle fastened to his saddle, he again started homeward, he smiled faintly to himself, and wondered why he had done it. Perhaps, after all, by this time their guest had made preparations for her departure. And this wild woman with her lowering looks and her muttering speech, would she be any addition to their already curiously assorted family?

A fierce rebellion, often there before, arose in his breast at the Power, whether God or what, that made and kept going a universe so filled with lives awry and hearts of bitterness and sorrow. Not even the breath of the morning, nor the rich notes of wild birds, could quite dispel this from his heart. A sky like that above him, so peerless, and earth like this around him, so matchless, and only lives like his and Stephen's and that dark-faced old hag's to enjoy them. He ran over the whole rough crew of friends who sometimes congregated with them, and saw no good in any.

Still, there was Margaret Halstead. She seemed a fitting one to place amid beauty and joyous surroundings. She would not mar a scene like that this morning with anything her heart or life contained.

Yes, there was Margaret. But it might be only seeming. Perhaps she was like them all. Doubtless she was. It remained to be seen what Margaret really was. But what were they all made for anyway?

The old question that had troubled Philip for a long, lonely time; and he drew his brows in an unhappy frown as he came to a halt at the only home he now owned.

Chapter 4

When Margaret Halstead came to the door a little later to view the morning and look by daylight upon the new land into which she had come a stranger and a pilgrim, she still carried with her the atmosphere of her Eastern home. She had changed the long, dark, close-fitting travelling-gown of the night before to a simple gown of light percale which she had wisely brought in her hand-baggage; and, though the garment was plain and of walking length, and must have occupied little space in the satchel, it hung with a grace and finish unknown in those parts; and there was still about her as she moved that soft atmosphere of refinement.

She opened the door wide, and stood for a moment enframed. The dark, big-boned creature who was huddled on the steps sprang up and gazed at her in wonder. Her eyes had never met a sight like this before. The golden hair, touched with the sunshine into finer threads of spun glass, the blue eyes like rare stones that hold the colors of a summer night, the fair face, the pleasant mouth, the graceful form in the soft blue cotton gown, made a picture for which an angel might have sat.

Margaret looked at the woman in amazement, and then at the dirty bundle that lay upon the steps at her feet.

"Who are you?" she asked after a moment of silent scrutiny between the two.

"Man come get. Say heap work. Man say big pay."

"O, my brother has been after you. I see. He brought you here this morning before I was awake. That was kind of him. And I thought he was asleep yet."

She was thinking aloud rather than speaking to the woman. Philip, coming around the corner of the house, heard and halted, and his lips settled sternly. A curious expression crossed his face, and then he turned and went back to the other side of the house without being seen. Let her suppose this was the work of her brother if she would. It ought to have been. It was as well she should think so.

But Margaret was grappling with the problem of breakfast, with the addition of this unknown quantity who had come to assist her. Would it be possible for those grimy, greasy hands ever to be clean enough to touch food that was to be eaten by them?

She hit upon the plan, however, of setting the newcomer at some much-needed scrubbing about the doors and windows until they should have breakfast out of the way, and she drew a sigh of relief as she looked about the one living-room and noted how large it was. The woman would not have to be in too close proximity to them while they ate. That was one thing to be thankful for.

She smiled to herself as she hastily laid the table. It was nice of Stephen to go out so early in the morning and get a woman to help. It was dear of Stephen! He was going to justify her utmost ideal of him, she felt sure.

They all felt a strain of embarrassment over them during breakfast. The morning light displayed the crudities of the rude home. Margaret's beauty showed in stronger contrast as she moved about in her dainty blue and white, and seemed some rare bird of paradise dropped into their midst. The two young men in their dark flannel shirts felt ill at ease. They were all facing the problem of what was to be done next.

Margaret felt that the crucial moment for the desire of her heart was coming, and she must walk carefully. She realized, more than did they, the changes it would make in their lives if she remained here as she wished. As for her companions, it seemed to them by the light of morning wisdom an impossibility that she should stay, and they discovered to their own surprise that there was a growing disappointment in their hearts. She had given them a peep into their former lives, and they would turn from it now the more reluctantly.

At last Margaret ventured.

"I don't intend to be a bit of bother when I get settled," she said brightly, "and I will be as patient now as can be; but I would like to know when you think it will be possible for my things to be brought up."

The silence grew impressive. Stephen looked at Philip, and Philip looked into his plate. Margaret watched them anxiously from the corners of her eyes. At last Philip spoke.

"How many things are there?" he asked, merely to make time and give Stephen a chance to tell her what he knew he ought to tell, that this was no place for her to stay.

Margaret would rather her brother had taken the initiative. It was awkward to have to ask favors of a stranger. She wondered how much of a partner he was anyway, and what right he had in the house. Could it be possible that he was part owner? If so, it was more complicated than she had expected.

"O, I'm afraid there are a good many," she answered humbly. "You see I had to bring them or sell them. There wasn't any good place in town to store them where I felt sure they would be safe. It is just a little country town, you know. And some of the things I love. They belonged to my old home. I thought Stephen would like having them about him again, too." She glanced wistfully over at her brother. These old things had been part of the ammunition she had brought with which to fight her battle for the winning of her brother.

"Of course!" said Philip brusquely, scowling across at Stephen. He was disgusted with Stephen for not being more brotherly.

"And there's my piano!" said Margaret, brightening at this slight encouragement. "I couldn't leave that!"

"Certainly not!" said Philip, looking about at the rough room in a growing wonder of what was coming to it. The impossibility of it all! A piano in the wilderness!

"Great Scott!" ejaculated Stephen, looking up at last, and struggling to express his feelings. "What did you do it for? You can't put a piano and things in here! Think of a piano in this barn!" and he waved his hands eloquently toward the silent, dejected walls.

"O we'll make something besides a barn of it, Stephen," said Margaret, laughing almost hysterically, she was so glad he had spoken at last, even if it was only to attempt a veto to her plans. "I thought it all out this morning when I woke up. This room is lovely, it is so large. It needs a few more windows, perhaps, and a fireplace to make it perfect; but unless you are very much attached to this primitive simplicity you won't know this place after I get it fixed. Just wait till my materials come, and we'll have a real home here. Couldn't you boys build a fireplace, the old-fashioned kind, with a wide chimney in the room? Isn't there any rough stone around here? It would be grand to sit around winter evenings while I read aloud to you, or we all sing. It ought to go right over there!" and she indicated a space between two windows rather far apart, and directly opposite the front door.

"No doubt!" said Philip, looking blankly at the wooden box that now occupied that position and trying to imagine a great stone fireplace in its stead. His fancy failed him, however. He could not see an angel in a bit of rough marble. But the picture of the reading aloud around the open fire on winter evenings, and the music, was alluring.

"Charming," he added, seeing that the weight of the answers all fell upon him. "I never built stone chimneys for a living, but I think I could assist if you would be so good as to direct the job, Miss Halstead. I can't bring my mind to comprehend anything in this room being lovely, but if you say so I suppose it is possible."

"Great Scott!" ejaculated Stephen again in amazement. He was not certain whether Philip was in earnest or not.

"And the piano ought to stand there," said Margaret after the laugh had subsided.

"Certainly," answered Philip again, more amazed than ever. "But might I inquire what you would do with the stove? You couldn't cook on the piano, could you? Or would you expect to use the fireplace?"

The old half-breed peered in from the window she was washing to see what all the laughter and shouts meant. This seemed to be an exceedingly jolly household into which she had come. She had not heard sounds so light-hearted and merry, so utterly free from the bitter mirth that tinged most of the jollity in this region, in all her life, not since she was a little child and played among the care-free children.

"The stove," said Margaret, "must go into the kitchen, of course."

"Ah!" said Philip meekly. "Strange I didn't think of that. Now, where, might I inquire, is the kitchen?"

Margaret arose and went to the back window, and the two followed her. "It ought to be right here," she said, "and this window should be made into a door leading to it. What is that little square building out there? Can't we have that for a kitchen?"

"That edifice, madam, was originally intended for other purposes, the housing of certain cattle or smaller animals, I forget just what. It isn't of much use for anything. It is in a tumble-down condition. But, if your fairy wand can transform it into a kitchen, so it shall be."

"Say, now that's an idea, Phil!" said Stephen interestedly.

"Then we could use a corner of this room for a dining-room, you know," said Margaret, turning back to the house again. "I have a pretty little cupboard with glass doors that will just fit into that corner, and there are screens and draperies. It will be just charming. I've always wanted to fix up a lovely big room that way. Can't you imagine the firelight playing over the table-cloth and dishes?"

"We haven't seen a table-cloth in so long I'm afraid it would be a strain on our minds to try to do that," said Stephen bitterly. All this talk was alluring, but wholly impossible. Such things could never come into his life. He had long ago given over expecting them. A look of hopeless longing went across his face, and Philip saw and wondered. He had felt that way himself, but somehow it had never seemed to him that his comrade would understand such feelings, he seemed so happy-go-lucky always.

"But what would you do with the roughness of everything?" asked Philip doubtfully. "Pianos and corner cupboards wouldn't like to associate with forests of splinters."

"O, cover them" said Margaret easily, as if she had settled that long ago. "I brought a whole bolt of burlap for such things. It is a lovely leaf-green, and will be just the thing for a background. I don't suppose I have enough; but I can send a sample to New York, and have it here before we need it. I've been thinking this morning what beautiful moulding those smooth, dry corn-stalks would make tacked on next the ceiling. You see, when the walls are covered with something that makes a good background, this will look like a different place."

"You see, Steve, that's what's the matter with you and me. We've never had a suitable background," said Philip slowly.

And thus it was that, amid laughing and questioning, Margaret won her way, and finally saw Philip go off with two horses and a large wagon. She was much troubled that Stephen had not gone with him. It seemed so strange when he was her brother, and Philip would need help, surely, in loading up the furniture. Philip certainly was a queer man. Why did he presume to dictate to Stephen, and, strangest of all, why did Stephen sulkily submit? When she knew her brother better, she would find out, and spur him on to act independently. Again she wondered uneasily whether Philip was not a hindrance to her plans. A man who could so easily command her brother was one whose influence was to be feared.

So Stephen stayed behind, followed his sister about, and did what she asked him to do. In the course of the morning much scrubbing and putting to rights was done, and a savory dinner was under way in spite of the marked absence of needed culinary utensils.

Philip Earle drove away into the sunshine at high speed. He was determined to make all the time he could. He felt uneasy about Stephen, lest he should mount his horse and come after, in spite of injunctions to stay about the house and take care of his sister until they got things into some sort of shape. There were more reasons than one why Philip should be uneasy about Stephen to-day. Nothing must be allowed to happen to startle the newcomer on this her first day. Perhaps she would be able to make things much better. Who knew? It certainly would be great to have something homelike about them. Though it would be all the worse when she would get tired of it, — as of course she would sooner or later, — and take her things and herself off, leaving them to their desolation once more. But Philip would not let himself think of that. With the gayety of a boy of fifteen he called to his horses and hastened over the miles to town.

Margaret and Stephen went out to walk around the house, and plan how the kitchen could be brought near enough for use. Margaret suggested, too, that there ought to be another bedroom built on the other side of the house. She tried to find out how much of a share in things Philip owned, but Stephen was non-committal and morose when she talked of this, and did not seem to take much interest in any changes she would like to make in the house; so she desisted.

She wondered why he acted this way. Could it be that Stephen was short of money? She knew that he had a good sum left to him by his own mother, and her father had also left certain properties which had gone to him at the death of her mother. Could it be that they were tied up so that he could not get at the interest, or was it possible that he had lost some of his money by speculation? Young men were sometimes foolhardy, and perhaps that was it, and he did not like to tell her.

Well, she would just be still on the subjects that she saw he did not wish to talk about, and work her way slowly into his confidence. She had accomplished even more than she had hoped for right at first, for Stephen's letters had not led her to think she would be very welcome, and she had come with a high heart of hope that she might first win his love for herself and then his life for God.

For several years now she had been praying for this stranger brother, until, when she was left in the world alone, she had come to feel that God had a special mission for her with him; and so she had dared to come off here alone and uninvited. She was not going to be daunted by any little thing. She would try to be as wise as a serpent and as harmless as a dove. Meantime she thought she understood Philip Earle somewhat, and she wished that he did not live in the same house with her brother. He might be interesting to try to help, taken by himself; but she was fearful that he would not help her with her brother.

Philip had succeeded beyond his wildest expectations in getting help to bring the freight that he found waiting in the little station. For Margaret had laid her plans well, and knowing the ways of delays on railroads, had shipped her household goods to this unknown land much in advance of herself, that when she arrived, there might not be so much possibility of sending her away, at least, until she had had opportunity to try her experiment. A girl with a little wider experience of the world, especially of the wild Western world, would not have dared do what she had attempted.

Two stalwart ranchmen Philip enlisted to help him, with their fine team of horses. They were the wildest of the wild men, who drank heavily, and gambled recklessly, and cared not at all that man's days are as grass and he is soon cut off, but took life as if they expected to hold it forever against all odds and have their wicked best from it.

Not a word said Philip about Stephen's sister to them. Something innate made him shrink from speaking of her to them. They were men such as he would not like to have his own sister know. Not that he objected to them himself. They were good fellows in their way. They could tell a story well, though not always of the cleanest sort, and they were fearless in their bravery. But they were men without any moral principles whatever.

Philip, as he drove back home, silent for the most part while the men talked, reflected that his own life was not faultless, and that in the three years that had passed since he came to this country to become a part of it his own moral principles had fallen quite perceptibly. He had not noticed it until to-day, but now he knew it. Somehow the coming of that girl had showed him where he stood. But he still knew what those principles were.

And these two men must, if possible, be kept from knowing that Miss Halstead had come.

But how could he manage that? Stephen ought to have been warned. What a fool he was not to have taken Steve out to the barn, and had a good talk with him before he went away, for Steve would never think to be careful. He had no idea of the part he ought to play in the protection of his sister.

The two men had joked him curiously on the amount and kind of furniture they were putting into the wagons, but Philip had only laughed and put them off with other jokes; and in the code of the wild, free life they accepted for the time, and questioned no more. They knew that when Stephen came he would tell all. Stephen could not keep a thing to himself when he got among his boon companions. They were a trifle curious to know why Stephen did not come along when he expected so important a shipment of goods, and they were exceedingly curious over the piano, feeling sure that either Stephen or Philip was about to be married and was going to try to keep the matter quiet. But they were obliged to content themselves with Philip's dry answer, "Steve couldn't get away this morning."

Just in sight of the house Stephen came out to meet them, still half-sulky that Philip had insisted on going away alone; and Philip said a few low words to him as he halted the forward wagon, the other two men being together on their own wagon just behind. Stephen demurred, but Philip's insistent tones meant business, he knew, and without waiting to do more than wave a greeting to the two in the other wagon, he walked reluctantly back into the house.

In his heart he was rebelling at Philip and at his sister's presence once more. He could see plainly that it was going to hamper his own movements greatly. His friends were good enough for him, and why should his sister be too good to meet them? If she would stay here, she must take what she found. But he did as Philip told him. He told his sister that he thought she had better go into her room and shut the door until the wagons were unloaded, as they were rough fellows that Philip had brought up with him to help, and she would not want to be about with them. He said it gruffly. He did not relish saying it at all. The men were his especial friends. Had it not been that he knew in his heart that Philip was right, he would not have done it at all.

Margaret wondered, but reluctantly did as he suggested, and went thoughtfully over to the window to look out.

She was right, then. Philip was wild. Stephen knew it. Stephen was trying to help him, perhaps, to reform him or something; and that was why he was so reluctant to speak about Philip's share in the household. And now Philip had brought some of his friends, some rough men that Stephen did not approve and did not wish her to meet, to the house; and he was trying to protect her.

It was dear of Stephen to care for her that way, and she appreciated it, but she felt that it was wholly unnecessary. She felt that her womanhood was sufficient to protect her from insult here in the house of her brother. She was not in the least afraid to be out there and direct where things should go. If Stephen was trying to help Philip to be a better man, then she ought to help, too. It would be another way of helping her brother to help what he was interested in. And these friends of his, could they not be helped, too? It was a pity for Stephen to feel so about it. She wished she had had time to argue with him, for she really ought to be out there to tell them where to place things. It would save a lot of trouble later.

Thus she stood thinking as she heard the stamping of the horses' feet about the front door, the creaking of the wagon-wheels as they ground upon the steps, and then the heavy footsteps, the voices of men, the thuds of heavy weights set down.

She wearied of her imprisonment the more that there was no window in her room from which she could watch operations; and at last, when she heard them discussing the best way of getting the piano out of the wagon, she could stand it no longer. She felt that she was needed, for they had made absurd suggestions, and her piano was very dear to her heart. She must tell them how the piano men in the East always did. It was ridiculous for her to be shut up here, anyway. Stephen might as well learn that now as any time. For an instant she knelt beside the gray cot and lifted a hurried prayer, — just why she knew not, for there was nothing to be afraid of, she was sure, — and then with firm hand she turned the knob of her door, and went out among the boxes and barrels of goods that were all over the room, until she came and stood framed in the sunny doorway, the brilliant noonday glare upon her gold hair and shining full into her eyes, her little ruffled sleeve falling away from her white wrist as she raised her hand to shield her eyes.

"Stephen, wait a minute," she called; "I can tell you just how to move that. I watched the men put it in the wagon when it started. It is very easy. You want two rollers. Broomsticks will do."

Chapter 5

There was sudden silence outside the front door. The two strangers turned and stared admiringly and undisguisedly. Stephen looked sheepishly triumphant toward Philip, and Philip drew his black brows in a frown of displeasure.

"My sister!" said Stephen airily, recovering himself first, and waving his hand comprehensively toward the two men. He felt rather proud of this new possession of a sister. His own eyes glowed with admiration as he looked at her trim form in its blue and white drapery framed in the rough doorway, one hand shading her eyes, and the animation of interest in her face.

But now Margaret was surprised. Why did Stephen introduce her if he had considered these men too rough for her even to appear in their presence? It was curious. Was he afraid of Philip? Ah! They must be friends of Philip's whom Stephen did not admire, and yet whom he had to introduce on his partner's account, and so he wished to evade it by keeping her out of sight. Well, what mattered it? A mere introduction was nothing. She would let them see by her manner that they were strangers still.

So she acknowledged Stephen's naming of them as "Bennett" and "Byron" with a cool little nod, that only served to increase their admiration. Perhaps the coolness of her manner was to them an added charm. Stephen rose in their estimation, being the possessor of so attractive a sister.

After she had given her wise, clear directions, — which proved to be exceedingly sensible ones, they could not but acknowledge, — she vanished into the house once more, but not, as they supposed, from hearing. She went quickly into Stephen's bedroom, from whose small window she could watch their movements. She intended to see that her directions were carried out and that piano safely landed in the proper place.

Just one short instant she was out of hearing as she opened the other room door, and closed it softly after her, and drew the torn paper that served as a window-shade slightly aside so that she could see out. During that instant Byron, who was famed among his associates for the terribleness of his oaths and the daring of his remarks, broke forth with a remark to Stephen, prefaced by a fearful oath. The remark was intended to convey the speaker's intense admiration of Stephen's sister, and Stephen himself would have been inclined to take it in the spirit in which it was meant; but Philip, standing close by with darkened countenance, laid a heavy hand on

Byron's shoulder, and said in low tones, which yet carried in them a menace, "That kind of talk doesn't go down here!"

It was just then that Margaret's ear became quickened to hear, and her intuition told her that she was the subject of the conversation.

"What's the matter with you, man?" said Byron, shaking off the hand. "Can't you bear to hear a woman praised? Perhaps you'd like a monopoly of her. But she don't belong to you — " with another oath; "and I say it again, Steve, she's a — "

But Philip's hands were at Byron's throat, and the word was smothered before it was uttered. Margaret dropped the paper shade, and stood back pale and trembling, she knew not why. Was Philip against her? Did he hate to hear her praised even, and did he wish her away, or was he defending her? She could not tell, though there had been something strong and true in the flash of Philip's eye as he sprang toward the other man, that made her fear lest she misjudge him.

What kind of a country was this to which she had come, anyway? And why, if there was need to defend her, had Stephen not been the one to do it, seeing it was Stephen who had warned her to keep away? It was all strange.

She sat thinking, on the hard little cot bed, looking around on the dismal room, and the pity of her brother's life appealed to her more strongly than it had yet done. She resolved to put away any foolish misgivings, and make a home here that should help him to live his life the best that it could be lived. She turned and knelt a minute beside her brother's bed, and asked help of her unseen Guide, a kind of consecration of herself to the mission that had brought her to this strange country.

Then she went once more to the window, and looking out saw the work of unloading the wagons going on as calmly as if nothing had happened. There was a firmness around Philip's mouth and chin that was not to be trifled with, and his eyes seemed to look apart from the others; but the rest were gayly at work, whistling, calling to one another merrily. Margaret watched them awhile. The one called Byron had a handsome face with heavy, dark waving hair, and big black eyes that were not true, but were interesting. She shuddered as she remembered the oath he had used to Philip and Stephen, a much milder one than the first, which she had not heard. The name of her Saviour, Jesus Christ! She had never heard it spoken in that way. It seemed to her the depth of wickedness. She had not yet dreamed of the depths to which wickedness can reach.

It rushed over her in a great wave of pity and sorrow as she watched the muscular arms lifting her furniture, saw the play of fun and daring on the handsome features, and thought that it was the name of his Saviour, as well as her own, he had used. His Saviour, and he did not know Him, did not recognize, perhaps, what he was doing. O, if he might be shown! If she might help to show him! It might be there would be a way.

And suddenly her mission widened, and took in Byron, Bennett, Philip, and an unknown company of like companions; and her heart swelled with the magnitude of the possibility that God might have chosen her to help all these as well as Stephen.

She watched a long time, and listened, too; but there were no more oaths, and no more fights. She studied the faces of the four men as they worked, especially the man who had spoken that awful word, and she prayed as she watched. It was a way that she had been acquiring during her last three or four years of loneliness. And by and by a plan began to open to her mind.

Then she went quietly out to see that the dinner she had started was doing as it should, and prepared to set the table for five instead of three.

By this time some packing-boxes and trunks were where they could be reached, and with Stephen's help she opened one containing some table-linen. It gave her much satisfaction to be able to have a table-cloth the first time she gave a dinner party in her new home.

The goods were all unloaded from the wagons and set under cover, and the two helpers were mopping their perspiring brows, while Philip drove his own wagon to the barn, when Margaret came to the door once more.

"Dinner is ready now," she remarked, quite as if they had all be invited, "and I suppose you would like to wash your hands before you come in. You will find the basin and towels out by the pump at the back door, Mr. Byron and Mr. Bennett." She had watched long enough from the window to know which was which, and she let the slightest glance of her eyes recognize each now, a glance that set them at an immeasurable distance. "And, Stephen, please hurry, because everything will get cold."

Stephen's eyes lit up with pleasure. This was the kind of thing he liked; but it was not what Philip would like, and he knew it. There was no telling but Philip would pitch the two guests out the door and down the hill when he came in and saw them preparing to sit down at the table.

They drew a long and simultaneous whistle when they entered the door together and saw the table draped in snowy white. They were none of them used to table-cloths.

Margaret had cleared a space around the table and arranged boxes for seats where there were not enough chairs; so there was room for all. Before each place she had laid a snowy napkin. To the young fellows so long unused to this necessity of civilization they looked of a dazzling whiteness, and each became immediately conscious of his own poor appearance. She had opened her trunk and found silver knives and forks and spoons, and all were set as she would have set the table in the East for a luncheon of a few friends.

She knew no other way. There was enough in this to awe the two wild Western cowboys, who under other circumstances might have proved to be unwelcome guests.

There was a touch of refinement, too, in the few green leaves and blossoms that Margaret had gathered in her morning tour around the house, wild blossoms, it is true, and nothing but weeds in the eyes of the men who daily and unheedingly trod over their like; but here, set in this snowy linen, held in a tiny crystal vase that had also been carefully packed in Margaret's trunk, they took on a new beauty, and were not recognized as belonging to the world in which they lived.

It was like the girl, impulsive and poetical, that she had kept the whole dinner waiting just a minute while she found that vase and added the touch of beauty to the already inviting table. Who knew but the flowers might speak to those men of the God who made them?

And the flowers lifted up their pink, dainty faces, and breathed a silent grace about that board at which they all sat down, creating a kind of embarrassment among the strangely selected company.

It was just as they were sitting down that Philip entered, and paused in the doorway at the sight, his brow darkening.

"Please sit over there, Mr. Earle," said Margaret, passing a plate of steaming soup to the place indicated; and Philip, hesitating, half-reluctant, sat silently down; but his eye ran vividly around the table like the threatening of lightning, in one warning glance.

Philip's look, however, was not needed. The spoons and the napkins and flowers, and above all the young woman, had awed for once the undaunted souls who were noted all about that region for their daring and wickedness. Margaret had rummaged among the tin cans on the shelf of the little cupboard in the corner, and had compounded a most delicious soup with the aid of a jar of beef-extract, a can of baked beans, and another of tomatoes. To be sure, its recipe was not to be found in any cook-book ever published; but it was none the less appreciated for that.

There was half a loaf of baker's stale bread, which she had toasted and cut into crisp little squares for the soup, and there was corn-meal wherewith she had made a johnny-cake or cornbread of flakiness and deliciousness known only to New England cooks. Not even the old mammies of the South could equal it.

It was not exactly a menu for an Eastern lunch party, but with the aid of another glass of jelly from a box hastily pried open it seemed a feast to the hungry young men who had been their own cooks for long, weary months of famine.

Bennett was tall and lanky, with freckled face, red, straight hair, and white eyelashes heavily shading light-blue eyes. He had a hard, straight mouth, and a scar over his left eye, and was known among his associates as a dead shot. His voice had a hard, cruel ring when he spoke. Margaret did not like his face.

She sat at her end of the table, pouring coffee, or slipping quietly over to the stove, waiting upon their needs, diffusing a softening, silencing influence about the table.

The old woman crept from her duties in the new kitchen which she was scrubbing and purifying, to peep inside the door, and wonder at the strange hush that hovered over the usually hilarious company. She knew the reputation of those young men, and could not understand their silence. Then she looked at the sweet presence of the girl as she presided over the meal, and shook her head, wondering again as she crept silently away.

It was after the last crumb was finished and they had risen from the table, — a mingled look, half of satisfaction in the meal, half of relief that it was over, in their faces, — that Margaret dared her part.

She had made up her mind to do it while she was preparing dinner, and her heart had thumped sometimes so hard that she had scarcely dared try to eat after she had decided upon it. Some rebuke must be given to the man who had uttered the name of Jesus Christ in that awful way. What she should say she did not know. "Lord, give me courage, give me words, give me opportunity!" had been the silent plea during the dinner-time.

And now, as she lifted her brave eyes, stern with the purpose she had in mind, they met the bold, handsome ones of Byron. He was trying to think up something appropriate to say to the hostess for giving them this delightful dinner. He was noted for his hilarious speeches; but the usual language in which he framed them would not be according to Philip's ideas, and he did not care to rouse Philip twice in a day. It would scarcely put him into this young woman's good graces to engage in a free fight with Philip Earle before her face.

Something in her troubled gaze embarrassed him as he lounged across the room to where she stood. He was conscious of Philip's forked-lightning glance upon his back, too, as he went; yet he swaggered a little more and held his head higher. He would not be put to shame before a girl. He ran his fingers through his abundant black hair, drew tighter the knotted silk handkerchief about his bronzed throat, and came gallantly forward with a few gay words of thanks on his lips, which were unusually free, for him, from profane garnishings.

He even dared to put out his great brown hand to shake hands with her. He had a fancy for holding that little white hand in his.

But Margaret looked at his hand, and then faced him steadily, putting her own hand behind her back.

They did not see Philip, his eyes like a panther's, unconsciously move toward them. Bennett and Stephen drew off by the door to watch what would come.

Her voice was very low, but clear. Philip, standing behind Byron, could hear every word she said; but the two by the door could not.

"Mr. Byron," she said, and there was pain in her voice. "I cannot shake hands with you. You have insulted my best friend."

The red flashed up under the bronze in the young man's cheek, and he drew back as if struck.

He stammered and tried to find words.

It was nothing but a passing word, a flash, he said; Philip and he were as good friends as ever. He did not know, or he would not have spoken. He would apologize to Philip.

Margaret caught her breath. She had not expected to be misunderstood.

"I do not mean Mr. Earle," she answered quietly and steadily; "he is but a new acquaintance. I mean my best friend. I mean Jesus Christ, my Saviour. I heard you speak his name in a dreadful way, Mr. Byron."

She lifted her eyes to his now, and they were full of tears.

The man was dumb before her. What had been a flash of anger and embarrassment grew into shame, deep, overpowering. He had nothing to say. He had never met a thing like this face to face before. It was not something he could point the barrel of his revolver at, nor could he grapple with it and overcome. It was shame, and he had never met real shame before.

The fire in Philip's eyes went out, and he turned half away, as if from something too holy to look upon. He had seen the tears in the girl's eyes, and the real trouble in her voice. Into his own heart Rebuke had sent a shaft as it passed to meet this other man whose guilt was greater.

At last the careless lips, so deserted of all their gay, accustomed words, spoke.

"I did not know—" was all he could say, and he turned and stumbled out of the room, not looking back.

And Margaret, trembling now, with the tears blinding her, took refuge in her room.

Chapter 6

The next few days were strenuous ones in the house of the unbidden guest. Philip and Stephen arose early and retired late, and did their regular work at odd times when they could get a chance, while they entered like two boys into the plans of their young commander.

They moved the little cattle-shed near to the house and floored it with some lumber that had been lying idle for some time. They took down the cook-stove and set it up in the new kitchen, where it soon shone out resplendent in a coat of black under the direction of Margaret and the wondering hand of the old woman.

A box of kitchen utensils which Margaret had considered indispensable to her own career as a housekeeper, and was now thankful she had not left behind, was unpacked, and soon there began to appear on the table wonderful concoctions in the shape of waffles and gems and muffins, which made each meal the rival of the last one, and kept the two young men and the old woman in a continual state of amazement.

Into the midst of all this work came the first Sabbath of Margaret's new life.

A storm had burst in the night, and was carrying all before it, seeming to have made up its mind to stay all day; so there was nothing to do but stay in the house as much as possible.

At the breakfast-table Stephen began to speak of the work they would do that day, and to say what a shame it was raining, as they could not work on a little room to accommodate the old woman, who had now to hobble home at night to her shanty a mile and a half away.

"You forget what day it is, Stephen," said Margaret, smiling. "You couldn't work if it didn't rain. It is Sunday, you know."

Stephen looked up in surprise. He had almost forgotten that Sunday was different from any other day, but he did not wish to confess this to his sister. He drew his brows, scowling, and answered, "O, bother, so it is!"

Then Philip scowled too, but for a different reason, and looked anxiously at the sky to see whether it was really to be a rainy Sunday. He grew suddenly thankful for the rain. But what would he do with Stephen all day?

They were compelled to do some work, after all, for the old woman did not hobble over at all that day, and no wonder: the rain came down in sheets; thunder rumbled; and lightning flashed across the heavens; and Philip blessed the rain again.

"Go into the kitchen, Steve, and wash those dishes," said Philip laughingly, "and I'll help. We're a lazy lot if we can't do the work one day out of seven for our board. It is enough for Miss Halstead to do the cooking." And so they worked together, and Philip hunted around, and managed to make work, little things that Stephen must do at once, and which Margaret kept telling them could wait until the morrow; but Philip insistently kept Stephen helping him at them till dinner was out of the way and it was nearly five o'clock.

The sky was lighting up, and showed some signs of clearing.

Stephen wandered restlessly to the door, and looked down the road, and then at his watch.

Philip was on the alert, though he did not have that appearance. He glanced at the big piano-case still unopened.

"Miss Halstead," he ventured, "why didn't we open that piano yesterday? If we should knock off a couple of those front boards and get at that keyboard, don't you think you might play for us a little, and while away the rest of this day? Steve will be off to gayer company than ours if you don't amuse him."

He laughed lightly, but there was a troubled something in his voice that caused Margaret to follow his glance toward her brother. She saw the restlessness in his whole attitude, and took alarm. Was it for one or both of the young men she was troubled? She could not have told.

"O, yes, if you can do it easily," said Margaret eagerly. It would be a delight to her to touch the keys of her piano again; it would drive away any lingering homesickness.

Philip's voice again called Stephen's wandering attention, and soon their united efforts brought the row of ivory and black keys into view.

Margaret, seated on a kitchen chair, touched strong, sweet chords while the two young men settled down to listen.

Sweet Sabbath music she played from memory, a bit from some of the old masters, a page from an oratorio, a strain from the minor of a funeral march, a grand triumphant hymn. Then she touched the keys more softly, and began to sing low and sweetly; and by and by there came a rich tenor and a grumbling bass from the two listeners as she wandered into familiar hymns that they had sung as little boys.

The rain came on again, and it grew darker, and still they sang, until at last Philip drew a sigh of relief, and realized that it was bedtime and Stephen had not gone to the village. Then Margaret stopped playing, and they all went to get a lunch before retiring.

Margaret, before she slept that night, asked a blessing again on the work she hoped to do, and never dreamed that already she had been used to keep the brother for whose sake she had come this long journey.

After they finished the old woman's room Philip came in with his arms full of great rough stones, and announced that he was ready to begin the fireplace, and he thought it would be best to get the muss and dirt of plaster out of the way before they put things to rights in the living-room.

Margaret had almost forgotten the doubts she had about Philip when she first came, and his strange actions on the morning after her arrival, and was prepared to accept both the young men as good comrades, or brothers. Laughingly they all went to work, Margaret drawing the outline of the fireplace that she thought should be built, and Stephen mixing mortar while Philip brought in stones from a great pile that had been collected by the former owner of the place to build a fence.

"There's nothing like being jack of all trades," said Stephen as he slapped on some mortar with the blade of a broken hoe, and settled into it a great stone that Philip had just brought in.

Margaret's eyes shone as she watched the chimney being built. She saw in her mind's eye a charming room, and she was anxious to get it into shape before another Sabbath, that they might have a quiet, restful time. While she had been playing and singing the night before, there had been revealed to her ways in which she might point the way to her Saviour, and she longed to begin.

There was much to be done in teaching the strange servant new ways, and in keeping clean the things they used every day: but Margaret was one of those whose hands are never idle, and she had put her whole soul into the making over of her brother's home; so she accomplished much in her own way while the young men worked at masonry and the stone fireplace grew into comely proportions.

By the time it was finished she had rooted out from the boxes and barrels most of the things she would need in the immediate arrangement of this living-room, and had cut and sewed cushions and fixings ready to put into place when the time came, so that the work of refurnishing went rapidly forward. Indeed, the two helpers became fully as eager to see the room finished as was the young architect.

Margaret had bought a number of things before she left the East that she thought she would be likely to need in arranging her own room, which she wanted to make as pretty as possible to keep her from getting homesick. All this plan she now abandoned, and set herself to put these pretty things into the adornment of the great, bare living-room which she meant should be the scene of her labors.

Among other things there were bright materials for cushions, and there were rolls of paper enough to hang the walls of a reasonably large room. A careful calculation and much measurement soon made it evident that this paper would cover the most of the walls of this room, which was the size of an ordinary whole house without any partitions. She puzzled a while to know whether she should risk sending for more, but finally a bright idea occurred to her as she looked at the large bundle of green burlap that was lying in the box with the paper. This she had intended for draperies, or floor covering, if necessary, or maybe covering for a chest or a cushion. Now all was plain before her.

The paper had an ivory ground on which seemed to be growing great palms as if a myriad of hothouses had let forth their glories of greenery. There was enough of this paper to cover the two sides and front of the room. That was delightful. It would look as if the room opened on three sides into a palm grove. On the back end, in the centre of which was the great stone fireplace, she would put the plain moss-green burlap, fastened along its breadths with brass tacks. Two or three good coats of whitewash would give the ceiling a creamy tint, and she could cut out a few of the palms from the paper to apply in a dainty design in the centre and corners.

The two young men looked bewildered when she tried to explain, and she finally desisted, and issued her directions.

They covered the back of the room first; and, when the mossy breadths were smoothly on over the rough boards, fastened at intervals with the gleaming tacks, the old stone fireplace stood out finely against the dark background.

"Now, if you have any guns and things, that is the place to put them," said Margaret, pointing to the wall about the fireplace, and Philip proudly brought out a couple of guns, and crossed them on the wall to the right, while Stephen fastened a pair of buffalo-horns over the door to the left that led into the new kitchen. This side of the room was at once denominated the dining-room, and Margaret unwrapped a handsome four-panel screen of unusual size, wrought in black and gold, and stood it across that corner.

They turned with avidity to follow her next directions, having more faith in the result than they had before. And another day or two saw the walls papered and the ceiling smiling white with its green traceries here and there.

It did not take long after that to unpack rugs and furniture. Margaret had brought many things from the old home, rare mahogany furniture and Oriental rugs, that a wiser person might have advised her to leave behind until she was sure of making a home in this far land. But the girl rejoiced in the beauty of the things she had to give to her "life-work," as she pleased to call it, and had brought everything with her that she intended to keep at all.

The rough old floor with its wide cracks and unoiled boards did not look too bad when they were almost covered with a great, soft rug of rich, dark coloring, and set off here and there by the skin of a tiger or a black bear, or by a strip of white goat-skin.

A wide, low seat, covered with green and piled with bright cushions, ran along the wall to the right of the fireplace. In the corner beyond the window was a low bookcase, which Margaret had intended for her own room, and again beyond her bedroom door another low bookcase ran along to the other bedroom door. These doors were hidden by dark-green curtains of soft, velvety material; and no one would have suspected the rough, cheap doors behind them. By each one there stood on the top of the bookcase, half against the green of the curtain and half mingling with the lifelike palms on the wall, a living palm in a terra-cotta jardiniere, which made the pictured ones but seem more real.

The piano stood near the front of the room, across the right-hand corner; and a wide, low couch invited one to rest and listen to the music.

The rest of the room that was not dining-room was filled with easy chairs, a large, round mahogany table with a most delightful reading-lamp in the middle, and more books, while Stephen's old writing-desk stood across the left-hand front corner.

It was all most charming to look upon, this finished room, when the weary workers at last sat down to a belated supper Saturday evening, and realized what they had accomplished during the week.

There was much to be done yet. Margaret, as she ate her supper, glanced around, and planned for a row of little brass hooks against the wall, whereon should hang her tiny teacups, and wondered how she should manage a plate-rail for the saucers, in this country without mouldings. The little glass-faced buffet that was to hold the china still stood on the floor in the corner, waiting its turn to be hung, and the pictures were as yet unpacked; but there was time enough for that. There was a room in which to spend the Sabbath, and she prayed that her work might now begin.

Softly there crept up through the darkness of the sky the dawn of another Sabbath day, and Margaret arose with eager anticipations. In the first place, she meant to make Stephen, and Philip, too, if possible, go with her to church. That, of course, was the right place in which to begin the Sabbath.

Before she left her room she laid out upon her bed the things she would wear to church, choosing them with care that she might be neatly and sweetly attired in the house of the Lord, and that she might be as winsome as possible to those she wished to influence.

She did not acknowledge even to herself that she had some doubt in her mind as to whether she should accomplish making Stephen and Philip attend church, for she meant to accomplish that in spite of all obstacles.

Nevertheless, she went about her self-set task with great care and deliberation, prefacing her request with the daintiest breakfast with which they had yet been favored.

It was just as they finished that she brought forward the subject that was so near to her heart and about which she had been praying all the morning.

"Stephen, what time do we have to start for church? Is it far from here? You don't go on horseback, do you?"

Stephen dropped his knife and fork on his plate with a clatter, and sat back in astonishment; and there was a blank silence in the room for some seconds.

Chapter 7

"To church!" Stephen uttered the words half mockingly. "What time do we start! Well, now, Phil, how far should you say it was to the nearest church?"

A mirthless laugh broke from Philip. It was involuntary. A wave of bitterness rolled over him as a wave of the ocean higher than the others might break over the head of one who was bravely trying to breast the tide. As soon as he had uttered the laugh he was sorry, for he felt the shock this would be to Margaret even before he saw her start at his harsh laughter.

These two young men were alike in the bitterness that each carried in his heart, but Stephen's had been caused by the hardness of his heart toward his earthly father, while Philip had hardened his heart, for what he considered just cause, toward his Father in heaven; and of the two his bitterness was the more galling.

Philip checked the laugh, which had really been but the semblance of one, and answered steadily with his eyes on his plate, "About forty miles by the nearest way, I should judge."

Stephen's eyes were twinkling with fun as he tipped his chair back against the wall and watched his sister. He had no inkling of the desolation this would bring to her, and he could not understand, perhaps did not notice, the whiteness of her face as she looked at him, only half comprehending. It was given to Philip, the stranger, to feel with her the appalling emptiness of a country without a church. Dismay dropped about her as a garment.

"But what do you do?" she faltered. "Where do you go to service on Sunday?"

"Same as any other day," laughed Stephen carelessly. " 'The groves were God's first temples,' " he quoted piously; "suppose we go out in search of one. This will be a first-rate day for your first lesson in riding horseback. It won't do for you to stick in the house at work all the time."

But Margaret's face was flushed and troubled.

"Do you mean you don't go anywhere to church?" she asked pathetically. "Is there no service in the town? Are there no missionaries even, out here?"

"There isn't even a town worth speaking of, Miss Halstead," answered Philip, feeling that some one must answer her earnestly. "You do not know what a God-forsaken country you have come to. Churches and missionaries would not flourish here if they came. You will not find it a pleasant place to stay. Men get used to it, but women find it hard."

She lifted her troubled eyes to his, wondering in an underthought whether he was hinting that she should go back where she came from; but she saw in his kind face no eagerness to get rid of her, as his eyes met hers. She turned sadly toward the window, looking out on the stretch of level country away down the hill, thinking with despair of the place to which she had come and the hopelessness of carrying out her plans without the aid of a church and a minister.

She had thought her part would be simply to make a good home for her brother, to speak a quiet word when opportunity offered, and to use her influence to put him under the power of the gospel. But out here it seemed there was no gospel, unless she preached it. For this she was not prepared.

Perplexed and baffled, she hardly knew with what words she declined her brother's urgent request to go riding with him, to which were added the most earnest solicitations of his partner when he saw that Stephen was not going to succeed. She wondered afterwards at the anxiety and annoyance in Philip's eyes when she told him firmly that she did not ride on Sunday, and would rather stay quietly at home. It seemed strange to her that he should try to interfere between her and her brother. Then she went into her little log room and shut the door, and knelt in disheartened prayer beside her bed. Had she, then, come out on a fruitless mission? For what would it avail if she did bring palm-covered walls and pianos and books into her brother's life, if there were no means by which he could be brought to see the love of the Lord Jesus Christ?

She was scarcely roused from her disappointed petitions by the sound of a rider leaving the dooryard. She wondered idly whether it were Philip, but soon she heard another horse's quick tread, and, going to the window, was just in time to see Philip fling himself upon his horse and ride at a furious pace off down the road.

Quiet settled down upon the house, and Margaret realized with disappointment that both the young men had gone away. Why had she not tried to keep Stephen with her? Perhaps he would have listened to her while she read something, or she might have sung. Philip, it was quite evident, had intended going off all the time, and was only anxious to get her and Stephen out of the way so that he could do as he pleased. The tears came into her eyes, and fell thick and fast. How ignominiously had she failed! Even the little she might have done she had let slip by because of her disappointment that God had not arranged things according to her expectations. Perhaps it might have been better for her even to go on the ride with Stephen rather than for him to go off with some friends who never had a thought of God or His holy day.

Thus reflecting, she read herself some bitter lessons. She had forgotten to ask for the Spirit's guidance, and had been going in her own strength; or she might have been shown a better way and been blessed in her efforts.

By and by she went out where the old woman sat outside the kitchen door, mumbling and glowering at the sun-clad landscape. Perhaps she might essay a humble effort with this poor creature for a Sabbath-day sacrifice.

"Marna, do you know God?" she asked, sitting down beside the old woman and speaking tenderly.

The woman looked at her curiously, and shook her head.

"God never come at here," she answered. "Missie, you—*you* know God?"

"Yes," answered Margaret earnestly. "God is my Father."

"God your Father! No. You not come off here; you stay where you Father at. God, you Father, angry with you?"

"No, my Father loves me. He sent His Son to die for me. God is your Father, too, Marna."

The old woman shook her head decidedly. "Marna have no father. Fathers all bad. Fathers no love anybody but selves. Brothers no much good, too. All go off, leave. All drink. I say, stay 'way. No come back drunk. Knock! scold! hate! I say stay 'way! Drink self dead!"

Marna was gesticulating wildly to make up for her lack of words. Suddenly she turned earnestly to the girl, with a gleam of something like motherliness in her wrinkled, wicked old face.

"What for Missie come way here? Brothers no good. All go own way. Make cry!" and Marna's work-worn finger traced down the delicate cheek, which was still flushed with the recently shed tears.

Margaret instinctively drew back, but she did not wish to hurt the old woman's feelings; so she answered in as bright a tone as she could summon.

"Brothers are not all bad, Marna. Some are good. My brother was lonely here, and I came to take care of him."

" 'Take care! Take care!' " muttered the old woman. "And who 'take care' of Missie? Men go off, stay all day. Drink. Come home drunk! Ach! No, no, Missie go back. Missie go off while men gone. Not see brothers any more."

Margaret was half frightened over this harangue; but she tried to be brave and answer the poor creature, though her heart misgave her as a great fear began to rise.

"No, Marna," she said, smiling through her fear; "I cannot go back. God sent me, and until He tells me to go back I cannot go."

"God love you and send you here? Then He never come here. He don't know—"

"Yes, He knows, Marna, and He is here, too," she answered softly, as if reassuring herself. "Listen!"

And Margaret began at the beginning of the story of the cross, and told it all to the wondering old woman as simply as she knew how. But, when she had finished, the listener only shook her head, and murmured:

"No, God never love Marna. Marna have bad heart. No love for good in heart. No heavenly Father love."

It was time to get dinner ready, and Margaret arose with a sigh, a great depression settling on her heart. Not even to this poor old woman could she show the light of Christ.

She gave herself to the preparations for the noon-day meal for a little while, thinking soon to hear the sound of horses coming up the road; but, though the dinner got itself done and sent forth savory odors on the air, and Margaret stood with anxious, wistful eyes shaded with a hand that had grown strangely cold with a new fear, there came no sound of horses.

The girl ate a few mouthfuls, and had the dinner put away. The old woman went about muttering:

"Men no come. Men off. Have good time. Missie cry. Missie go home. Not stay."

The stars came out thickly like sky-blossoms unfolding all at once, and the sky drew close about the earth; but still there came no sound of travellers along the long, dark road.

Margaret went in at last from her vigil on the doorstep and lit the great lamp. It was a disappointing Sabbath. It was more than that; it seemed a wasted Sabbath. She might much better have been riding with Stephen if perchance she might have said some helpful thing to him. And the old woman rocking and muttering to herself in the back doorway, what good had she done to her?

At last she could bear the silence and her fears no longer.

She called to Marna to come in. "Sit down," she said gently. "I will sing to you about Jesus."

Marna sat down with folded hands on a little wooden stool, and listened while Margaret sang. She chose the songs that were in simple language, that told of Jesus and His love; songs that spoke to weary, burdened ones and bade them rest; songs that told of forgiveness and a Father's love.

A long time she sang; and then, yearning for a help, she knew not what, feeling as if she must have a companionship in her need, she came over to the old woman, took her hand, and drew her down beside the fireplace seat.

"Come," said she. "We will talk to God."

Wonderingly, half fearfully, the old woman knelt, watching the girl with wide-open eyes the while; and Margaret closed her eyes, and said:

"O God, show Marna how her Father loves her. Make Marna love God. Make Marna good, for Jesus' sake."

As under a spell the old woman stood up; her eyes, half frightened, half fascinated, were upon the girl's face.

Margaret smiled and said good-night, but Marna went out under the stars, and muttered wonderingly, "Make Marna good?" as if it were a thing that had to be and she could not see how it could be.

Then Margaret locked the door, and turned out the light, and sat down at the window to watch and pray. During that time there was revealed to her a part of what she might do in this land without a God or a temple. Out of her darkness, her fear, and her feebleness came a strength not her own.

It must have been long past midnight—her watch had run down and she could not tell—when at last faint sounds came slowly up the hill; and silently, slowly there crept past her window and wound around the house to the barn two horsemen, strangely close together. One seemed to be supporting the other. They spoke no word; but one of them turned his head as he passed her window, and looked, though she could not tell which one it was.

Neither of them came to the house that night, though she lighted the lamp and waited awhile for them. She concluded they did not wish to disturb her.

Then, not caring to take off her clothes, she lay down and wept. After all the long, hard day the tension was loosened at last, but what yet did she know? Was one of her new-found fears dissipated? Was she sure that Stephen had come home with Philip, and was now in the barn lying in the hay? Was she sure that it had been Philip? They might have been two tramps—but no. Tramps would not come to a desolate land like this. They would tramp to more profitable places for plying their beggarly trade. Somehow for herself a strange peace settled down upon her. She was not afraid that anything would happen to her. She feared only for her brother—and—yes, she must admit it—for his friend. For, after all, he was her brother too, in a larger, broader sense, but still the son of her heavenly Father.

And those words of Marna's, what had they meant? Did the two with whom she had come to make her home, drink? And, if so, how could she ever hope to help and save them, just she alone in that country without a church? For the absence of a Christian church and a Christian minister seemed to leave her most inexpressibly alone.

And yet not alone, for out of the darkness of her room came the words to her heart, "And lo, I am with you alway."

Then she prayed as she had never prayed before, prayed until her soul seemed drawn up to meet the loving Comforter, Strengthener, and Guide. In that consecration hour she laid down herself, her fears and wished, and agreed to do what God would have her do here in this lonely place, against such fearful odds as might be; herself alone with God.

Out in the hay lay Philip, body and mind weary with the fight of the day, in which he had not won, yet too troubled to sleep now that he had the chance.

With anxious eyes he peered through the darkness toward the house, and wondered how it had fared with the one who had waited all day while he had been in the forefront of battle. Was she frightened at being left so late alone? Had she seen them when they came in? Had she guessed at all what the trouble was, or had she coupled them both in deserting her? Philip's heart was very bitter to-night, and against God. He felt like cursing a God who would let a woman, and so fair a woman, suffer. Poor, straying child of God, who knew not the comfort of trusting and leaning on the everlasting arm; who knew not that even suffering may bring a beauteous reward!

Chapter 8

Stephen slept late the next morning; and when he came heavy-eyed and cross to the breakfast-table, he complained of a headache. But Philip sat silent, with grave lines drawn about forehead and mouth. He was too strong a man to show the signs of fatigue or loss of sleep in any other way.

Margaret had come out from the horror of the night with peace upon her brow, but her eyes looked heavy with lack of sleep. Philip gave her one long look while she was pouring the coffee, and saw this. It angered him to think she had suffered.

Margaret was sweetness itself to her brother. She insisted upon his lying down on the long seat by the chimney, while she shaded his eyes from the glare of the morning, and brought a little chair near by, and read to him. When he turned his head away from her entirely because for very shame he could not face this kindness, and know what in his heart he really was, she laid the book aside, and, bringing a bowl of water, dipped her cool, soft hand in it, and made passes back and forth across the temples that really throbbed in earnest.

Something was working in his easily stirred heart, something that went beyond the mere surface where most emotions were born and died, with him; and, as her hand went steadily back and forth with that sustained motion that is so comforting to sick nerves, he reached up a shaking hand, and caught hers, and his voice choked as he said,

"You are a good girl, — a good sister!"

Then Margaret stooped over, and kissed his lips, and murmured softly, "Dear brother, now go to sleep; and, when you wake up, you will feel better."

Stephen had much ado to keep back the moisture that kept creeping to his eyelids with stinging, smarting stealth; and he was glad when she finally thought him asleep and tiptoed away. Not for long years had he felt a lump like that that was now growing in his throat till it seemed it would burst. But by and by the quiet and the darkness brought sleep; and Philip, looking anxiously in, went out quickly with a relieved sigh.

The dinner was late that day, for Stephen slept long, and Margaret would not have him disturbed. But when it came it was delicious. Strong soup seasoned just right, home-made bread, delicious coffee, and a quivering mound of raspberry jelly, cool and luscious with the flavor of raspberries from the old New England preserve-closet. It was marvellous how many things this sister could make from canned goods and boxes of gelatine. There seemed to be no end to the variety.

But Stephen was restless as the dinner neared its close, and Philip looked anxiously toward him.

Stephen shoved his chair back with a creak on the floor, and said crossly that he believed he would ride down to the village for the mail. He needed to get outdoors; it would do his head good. Philip frowned deeply, and set his lips for a reply; but before he could speak Margaret's sweet voice broke in eagerly.

"O, then, give me my lesson in riding, Stephen, please. It is a lovely afternoon, and will soon be cool. I don't want to be left behind again. I was sorry I had not gone with you yesterday. Please do; I am in a great hurry to learn to ride so I can go all about and see this country."

Philip's face relaxed. He waited to see what Stephen would do, and after a bit of coaxing Stephen consented, although Philip felt uneasy yet.

The horses were saddled and brought to the door, and Philip held the bridle of the gentler horse while Stephen helped his sister to mount, giving elaborate advice about how to hold the reins and how to sit. Then they were off.

"Go the east road, Steve!" called Philip as they rode away from him; but Stephen drew his head up haughtily, and did not answer. Then Philip knew he had made a mistake, and he bit his lip as he turned quickly toward the barn. There was still another horse on the place, though it was not a good riding-horse, and had some disagreeable habits, which left it free generally to stay behind when there was any pleasure riding to be done. Philip flung his own saddle across her back now, and, hardly waiting to pull the girths tight, sprang into it and away after the two, who were turning westward, as he had been sure Stephen would do after his unfortunate remark.

He urged the reluctant old horse into a smart trot, and soon caught up with the riders, calling pleasantly:

"Made up my mind I would come along too. It was lonely staying behind by myself."

Stephen's only answer was a frown. He knew what Philip meant by following. His anger was roused at Philip's constant care for him. Did Philip think him a fool that he couldn't take care of himself with his sister along?

Margaret, too, was a little disappointed. She had hoped to get nearer to her brother during this ride, and perhaps to find out where he had been the day before, and have a real heart-to-heart talk with him. But now here was this third presence that was always between her and her brother, and hindered the talk.

Philip, however, was exceedingly unobtrusive. He rode behind them or galloped on before, dismounting to gather a flaming bunch of flowers, and riding up to fasten them in the bridle of the lady's horse, and then riding on again. Stephen ignored him utterly, and Philip gayly ignored the fact that he was ignored. Margaret came to feel his presence not troublesome, and in fact rather pleasant, hovering about like a guardian angel. Then she laughed to herself to think of her using that simile. To think of an angel in a flannnel shirt, buckskins, and a sombrero!

It was Philip's quiet hint — no, not a hint, merely a suggestion that a certain turn would bring them to a view of the river — that caused Margaret to plead for going that way just as they had come to a critical turn in the road. Stephen, all unsuspecting, turned willingly, thinking they would go back soon and find their way to the village; but wary Philip tolled them on still further until the town with its dangers was far behind them. Then Stephen awoke to the plot that had been laid for him, and rode his horse sulkily home; but the deadly fiend that slumbered within him was allayed for the time, and he went to his room and slept soundly that night.

There was plenty of work to be done yet upon the house. Philip surprised them all a few days later by driving up to the door before breakfast with a load of logs, several men and another load of logs following after him. The sound of the axe, saw, and hammer rang through the air that day, and by night a good-sized addition of logs, divided into two nice rooms, was added to the right-hand side of the living-room.

Margaret's eyes shone. It was just the addition she had spoken of to Stephen, to which he had seemed so opposed. Her heart swelled with gratitude toward him. It seemed she did not yet understand this brother, who was sometimes so cold, but who yet was trying to do all in his power to please her. She watched the work some of the time, and was surprised to find that, while Stephen worked with the rest, he yet took all his orders from Philip as did the others, and seemed to expect Philip to command the whole affair. It was still more strange that all the orders were just what she had suggested to Stephen on the first walk around the house.

It was as they were coming to the supper-table that evening that she attempted to tell her brother how good it was of him to do all these things that she suggested. She thought they were alone; but Philip had come in behind them while they were talking, and Stephen saw him. The back of Stephen's neck grew red, and the color stole up around his golden hair as he said laughingly:

"O, thank Phil for that. He's the boss carpenter. I couldn't build a house if I had to stay out in the rain the rest of my life."

Margaret looked up brightly, and gave Philip the first really warm smile he had received from her, a smile that included him in the family circle.

"I will thank him, too," she said and put out her hand to grasp his large one, rough with the handling of many logs. But she left her other hand lovingly on her brother's shoulder, and Stephen knew she had not taken back the gratitude she had given him. It somehow made him feel strangely uncomfortable.

In a few days the addition to the house was in good order and the windows draped in soft, sheer muslin.

There seemed to be good cheer everywhere. The three householders took a final survey of the premises before the sun went down.

"If we could only grow bark on the outside of the old boards on the main part of the house!" said Margaret wistfully."

"Nothing easier," answered Philip quickly. "It shall be done."

"What do you mean?" asked Margaret.

"Why, cover it with bark," answered Philip. "Steve, get up early with me in the morning, and we'll strip enough bark down in the ravine to cover one side of this front before breakfast."

"Won't that be beautiful?" said Margaret, clapping her hands child-ishly, and the stern lines in Philip's face broke into a pleased smile. He was glad he had suggested it. What was it about this girl that always made one feel glad when he had done her a favor? Other girls he had known had not been that way.

That night he slept in the house for the first time since Margaret came to live there. The front room of the addition was fitted up for him. Margaret had just found out that his only bed had been in the hay, and that he had permanently and quietly given up his room to her. She had supposed before that there was a room over the barn, large and comfortable, which he called his own, though she had indeed thought little about it. She took especial pains with the furnishing of Philip's room. She felt it was due to him for turning out of his own for her. It was not difficult to make it beautiful. There was enough fine old mahogany furniture left. She picked out the hand-somest things, and arranged them attractively. She had not yet fixed up her own room further than to have her own bedstead set up in preference to the hard little cot, but she wanted to make Philip's as attractive as possible.

As a final touch she went to her room, and unpinned from her wall the photograph of the sweet-faced woman with the white hair, and framing it in a little leather case of her own, set it upon the white cover of Philip's bureau. And it was his mother's eyes that looked at Philip in the morning as he opened them for the first time in his new abode. He lay for a moment, looking at the picture, wondering how it got there, blessing the thoughtful-ness that had so placed it, wondering what his mother would think of him now in this strange, wild life. Wondering, too, what she would think of the girl who was bringing to pass in this desolate house such miracles of change. He touched the smoothness of the sheet and the pillow-case, and realized that he had missed such things as these for a long time, and had not known it.

Those were busy, happy days. At times Stephen seemed to be wrought up to the same pitch of enthusiasm and violent effort that kept the other two at work. He did not seem to want to stop for his meals even, until all was finished. And one night, when they were standing off, looking at the almost completed outside of the house, he said,

"We ought to have a housewarming when it gets done."

"Certainly," said Margaret. "We will do it by all means. How soon can we have it, and whom will you invite?"

But, as she turned to go into the house, she caught that look of disapproval on Philip's face, the look she had not seen for several days, and wondered at it.

"Let's have it next Sunday," said Stephen enthusiastically. "It's getting cooler weather now, and by evening we can have a fire in that jolly new fireplace of Phil's. And we'll ask all the fellows, of course."

Philip stood still, aghast. If Margaret had not been there, he would have fairly thundered. But his tongue was tied. This must be managed, if possible, without letting her know what a precipice she was treading near. She would be overcome if she knew all.

"Is there no other day but Sunday, Stephen, dear?" asked Margaret, and her troubled voice was very soft and pleading. "You know I always make the Sabbath a holy day and not a holiday. I would much, *much* rather have it some other time."

She did not say no decidedly to his proposition, remembering her Sunday's experience when she had declined to ride with him. Perhaps there was some way out of the perplexity better than that. She would not antagonize her brother yet, and she would ask her Guide. There surely would be a way.

"No, there isn't any other time when they all can come," answered Stephen shortly. "But of course if you have your puritanical notions, I suppose it's no use. I can't see what harm it would do for the boys to be here that day more than any other day. You can go off into your room, and pray if you want to; and the boys won't be doing any worse than they would do down in the village carousing round."

Stephen was angry, and was forgetting himself. Philip's cheeks flamed with indignant pity for the girl who winced under her brother's words.

"Oh, Stephen, *don't*, please! Let me think about it. I want to do what you wish if there is a right way." She spoke pleadingly. There were tears in her voice, but her eyes were bright and dry.

"Well, then, do it," said Stephen sulkily. "It won't hurt your Sabbath to give us some tunes on the piano. The boys will like that better than anything else. They don't hear music about here."

Margaret looked up troubled, but thoughtful.

"I'll think about it to-night, Stephen, and tell you in the morning. Will that do? I'll really try to see if I can please you."

Stephen assented sulkily. He had very little idea she would do it. He remembered her face that Sunday when she declined to ride with him. He set her down as bound by prejudices and of very little use in such a country as that.

But Philip, troubled, hovered about the door.

"Miss Halstead," he called pretty soon, "the moon is rising; have you noticed how bright the stars are? Come out and look at them."

"Come, Stephen," said Margaret.

"What do I care for the stars?" said Stephen sulkily, and he went into his room and shut the door.

Margaret's eyes were filled with tears, but she winked them back, and came to the door, anxious to get to the kindly starlight that would not show her discomfiture.

"Miss Halstead, I beg you will not think of doing what Steve asks," said Philip low and earnestly.

"Why not, Mr. Earle? Have you any conscientious scruples against company on Sunday?" Her voice was cold and searching.

"No, of course not," said Philip impatiently.

"Then why? You spent all day one Sunday off somewhere, presumably on a pleasure excursion."

"It was anything but a pleasure excursion, Miss Halstead," said Philip, his face growing dark with anger in the starlight. "But that has nothing whatever to do with the matter. I beg you will not do this for your own sake. You do not know what those fellows are. They will not be congenial to you in the least."

"Does that make any difference if they are my brother's friends?" Margaret drew herself up haughtily. "I thank you for your advice, Mr. Earle; but this is my brother's house, and of course I cannot stop his having guests if he wishes. I do not like company on Sunday; but, if they must come, I shall do my best to make it a good Sunday for them. More than that I cannot promise. Do you think I can?"

There was a mixture of coldness and pleading in her voice which would have been amusing at another time. But she had silenced Philip most effectually. He bit his lips, and turned away from the house to walk out into the starlight with his vexation.

Chapter 9

Margaret slept but little that night. A great plan had come to her, born of anxiety and prayer. At first she thought it seemed preposterous, impossible! She drew back, caught her breath, and prayed again; but over and over the idea recurred to her.

It was this. Perhaps God had sent her out here into these wilds to witness for Himself, yes, even among rough men like the two that had taken dinner with them that first day after her arrival.

Could she do it? Could she make that proposed Sunday gathering into a sanctified, holy thing? She, who had never spoken in public in her life, except to read a low-voiced essay from a school platform? She, who had always shrunk from doing anything publicly, and let honors pass her rather than make herself prominent? She who had never been taught in ways of Christian work, other than by her own loving heart?

Could she do it?

And *how* could she do it?

The utmost she knew about Christian work was learned in the class of boys she had taught in Sunday school at home. But they had been boys, most of them still in knee-trousers, and under home discipline. They had loved her, it is true, and listened respectfully to her earnest teaching. Even their mischief had given way before her hearty, trusting smile. They had learned their lessons, and thought it no disgrace to answer her questions. They had come to her home occasionally, and seemed to enjoy it, and she had talked with several of them about holy things. Two she had labored with and knelt beside while she heard their first stumbling acknowledgment that God was their Father and Jesus Christ their Saviour.

But this was all very different from bringing the gospel to a lot of men who knew little and cared less about God or their own salvation. She shuddered in the dark as she remembered the sound of that awful oath that Byron had let fall. How could she do it? Was it right and modest for her to try?

Then out of the night she seemed to feel her Saviour's eyes upon her, and to know that such things must not count against the great need of souls when she was the only one at hand to succor. And she bowed her head, and answered aloud in a clear voice.

"I will do what you want me to do, Jesus; only let me help save my brother."

The sleeper in the next room stirred, and started awake at the unusual sounds, and thought over the words he had heard, trying to put a meaning to them, but thought he had dreamed; so he slept again, uneasily.

After Margaret had said, "I will," to her Master the rest came easily. The plan, if it was a plan, was His. The Spirit would guide her. She had asked for such guidance. If it was of God, it would be crowned with some sort of success. She would be made to understand that it was right. If it was her own faulty waywardness, it would fail. It surely could do no harm to try to have a Sunday-school class of any of Stephen's friends who would come; and, if they refused or laughed at her, why, then she could sing. The gospel could always be sung, where no one would listen to it in other form. It would be a question of winning her brother over, and that might be difficult.

Stay! Why need she tell him? Why not take them all by guile, and make the afternoon so delightful to them that they would want to come again? Could she?

Her breath came quickly as the idea began to assume practical proportions and she perceived that she was really going to carry it out. She had ever a spirit of strong convictions and impulsive fancies; else she would have stopped right here. But perhaps in saying that too little weight is given to the fact that she had given herself up to the guidance of One wiser that herself.

Just before the stars paled in the eastern sky she lay down to rest, her mind made up, and her heart at peace. As for Philip's words of warning, she had forgotten them entirely. Philip she did not understand, but neither did he understand her.

The two young men were both surprised the next morning when she told them, quietly enough, that she would be glad to help them entertain their friends on Sunday afternoon, provided they would allow her to carry out her own plans. She thought she could promise them a pleasant time, and would they trust her for the rest?

It was very sweetly said, and her dainty morning gown, a touch of sea-shell pink in it this time that made her look like an arbutus blossom in the greenery of the room, sat about her so trimly that her brother could but admire her as he watched her put the sugar into his coffee.

It must be admitted that Stephen was surprised, but he was too gay himself to realize fully the depth of earnestness in any one else; so he concluded that Margaret had decided to let her long-faced ideas go, and have a good time while she was here; and he resolved to help her on with it. She was certainly a beauty. He was glad she had come.

But Philip's face darkened, and the little he ate was quickly despatched. After that he excused himself, and went out to the barn. He was angry with Margaret, and he was troubled for her. He knew better than she what she was bringing upon herself; moreover, her brother, who should have been a better protector of so precious a sister, knew even better than he. Why did not Stephen see, and stop it?

But Philip forsaw that matters had gone too far for it to be wise in him to say a word to Stephen. Former experience had taught him that Stephen took refuge from pointed attacks in flight to his companions in the village, which always ended in something worse.

Philip was so angry that after he had done all the work about the barn-yard that was ready for him he concluded to take himself away for a while. There was enough in the house to keep Stephen busy and interested for the day. The fear that had made him keep guard ever since the arrival of Margaret Halstead was for the time dominated by his anger at both brother and sister; and he took his revenge in going off across the country many miles on a piece of business connected with a sale of cattle which he had proposed to make for some time, but had put off from week to week.

He did not stop to explain to the household except in a sentence or two, and then he was off. Margaret noticed the hauteur in his tones as he announced his departure at the door, but so full was she of her plans for Sunday that she took little heed of it. It did not matter much about Philip anyway. He was only an outsider, and, besides, he would feel differently, perhaps, when Sunday came.

Philip's anger boiled within him, and grew higher and hotter as he put the miles between himself and the cause of it. He wished himself out of this heathenish land, and back into civilization. He decided to let people take care of themselves after this. Of what use was it to try to save this girl from a knowledge of her brother's true self? She was bound to find it out sooner or later, and she would perhaps only hate him for his effort.

But Stephen, after teasing his sister to discover what plan she had for the entertainment of their guests, made up his mind to make the most of Philip's absence, and get his guests well invited before that autocrat interfered. It was marvellous that he had not done so already. Therefore he slipped away to saddle his horse while his sister was busy in her room, and, only leaving a message with Marna, rode away into the sunlight, as gay of heart as the little insects that buzzed about his horse, and with less care for the morrow than they had.

Margaret was disappointed to find her brother gone when she presently came out, for she had planned to get him to do several little things about the house that morning, and while he was doing them she had intended to sound him on the friends he would invite. She wondered whether there were many and whether among them there would be any who could help her in the work of establishing her Sunday school. There must be some good women about there. Surely she could get a helper somewhere.

But perhaps this first time it would be only two or three of Stephen's best friends. He had spoken of "the fellows," and it would be better not to have any complications of womankind till she was well acquainted and knew on whom she could count for help. She admitted to her own heart, too, that she could open up the plan to them, and teach a class in her own way, better stilling the flutter of her own frightened heart, if there were no women or girls about to watch.

She was disappointed, it is true, but after a moment she reflected that perhaps even Stephen's absence was an advantage. She would take this quiet hour to study up a lesson and plan her programme, though it would be much easier if she knew just what kind of scholars she was to have. She spent a happy morning and afternoon planning for the Sunday, and only toward night did she begin to feel uneasy and hover near the door looking down the road.

Marna came in, shaking her head and muttering again, and it required all Margaret's faith and bravery to keep her heart up.

The night closed down like that other night when she had kept a vigil, and still neither of the young men appeared. Margaret wished that Philip would come, so that she might reassure herself by asking where he supposed Stephen had gone and when he would return. She acknowledged to herself that after all there was something strong and good to lean upon in Philip.

She prayed much that evening, and by and by lay down and tried to sleep. After several hours of restless turnings she did finally fall into an uneasy sleep.

But, when the morning broke with its serene sunshine, and neither of the two men had returned, she grew more restless. In vain did she try to settle to anything. She constantly returned to look off down the road.

Marna said little that day; but Margaret remembered her former words, and her old anxieties returned to clutch her till she was driven to her knees. As she prayed, a great, deep love for her new-found brother grew and grew in her soul till she felt she must save him, for instinctively she knew that he needed saving more than many.

And the second day wore away into the night, but still they had not returned.

Margaret lived through various states of mind. Now she was alarmed, now indignant that they should treat her so; and now she blamed herself for having come out here at all. Then alarm would succeed all other feelings, and she would fly to her refuge and find strength.

When the third day dawned and seemed likely to be as the others had been, she questioned Marna as to where she thought they could have gone; but the old woman shut her lips and shook her head. She did not like to tell.

She had watched the young girl long enough to have a tender feeling of protection toward her.

This third day was Saturday. Margaret had had some wild ideas of trying to saddle the horse and go out into the strange, unknown country to seek knowledge of her brother; but her good sense told her that this would be useless. She must wait a little longer. Some news would surely come soon. Resolutely she sat down to study the Sunday-school lesson just as if nothing had happened to disturb her, and to plan out everything for the morrow, trying to think that her brother would surely return for Sunday; but her heart sank low in trouble as the night came on once more, and she left her supper, which Marna had carefully prepared, untasted on the table while she stood by the dark window looking down the road.

Philip's anger had carried him far toward his destination. When at last it cooled with his bodily fatigue, and he began to reflect on the possibilities of what might happen during his absence, he would have been minded to turn back, but that his horse was weary and the day was far spent. Besides, it would be foolish to go back now when he had almost accomplished that for which he came. A few minutes with the man he sought would be all he needed, and perhaps he could exchange horses, or give his own a few hours' rest and then return. He hurried on, annoyed that it was growing so late.

There was some difficulty in finding the place, after all, for several old landmarks had been removed by a fire, and it was quite dark before he reached the lonely ranch of the man with whom he had business.

He had not known his own strong desire to return until he discovered how he was to be hindered. He found that the man whom he sought had gone to another ranch a few miles further on, and would probably not return for three or four days. It would be ridiculous to turn back and have his long journey for nothing. He must press on now and accomplish what he had come for. He got a fresh horse, and, taking only a hasty supper, spurred his horse forward through the darkness, trusting recklessly to his own knowledge of the country to bring him to the desired point.

Of course he lost his way, and brought up at the place the next morning when the sun was two hours high, only to find that the man whom he had come in search of had started back the afternoon before, and must be at home by this time.

Another delay and another fresh horse, and he was on his way back, too weary to realize how long a strain he had been under. And, when he reached the first ranch and found his man, he was so worn out that he dared not start home without a few hours' sleep. So, the business disposed of, he lay down to sleep, his mind tormented the while by thoughts of Stephen and his own discarded trust.

But worn nature will take her revenge, and Philip did not awake until almost sunset on the second day. Then his senses came back sharply with a vision of Margaret, a dream perhaps, or only his first waking fancies. She seemed to be crying out in distress and calling: "My brother! Stephen! O, save him, Philip!" And with the sound of that dream voice there came a great desire in his heart to hear her speak his name that way.

But he put this from him. He tried to remember that he had been angry with her, and that this whole thing was her fault anyway for not following his advice, and then he remembered that she had no knowledge or reason to follow his advice — a stranger. What did she know of him and his reasons for what he had said? In some way she must be told, but how could he tell her?

All these thoughts were rushing through his mind as he went out and was hunting up his own horse, hastily preparing to go home. He would not have stopped for something to eat even, had his host not insisted. Then it was only because the reasonableness of this act appealed to him that he finally yielded and ate what he was given.

And all the long miles back, most of it in darkness, Philip was thinking, thinking, cursing himself for a fool that he had left Stephen alone with his sister, almost cursing God that such a state of things was possible.

It was toward morning when he neared the handful of buildings that constituted the village near their home. The horse quickened his pace, and familiar things seemed to urge the travellers forward. Distant discordant sounds were in the air. A pistol-shot rang out now and again. But that was not unusual. Shots were as common as oaths in that neighborhood. They were a nightly occurrence, a part of a gentlemen's outfit, like his generosity and his pipe. Nearer the sounds resolved themselves into human voices, the deep bark of dogs, singing, the clinking of glasses, a slamming shutter, the gallop of a rider whirling home after a night of revelry, to strike terror to the heart of any who waited for him.

The muscles around Philip's heart tightened as a sickening thought came to him, and he put spurs to his willing beast, making the road disappear rapidly behind him.

Near the one open house in the village, where lights were still burning and whence the sounds came, he drew rein, and the patient horse obeyed, having felt that anxious check to his rein before. Close under the window he stopped. Listening and then rising in his saddle, he looked to make sure of what his heavy heart had already told him was true.

There in the midst of the room, on a table, his golden curls all dishevelled, his jaunty attire awry, his fine blue eyes mad with a joyless mirth, and his whole face idiotic with absence of the soul that lived there, stood Stephen. He had evidently been entertaining the company, and he was speaking as Philip looked.

"Jes' one more song, boys!" he drawled. "I got a go home to my sister. Poor little girl's all alone, all aloney. Zay, boys, now that's too bad, ain't it?" His voice trailed off into unintelligibility.

A great anger, horror, and pity rose within Philip. Pity for the sister, anger and horror over her brother. He had seen Stephen like this before, and had sadly taken him away and brought him to himself, excusing him in his heart; but he had never before felt more than a passing disgust over the weakness of the man who put himself into such a condition. He had gone on the principle that, if Stephen liked that sort of thing from life, why, of course he had a right to take it; but he had always tried to save him from himself. Now, however, the thought of the sweet, trusting girl alone in the night waiting for him — how long had she waited? — while the brother she had come to help and love bandied her name and her pity around among a set of drunken loafers — Philip stopped his thoughts short, and sprang into action.

Not in the quiet, careless way in which he usually entered upon such scenes and took possession of his partner did he come this time. His soul was roused as great men's are when they have a deed of valor to perform.

He strode into that maudlin company, and dashed men right and left. They rose from the floor in resentment, or reeled against the wall, and shook trembling fists, and felt for ready weapons; but Philip's wrath was mighty. They quailed before him. One word he uttered between set teeth and white lips.

"Fiends!"

Then he grasped the shrinking Stephen firmly, and dragged him from the table and from the room before the fiery men around him had realized and drawn their revolvers. One or two wild shots whistled harmlessly into the air after him, but he and Stephen were gone.

He put Stephen — already in a senseless state — upon his horse, and took him to a shanty where he knew that no one was living now; and all the rest of that night and through the brightness of Saturday he stayed guard over him.

Stern lessons of life he read to himself as he sat there watching the tainted beauty of the face lying before him. All Stephen's gay, winning qualities were hidden behind the awfulness of what the man had become. He had never seen it so before. He had simply borne with Stephen till he came out of one of these states and became his gay, companionable self again. Now all at once Philip looked with disgust upon him. And the difference was that up on the hill five miles away there sat a sweet, pure woman, whose trust and freely lavished love the man before him had basely betrayed.

When Stephen had slept long, Philip brought water, bathed his face, and made him drink. He was determined to make Stephen perfectly sober, and he was anxious to do this as soon as possible, that they might get home and relieve the anxieties of the girl who waited there. But it was a stern face that Stephen looked into from time to time, and it was a silent journey that they took that night when darkness had come down to cover them. Only one sentence Philip spoke as they neared the house, and it was in a tone that Stephen was not likely to disregard.

"Be careful what you say to your sister!"

Then Stephen wondered what had happened since he left home, and how many days he had been away, and sat soberly trying to think as he rode up to the house.

Margaret's white face met them at the door, and Philip spoke first, his tone anxious and earnest.

"I am afraid you have been lonely, Miss Halstead. I am sorry it happened so. You see, Stephen thought he must come after me, and we were delayed by the absence of the man we went to see. The ride was too much for Stephen. He is played out, I am afraid. He ought to go right to sleep. If you have any coffee there, I will carry him in a cup. It will do him good. No, he isn't sick, just used up, you know. Nothing to worry about."

Philip's voice was quite cheerful. If Margaret could have seen his face, she would have wondered at his tone. But Margaret had been sitting in the dark, and it took some minutes to light the lamp with her trembling fingers, shaking now from the relaxation of the strain.

"Hope I didn't scare you, Margaret," Stephen spoke, his gay, easy manner settling upon him like an old coat he had plucked from its familiar nail and fitted on. "You know one must not wait where duty calls. But I'll take Phil's advice, I guess, and turn in. I feel mighty seedy. All knocked up with the long ride."

Philip was soon back from caring for the horses, and took the smoking coffee from Margaret's hand. As she handed it to him, she looked into his face.

"How about you, Mr. Earle? You look as if you needed the coffee more than Stephen," she said kindly.

The tender tone was almost too much for Philip after the grim strain he had passed through. It had in it a note of his mother's voice when he used to come home with a bruise from a fall or a fight. He smiled faintly, and said most earnestly,

"Thank you!"

And when he came out from Stephen's room he found that she had set him a tempting supper on one end of the table.

She hovered about, waiting upon him till he was done, and told him to sleep late in the morning when she said good-night. Then she went to her room, buried her face in the pillow, and cried. She did not know why she was crying. It was not from trouble. Perhaps it was relief. When she grew calm, she thanked God for saving her from some nameless trouble that she felt, but did not understand, and begged of Him again, help for the morrow and the work she was going to try to do for Him.

Chapter 10

The healing of sleep settled down upon the little household late that Saturday night, and lasted far into the morning.

When Margaret awoke, the sun shone broad across her floor, and a sense of relief shone into her heart. As she went about her preparations for the day, an awe settled down upon her in remembering what she was going to try to do for Christ. She dared not think of any words she would speak, and she had not yet made up her mind how she would set about it to introduce her plan to the expected guests. She shrank as she remembered Byron's bold, handsome eyes, and wondered whether he would be among those invited, or whether he was Philip's friend alone. She shut her own eyes, and prayed that she might put away such thoughts and think only of the message she had to bring.

The two young men literally did as she told them, and did not awake until almost noon. Margaret had kept their breakfast waiting until it was too late, and then she hastened the dinner preparations; and so the first meal they ate together was dinner.

After dinner Philip hastened to the neglected horses, and to see after some matters at the barn, and Stephen threw himself upon the couch. The day was chilly, and Marna had kindled a fire on the hearth. It crackled pleasantly, and Stephen was feeling the relief that comes after a throbbing headache has ceased. He took up a book from his sister's case, and began to read. He seemed to have forgotten all about his company, and Margaret thought perhaps he had not invited them after all, and it would be best not to speak about it. He was tired, and it would be much better for him.

There was immense relief to her in the thought that her task, which at times assumed proportions impossible, would be put off indefinitely. And yet there came a strange pang of disappointment, for her careful study of the lesson had revealed to her hidden blessed truths which the Spirit had made her long to impart to others. She wondered whether she could muster courage to suggest to Stephen that he and she, and perhaps Philip, too, if he liked, study the lesson together. She was sitting shyly by the piano, looking at her brother behind his book, and meditating whether she should ask him about it, when the door burst open most unceremoniously, and three young men stood upon the threshold.

To be sure, they knocked uproariously upon the opening door, and their greeting was loud and hilarious. Margaret arose, startled. But they stopped as suddenly as they had begun, and looked about upon the strange, changed place. This was a room with which they were unacquainted, many times as they had ascended the hill to make good cheer for Stephen. And the woman who stood silent by the piano was a lady, and was beautiful beyond any question.

It was as if they had come expecting summer weather, and were suddenly plunged into a magnificent snowbank. They stood embarrassed and for the moment silent, just as the other two strangers had stood, a little while before. All the effrontery of their brave, outlandish Western attire deserted them. The instinctive feeling of each man was self-defence, and involuntarily their hands sought the place which held the inevitable weapon. Not that they meant to draw it, only to feel the cold, keen protection of its steel assuring them.

They had been gentlemen born, these three, at least in appearance, but had long ago forgotten what that word meant. Perhaps it was the harder for them, therefore, to understand the beauty of purity and art, having once known it and wandered so far from its path, than if they had never seen it.

They were wordless for the moment, not knowing how to occupy the new position.

Stephen came airily forward. He was glad Philip was out of the way for the time. He hoped he would remain away until things were well going.

"Welcome!" he said with a wave around the place as if it were a palace and he the king. "My sister, Margaret Halstead, gentlemen. Margaret, this is Bowman, and Fletcher, and Banks."

Margaret bowed in a stately way she had, which made her seem much taller than she really was, and kept at a distance any man whom she chose to keep so. Nevertheless, there was in her manner a smile of welcome, which seemed to the three strangers something like a cold bit of sunshine that had fallen their way and charmed them, but did not belong to them.

They came in and sat down, trying to assume their natural voices and easy speeches; but a mist of convention was enveloping them round, which they could not drive away. All but Banks.

Banks was small, slightly hard of feature, with an unfeeling slit of a mouth and hateful, twinkly black eyes that were not large enough to see anything wonderful. He carried about him an ill-fitting self-complacency that belonged to a much larger man. His collegiate career had been cut short by his compulsory graduation to an inebriate asylum and later to the West.

Banks essayed a remark to Margaret which would have caused Philip to sling him out the door if he had been there. It was complimentary and coarse in the extreme. Fortunately Margaret did not understand it, and stood in dumb amazement at the shout of laughter that was raised. She was glad when the door was darkened again by other guests, for she felt there was something painful in the atmosphere. She looked for Stephen to stand beside her; but he was already slapping shoulders with a newcomer, and her gaze met Byron's bold eyes bent in admiration as he came forward and attempted to take her hand by way of greeting, having a desire to show to the others his superior acquaintance with the queen of the occasion. But Margaret drew her hand behind her, and held him back with the gentle dignity of her greeting. He felt that she had not forgotten their last meeting and the words she had spoken to him. Her glance reminded him reproachfully of it. He saw he must not expect to be her friend with that between them. The blood stole up his swarthy cheeks, and he stood back conquered, to see Bennett—whom he knew to be no better than himself, but whom she did not know—greeted with a welcoming smile.

Bennett's white eyelashes fell beneath the glory of that smile, and his freckles were submerged in red. He sat down hard in a Morris chair that was several inches lower than he had expected, while Banks carolled out a silly song appropriate to the moment. This happened to be Bank's role, the bringing in of appropriate songs and sayings at the wrong minute, and causing a laugh.

Margaret looked about the room bewildered. The place seemed to be swarming with great, bold, loud, men. She remembered Philip's warning, and gasped. One moment more, and she felt that her head would be whirling dizzily. She must get command of the situation or fail. Surely her Strength would not desert her now, even though she had made a mistake. She lifted her soul to God, and wished while she prayed that Philip would come in. Philip somehow seemed so strong.

There were but seven men invited, though they looked so many. They were for the most part the pick of the country thereabout, at least among Stephen's friends. He had intended to be careful on Philip's account, for he knew Philip would not stand any one that would be outrageous. But Stephen's discretion had forsaken him with the first taste of liquor that passed his lips, and two had crept into the band worse than all the rest. Well for Margaret that she was strong in her ignorance of this.

"Well," began Stephen, and Margaret saw that now was her opportunity if she would not let this strange gathering slip from her control.

"My brother asked you to come this afternoon because he thought you might enjoy some music and reading," she said in a clear voice that commanded instant silence, "and I shall be very glad if I can give you any pleasure."

Then she smiled upon them like an undesired benediction, and each man dropped his eyes to his feet, and then raised them, wondering why he had dropped them.

"Won't you all sit down and make yourselves comfortable?" she went on pleasantly. "We should like to have you feel at home."

"Be it ever so humble, there no place like home," sung out Banks flippantly.

"Shut up, Banks!" said Bennett, turning redder, and glaring from under his white eyelashes at his neighbor.

"I want to get acquainted with my brother's friends, of course," went on Margaret, not heeding this accompaniment to her words. She had suddenly the feeling that she was holding a pack of hounds at bay, much as one feels when starting a mission school of wild street arabs. She must say the right thing at once and work quickly, or her cause would be lost.

"I don't know what kind of music you like best; so perhaps you will excuse me to-day if I play you my own favorites. I'm going to begin at once, please, so that we shall have plenty of time for them all, because by and by I want you all to sing."

They looked at her as they might have watched some new star in a theatre, wondering, awed for the minute by the strangeness, but not permanently. It takes a great deal to awe a Western cowboy.

Margaret turned with a sweep of her white draperies, and sat down at the piano. As she did so, she caught a glimpse of Philip standing in the doorway, his rugged face written over with disapproval and anxiety. It spurred her to do her best; and, laying her fingers upon the keys, she imparted her own spirit to them.

Some music lay upon the rack before her. It was not what she had intended to play first, but it would do as well as anything. She felt she must waste no more time in beginning, for Philip's face looked capable of almost any action if there was suffient cause.

It was Handel's "Largo" that sounded forth through the room with swelling, tender strain. She felt that perhaps it was not the right thing with which to hypnotize her audience, but she put her soul into it. If it were possible for music to express sacred things and true, then her music should do so. But, had she known it, music of any kind was so rare a treat and so unique that she might have played even a common scale for a few moments and had her audience until the strangeness wore away.

She gave them no time, however, to grow restless; for she glided from one thing to another, now a great burst of triumph, and now a tender sympathetic melody, and all of them connected in her own mind with sweet days of worship in her childhood's church at home. Instrumental music might not convey anything of a Sabbath nature to these untamed men, but it certainly could be no worse than no attempt at it, and she was feeling her way.

Philip stood like a grim sentinel in the doorway. The company felt his shadow and resented it, but were engrossed with the music at first. Philip could not let himself enjoy it. He stood as it were above it, and let it break like waves about his feet. He felt that he must, or some wave might ingulf them all.

He watched their faces as a great watchdog might eye intruders, mistrusting, lowering, a growl already in his throat.

The wonder of the spell the girl had cast about them had not yet touched him. He was guarding her.

Suddenly she felt the pressure of emotion too strong for her. With a chord or two she dealt "one imperial thunderbolt that scalps your naked soul," as Emily Dickinson has put it, and stopped.

They caught their breath, and, coming out from under the charm, turned toward Philip to take their revenge for his attitude.

But Margaret was all alert now. She felt the disturbance in the air. She moved quickly.

"You must be thirsty," she said, unconsciously using a term that meant more to them than she dreamed. "I'm going to give you a cup of tea. Stephen, call Marna to bring the kettle, please; and Philip, will you pass the cups?"

There was a gentle deference in her tone as she addressed Philip, almost as if she would ask his pardon and acknowledge that he was right about what he had told her.

There was something more also, a pleading that he would stand by here and help her out of this scrape into which she had allowed herself to go.

The soul of Philip heard and responded, and his quiet acquiescence sustained her all through the afternoon. It was as if there were some unspoken understanding between them.

The men watched her curiously as she moved about the room, collecting strange, thin, little dishes, the like of which some of them had never seen, and others had almost forgotten. There was enough of the unexpected and interesting about it to keep them moderately subdued, though a muttered oath or coarsely turned expression passed about now and again, and Banks tried a joke about the tea which did not take very well.

Margaret, however, was happily ignorant of much of this, though she felt the general pulse of the gathering pretty accurately.

The tea came speedily, for Marna had obeyed orders implicitly, and had been hovering near the door with a curious, troubled expression and shaking head. With the tea were served delicious little cakes of sugary, airy substance, olives, salted almonds, and dainty sandwiches.

The whole menu was just what Margaret would have used at home with her own friends. She knew no other way. Extravagant and unusual? O, certainly, but she did not realize this, and the very strangeness of it all worked for her anew the charm she had broken when she ceased to play, and kept the wild, hilarious spirits she would tame quiet till she had the opportunity for which she had been praying.

They vanished, these delectable goodies, as dew before the sun. The capacity of the company seemed unlimited. The entire stock of sweet, dainty things from carefully packed tin boxes that Margaret had brought with her would scarcely have sufficed to satisfy such illimitable appetites.

"They eat like a Sunday-school picnic," thought Margaret to herself, laughing hysterically behind the screen as she waited a minute to catch her breath before going out to try her hand at the most daring move of all her programme.

Then she looked across to where Philip stood watching her with faithfulness written in every line of his face, and saw that he was eating nothing. She motioned him to her, and gave him with her own hands a cup of tea. It was well she gave it behind the screen; for, had the others seen it, a bitter rivalry would have begun at once for favors from the lady's hand.

He took it from her as one might take an unexpected blessing, and drank it almost reverently, if such a thing can be.

Then he looked up to thank her; but she was gone, and he saw her standing, palm-surrounded, near the piano again, her soft white draperies setting her apart from the whole room, and her golden hair making a halo about her head, the rays of the setting sun just touched her with its burnished blessing like a benediction upon her work. Philip felt, as he looked, that she was surrounded by some angelic guard and needed no help from him. His stern expression relaxed, and in its place came one of amazement.

She was talking now in low, pleasant tones, as if these men were all her personal friends. Each man felt honored separately, and dropped his gaze, that the others might not know.

She was telling them in a few words about her home, and how she had come out there alone to her brother, now that she was alone in the world. She was putting herself at their mercy, but she was also putting them upon their honor as men, if they had any such thing as honor. Philip was doubtful about that, but he listened and wondered more.

Then she told them about the first Sabbath she had spent here, and how shocked and disappointed she had been to find no church or Sabbath services going on near by. She told them how she missed this, till they could not but believe in her sincerity, though such a state of mind was beyond their ken entirely; and she spoke of her Sabbath-school class at home, and how she loved the hour spent with them, until each man wished he might be a little boy for the time being, and offer her a class.

"I haven't asked my brother if I may," she said with a girlish smile, turning toward Stephen as he sat disturbed and uncomfortable in the corner. She felt intuitively that Stephen would count it a disgrace to be implicated in this manner, and thus honorably exonerated him. "But I am going to ask whether you would not be willing to help me make up for this loss I have felt. Perhaps some of the rest of you have felt it too."

Here she gave a quick, searching look about the circle of sunburnt faces.

"I wonder if you will help."

They straightened up, one or two, and looked as if they would like to assent, but Margaret went quickly on. She did not want to be interrupted now till she was done; else she might not have courage to finish.

"I am going to ask if you will help me have a Sunday school, or Bible service, or something of that sort. I will try to be the teacher unless you know of some one better—"

There was a low growl of dissent at the idea that any one could equal her, and Margaret flushed a little, knowing it was meant for her encouragement.

"We could not do much as they do at home in the East, but it would be keeping the Sabbath a little bit, and I think it would help us all to be better. Don't you?"

She raised her eyes, at last submitting the question to them, and the slow blood mounted in each face before her, while shame crept up and grinned over each shoulder. When had any one ever supposed that they wanted to be helped to be better?

"Now, will you help me?" She asked it in a sweet, pleading voice, and then sat down to wait their decision.

Chapter 11

But shame does not sit easily upon such as Banks. He roused himself to shake it off. He seldom failed in an attempt of that sort. He saw his opportunity in the intense silence that filled the room.

> "I am a little Sunday-school scholar, lah, lah,
> I dearly love my pa and ma, ma, ma, ma;
> I dearly love my teacher, too, too, too, too,
> And do whatever she tells me to—to, to, to,
> Teacher, teacher, why am I so happy, happy—"

He had chanted the words rapidly in his most irresistible tone, and he expected to convulse the audience and turn the whole gathering into a farce; but he had sung only so far when strong hands pinioned him from behind, gagged him with a handkerchief, and would have swiftly removed him from the place but that Margaret's voice broke the stillness that succeeded the song. Her face was white, for she realized that she had been made the subject of ridicule; but her voice was sweet and earnest.

"O, not that, please, Philip. Let him go," she said. "I'm sure he will not do it again, and I don't think he quite understood. I don't want to urge anything you would not all like, of course. I want it very much myself, though, and I thought perhaps you would enjoy it too. It seems so lonely out here to me, without any church."

She sat down, unable to say more, it must be left with God now, for she had done all she could.

Then up rose bold Byron. It was his opportunity to redeem himself.

"My lady," he began gallantly, "I ain't much on Sunday schools myself, never having worked along that line; but I think I can speak for the crowd if I say that this whole shootin'-match is at your disposal to do with as you choose. If Sunday school's your game, we'll play at it. I can sit up and hold a book myself, and I'll agree to see that the rest do the same if that'll do you any good. As for any better teacher, I'm sure the fellows'll all agree there's not to be found one within six hundred miles could hold a candle to you, so far as looks goes; and as for the rest we can stand 'most anything if *you* give it to us."

It was a long speech for Byron, and he nearly came to grief three times in the course of it because of some familiar oath that he felt the need of to strengthen his words.

Philip, as he held the struggling, spluttering Banks, glared at Byron threateningly during it all, and wondered whether he would have to gag the entire crowd before he was through; but Byron stumbled into his chair at last, and Margaret, to cover her blushes and her desire to laugh and cry both, put her hands up to her hot cheeks, and wondered what would come next. Then a wild, hilarious cheer of assent broke from the throats of the five other guests, and Margaret knew she had won her chance to try.

"O, thank you!" was all she could gather voice to say; but she put much meaning into her words, and the men felt that they had done a good and virtuous thing.

"Then we will begin at once," said Margaret, almost choking over the thought that she was really going to try to teach those rough big fellows a Bible lesson. "Mr. Byron, will you pass that pile of singing-books? And let us sing 'Nearer, my God, to Thee.' You must all have heard that, and I'm sure you can sing. Philip, please give this book to your friend, and release him so he can help us sing," and she actually was brave enough to smile condescendingly into Banks's mean little eyes.

Philip took the book, and let Banks go as he might have given a kick and a bone to a vagrant dog; but he looked at this most remarkable Sunday-school superintendent with eyes of wonder.

And they could sing. O, yes, they could sing! From their great throats poured forth a volume of song that would have shamed many an Eastern church choir. They sang as they would have herded cattle or forded a stream, from the glad, adventurous joy of the action itself; and more; they sang because they were trying to help out a lonely, pretty girl, who for some mysterious reason was to be helped by this most pleasant task.

As she played and listened to the words rolled forth, Margaret found in her heart a flood of uncontrollable desire that they all might know the meaning of those words, and sing them in very earnest.

The lesson, the same one that she would have taught, had she been at home with her class of little boys, began with the grand and thrilling statement:

"There is therefore now no condemnation to them that are in Christ Jesus, who walk not after the flesh, but after the Spirit."

They listened respectfully while she read the lesson in her clear voice. But the words conveyed very little to their minds, and it is doubtful, when she began to talk about a prisoner condemned to death and a pardon coming just in time to save him, whether they connected it in the least with the words she had been reading, or whether they even recognized them as the same she had read, when she repeated them later after having made the meaning clear.

It was simple language she used, with plain, everyday stories for illustrations; for she was accustomed to teaching little boys. But a doctor of theology could not have more plainly told the great doctrines of sin and atonement than did she to those men whose lives were steeped in sin, and to whom the thought of conviction of sin, or of condemnation, seldom if ever came.

They felt as if they had suddenly dropped into a new world as they listened, and some of them fidgeted, and some of them wondered, but all were attentive.

She did not make her lesson too long. For one thing, her own trembling heart would have prevented that. She had feared that she would not have enough to say to make the lesson of respectable length; but, when she began, the need of the souls before her appealed to her so strongly that she found words to bring the truths before them.

Philip watched her in amazement. She reminded him of a priestess robed in white, the palms behind her and her gold hair crowning her. He could think of nothing but Hypatia and her wonderful school of philosophy of old, as she opened up the simple truths. Looking about on the hard faces, softened now by something new and strange that had come over their feelings, he felt her power, and knew her way had been right; yet he feared for her, was jealous for her, hated all who dared to raise their eyes to her.

What power was it that made her able thus to hold them? Was it the mere power of her pure womanhood? Or the fascination of her delicate beauty? No, for that would have affected such men as these in another way. They would have admired, and openly; but they would not have been quiet or respectful.

Another thought kept forcing itself to his mind. If the God whom she was preaching, whom she claimed as her Father, should prove indeed to be the one true God, was he, Philip Earle, condemned? But this thought Philip put haughtily aside.

"I have been thinking," said the teacher, "as I sat here talking, how beautiful it would be if Jesus Christ were yet on the earth so that we could see Him. What if He should walk into that door just now?" and she pointed to the doorway where they had all entered.

Involuntarily each man lifted his eyes to the door, and Philip with the rest.

"He would come in here, just as He used to come into households in those Bible times, and we would make room for Him, and you would all be introduced."

Some of the men moved restless feet. Their thoughts were growing oppressive.

"And you would all see just what kind of a man, and a Christ, Jesus is," went on the sweet voice, "You could not help admiring Him, you know. You would see at once how gracious He is. You would not be—I hope—I think—none of you would be like those people who wanted to crucify Him—though we do crucify Him sometimes in our lives, it is true; but if we could see Him and know Him it surely would be different. He would call you to be His disciples, just as He called those other disciples of His, Philip and Andrew and Matthew and John and Peter and the rest."

Unconsciously Philip Earle flushed and started at his name. She had never called him Philip until that afternoon, and he thought for the moment she was speaking to him now.

There were others who looked conscious, too, for Bennett's name was Peter, and Fletcher's name was Andrew, and two others bore the name of John. Because of these little coincidences they were the more impressed by what she said.

"And what would you answer Him?" She paused, and there was stillness for just a minute in the room.

"I am going to tell you what I want for you all." She said it confidingly. "It is that you shall know Jesus Christ, for to know Him is to love Him and serve Him. And suppose as we study in this class that you try to think of yourselves as men like those disciples of old, whom He has called, and that you are getting acquainted with Him and finding out whether you want to answer His call. Because until you know Him you cannot judge whether you would care enough for Him for that. Will you try to carry out my fancy?"

She had struggled much with herself to know what she should do about prayer. It did not seem right to have a service without it, and she did not feel that she could pray. It was unlikely that the others would be willing to do so. She had settled on asking them all to join in the Lord's Prayer until she saw them, and then she knew that would not do. She even doubted whether many of them knew it. Her faint heart had decided to go without prayer, but now in the exultation of the moment she followed the longing of her heart to speak to her Father.

"Please, let us all bow our heads for just a minute and keep quiet before God," she said, and the silence of that minute, wherein seconds were counted out by great heart-beats, was one whose memory did not fade from the minds of the men present through long years of after experiences.

Awful stillness, painful stillness! Banks could not bear it. All his weak flippancy seemed singled out and held in judgment by it. He wanted to escape, wanted to break forth in something ridiculous, and yet he was held silent by some Unseen Power, while the terrible seconds rolled majestically and slowly around him.

"O Jesus, let us all feel Thy presence here, Amen!" said Margaret as if she were talking to a friend.

Then she turned quickly to the piano, and before the raising of the embarrassed eyes that dared not look their comrades in the face, lest they should be discovered as having been bowed in prayer, soft chords filled the room, and Margaret's sweet voice rang out in song.

"Abide with me," she sang; "fast falls the eventide."

The room had grown quite dusky, lighted only by the glowing fire in the fireplace, which Philip had quietly replenished from time to time with pine-knots that sent fitful glares upon the touched and softened faces of the men, while they sat rapt in attention to the music.

A few more chords, and the melody changed,

> "Weary of earth, and laden with my sin,
> I look at heaven and long to enter in;
> But there no evil thing may find a home,
> And yet I hear a voice that bids me, 'Come,'

> "So vile I am, how dare I hope to stand
> In the pure glory of that holy land?
> Before the whiteness of that throne appear?
> Yet there are hands stretched out to draw me near."

Soft chords came in here, like angel music that seemed to float from above them somewhere. It was a way she had with the piano, making it speak from different parts of the room and say the things she was feeling. The listeners half looked up as if they felt there were white hands stretched toward them.

The sweet voice went on:

> "It is the voice of Jesus that I hear,
> His are the hands stretched out to draw me near,
> And His the blood that can for all atone,
> And set me faultless there before the throne.

> "O Jesus Christ, the righteous! live in me,
> That, when in glory I Thy face shall see,
> Within the Father's house my glorious dress
> May be the garment of Thy righteousness.

> "Then Thou wilt welcome me, O righteous Lord;
> Thine all the merit, mine the great reward;

Mine the life won, and Thine the life laid down,
Thine the thorn-plaited, mine the righteous, crown."

"And now will you all sing a few minutes?" said their leader, turning toward them in the firelight, her fair face filled with the feeling of the prayer with which her song had closed.

"Philip, will you give us some light? Now let us sing 'I need Thee every hour' before you go home."

They growled out all their superfluous, bottled-up feelings into that song, and made it ring out, till Marna crept around and peered into the window to watch the strange sight. She stood there muttering in amazement, for such a miracle she never saw before. Perhaps Missie could work charms on even her, if she could make those wild fellows sit quiet there and sing that way.

And then they found themselves dismissed.

"I shall expect you next Sunday at the same time," she said, smiling, "and thank you so much for helping. It has been so good, almost like a Sunday at home. I have a delightful story and a new song for you next Sunday."

Greater marvel than all the rest, they went out quietly beneath the stars, mounting their horses in silence, and rode away. One attempt on Banks's part came to a dismal failure. Philip, standing at the door, heard the silly, swaggering voice rollicking through the night. "I dearly love my teacher, too, too, too, too," and Bennett's unmistakable roar, "Shut up, you fool, can't you?" as the song was brought to a summary close.

Byron had dared to linger a moment by the teacher's side, and with an expression almost earnest on his face had asked,

"Aren't you ever going to forgive me?"

"You must go to the One you insulted for forgiveness," answered Margaret gravely. "When you have made it right with Him, I will be your friend."

Then Byron dropped his boastful head, and walked away silent and thoughtful.

They turned, then, Philip and Margaret, and found themselves alone. They could hear Stephen slamming around in his room, the thud of first one boot and then the other thrown noisily across the floor. Stephen evidently was not in a good humor.

Margaret's face grew sad, and she realized that through the whole afternoon her thoughts had been more taken up with the others than with the brother she had come to try to save. Had the message reached him at all?

Seeing Philip standing in the door watching her, the look of wonder still upon his face, her expression changed. She went over to where he stood, and, putting out one hand, touched him gently on the coat-sleeve. "I did not understand," she said simply. "You were right. I ought to have listened to you."

He looked down at the little hand with finger-tips just touching the cuff of his sleeve, as if it had been some heavenly flower fallen upon him by mistake; and then he said, his voice all strange and shaking, "No, it was I who did not understand. You have been *wonderful!*"

Chapter 12

The days passed busily now. The queer little dwelling on the hill grew in beauty and interest with every passing hour. Stephen did his part, and seemed pleasant enough about it, although the first few days after the Sunday school he was strangely moody and quiet. Margaret could not tell whether or not he was pleased with what she had done.

And now she lured the two young men to gather around the hearth in the evenings while she read aloud to them in carefully selected books which touched their experiences of life and made them forget themselves for a little while. Margaret's power of song was equalled only by her ability to read well; and no dialect, be it negro or Scotch, was too difficult for her to enter into its spirit and interpret it to her readers. So long had they been out of the world that some of the best books about which people had raved for a few days and then forgotten had passed them by entirely. These were among her favorites, and now she brought them out and read them, while the two sat by and listened, much moved, but saying nothing except to laugh appreciatively at some fine bit of humor.

Thus she read "Beside the Bonnie Brier Bush," "A Singular Life," "Black Rock" and "The Sky Pilot"; and then went further back to George Macdonald, and chose some of his beautiful Scotch stories, "Malcolm," "The Marquis of Lossie," and "Snow and Heather." Over this last they were as silent as with the rest, but now and then Margaret noticed that Stephen covered his face with his hand and Philip turned his eyes away from the light while she was reading about the "Bonnie Man."

This sort of thing was all new to the two lonely fellows, who were used to making companions of the woods and fields and dumb beasts, and letting life go for little. This world of the imagination peopled life more richly. But ever when a book was finished Stephen would grow restless, and sometimes go off upon his horse, and Philip too would disappear. When they returned, — it might be late the same night, or after a day had passed, — Margaret could not tell which of the two, if either, had been the one who started first, and her heart grew heavy.

She rode with Stephen or with both of them quite frequently now, and was getting to be an expert horse-woman. She knew the ways about the country, and had seen some beautiful views. But not once had either of her escorts taken her near to the railroad station where she had arrived, nor pointed out what she fancied must be the semblance of a village. When she asked them, they always put her off, and more and more she wondered why.

With some trepidation she faced the next Sabbath, half fearful that her class would come again, half fearful lest they should not. But they came, every one, and brought two or three others along. There was not much need for Philip to stand guard, as he did, at the rear of the company, ready to spring should any slightest insult be offered to the teacher.

They had odd ways, these rough scholars of hers, and were as undisciplined as a company of city ragamuffins; but they respected the beautiful girl who chose to amuse herself by amusing them, and they listened quietly enough.

After the first wonder wore away they had the air of humoring her whimsical wishes. It pleased them to take it this way. It helped them to humble themselves into respectful attention. But ever, now and again, some word of hers would strike home to their hearts; and there would come that restless, noisy moving of the feet, that dropping of the eyes and avoiding one another's gaze, as each tucked his own past away within his breast, and fancied no one knew.

They grew to love the singing, and put their whole souls into the hymns they sang together; but they liked it more when Margaret sang to them the songs which sometimes brought back to them the days when they had been innocent and pure.

There was always, too, that solemn hush, that moment of silent prayer, before the one trembling but trustful sentence Margaret spoke to God. And sometimes, as the weeks went by, this or that man would find himself saying over in his own heart that sentence she had prayed the week before. It was not often she used the same sentence. Always it was something that touched the heart-experience or impressed the lesson-thought upon the mind.

The first prayer she had uttered in that house would always remain with Philip—"O Jesus, let us all feel Thy presence here." And, as he looked about the glorified room, it did seem as if a Presence had entered there, and come to stay. He often thought, as he sat waiting for the reading to begin in the evenings, of how that room had looked the night her letter came, and of how much he had hated the thought of her coming. Now, how light would go out of his life, should she go away! She did not know that. She never would, most likely. She was as far above him as the angels of heaven, but her coming had been as a gift from heaven. Would it last? Would she care to stay and keep it up? And Stephen, sitting on the other side of the hearth! Who could tell what were his thoughts as he alternated between his fits of moody silence and gay restlessness?

There came a day when Philip and Stephen were at work upon some fences, mending weak places where the cattle had broken them down. And in the afternoon Margaret put on a thin white dress with a scarlet jacket, and wandered out to where they were at work.

The day was bright and warm for late October, really hot in the sun. The light scarlet jacket was almost superfluous, but it served to intensify the scarlet in the landscape; and so she came, a bright bit of color into the prosaic of their work.

She had meant to talk to Stephen. In her heart she had been keeping some precious words she meant to say to him as soon as an opportunity offered. She longed to see him give himself to Christ. As yet she saw no sign that he had even heard the call to become a disciple.

But Stephen was in his most silent mood. He answered her in monosyllables, and at last gathered up his tools and said he was going to the other end of the lot. She saw it would do no good to follow him, for he was not in a spirit to talk; so, saddened and baffled, she walked slowly along by the fence toward the house. Until she came close to where he stood she had not noticed that Philip was working now right in the way where she would have to walk.

He stood up, and welcomed her with a smile, and offered her a seat on a low part of the fence, where the rails had some of them been taken down.

It came to her that perhaps her message to-day was for Philip rather than Stephen; so she climbed up and sat down.

He stood leaning against the supporting stakes near her, and the breeze caught a fragment of her muslin gown, and blew it gently against his hand. It was a pleasant touch, and his heart thrilled with the joy of her presence so near him. The muslin ruffle reminded him, with its caressing touch, of the wisp of hair that had blown across his face in the dark the night she had come.

A great, overpowering desire to tell her that he loved her came to him, but he put it aside. She was as cool as a lily dropped here upon this wayside, and talked with him frankly. But there was a something in their intercourse this afternoon more like their first brief talk about the moon than there had been since the night she came. She seemed to understand what he was saying, and he to interpret her feeling of the things in nature all about them. He dropped his tools, and stood beside her, willing to enjoy this precious moment of her companionship.

She looked across the fields to the valley, the other hills beyond, and a purple mountain in the distance, while he followed her gaze.

"You see a picture in all that," he said briefly, as if reading out her thoughts.

She smiled.

"Was it for all this that you gave up your home and friends, and came out here to stay?"

His face darkened.

"No," he said, "I was a fool. I thought life's happiness was all in one bright jewel, and I had lost mine."

"O," she said, looking at him searchingly, sorrowfully. "And, when you found out that was not so, why did you not go back?"

"Perhaps I was a fool still." He spoke drearily. He would not tell her the reason why he had stayed.

There was silence for a few minutes while each looked at the dreamy mountains in their autumn haze, but neither noted much of what was to be seen.

"There is a jewel you might have, which could not be lost. It is a pearl. The pearl of great price. Do you know what I mean?"

"Yes, I understand," he answered, deeply moved, "but I am afraid that would be impossible."

"O, why?" said Margaret, with pain in her voice. "Don't you care the least in the world to have it? I thought I saw a look of longing in your face last Sunday when we talked about Jesus Christ. Was I mistaken?"

Then she had been watching him and cared. Last Sunday! The thought throbbed in his throat with a delirious joy. He lifted his hand, and laid it firmly on the bit of fluttering muslin on the rail beside him. It was all he dared do to show his joy that she cared even so much.

"No, you were not mistaken," he said, his voice choking with earnestness. "I would give all I own to feel as you do , but I cannot believe in your Jesus as more than a man of history. If it were true, and I could believe it, I would be His slave. I would go all around the world searching for Him till I found Him if He were upon earth. But I cannot believe. I would not shake your sweet belief. It is good to know you feel it. It makes your life a benediction to every one you meet. Don't let my scepticism trouble you, or make you doubt."

"O, it couldn't!" said Margaret quickly, decidedly. "You could not shake my belief in Jesus any more than you could shake my belief in my mother, or my father, you know. Because I have known them. If you should tell me I had not had a mother, and she was not really good and kind to me, I should just smile, and pity you because you had never known her. But *I have*, you know. I do not blame you, for you have never known Jesus. You have not felt His help, nor almost seen Him face to face. You don't know what it is to talk with Him, and know in your heart He answers, nor to be helped by Him in trouble. You think I imagine all this. I understand. But you see I *know* that I do not imagine it, for *I* have *felt*. You may feel too, if you will."

"I wish I might," said Philip with a sigh.

" 'And ye shall find me, when ye shall search for me with all your heart,' " quoted Margaret softly, wistfully. "And there is another promise for such as you. God knew you would feel so, and He prepared a way. 'He that doeth His will shall know of the doctrine, whether it be of God—' "

"Do you really think that is true?" asked Philip, looking into her eager face.

"I know it is. I've tried it myself," she replied with emphasis.

There was silence broken only by the whisperings of some dying leaves among themselves.

"Won't you take that promise, and claim it, just as you would take a bank-bill that promised to pay so much money to you, and present it for payment? Won't you do it—Philip?"

She had never called him that before except the first day of the Sunday school. It seemed to have been done then as a half-apology to him for not following his advice. After that day she had gone back to the formal "Mr. Earle" when she was obliged to address him by name at all.

Philip started, and crushed the bit of muslin between his fingers.

He was deeply affected.

"How could I?" he said softly.

Margaret caught her breath. She felt the answer to her prayer coming.

"Just begin to search for Him with all you heart, as if you *knew* He was somewhere. You never have tried to find Him, have you?"

"No."

"Then try. Kneel down to-night, and tell Him just how you feel about it, just as you have told me. Talk to Him as if you could see Him. You may not feel Him right away; but by and by, when your whole heart is in it, you will begin to know. He will speak to you in some way, until you are quite sure. Take as many other ways to find out, too, as you can, all the ways there are, of course; not that it matters so much, though, about your mere reason's being convinced; for, when you have felt Him near, you will know against any kind of reasoning. But take the way of talking with Him. It is the quickest way to find Him."

"But should I not feel like a hypocrite, talking to One in whom I do not believe, of whose existence I have even no assurance?"

"No, for you said you wanted to find Him. It would be reaching out for what your heart desires, just as the untaught heathen do."

Philip flushed.

"You think I am a heathen," he said reproachfully.

"No, Philip, only a child of God, lost in the dark. I want you to find the way back."

"But suppose I do this, and nothing comes of it. Then you will be disappointed."

"What has that to do with it?" she said with a motion as of putting any thought of herself aside; "and something will come of it. No soul ever went to God in that way and nothing came of it. Besides, there is more you can do. There is the other promise. 'He that doeth His will.' After you have come to Him, and told Him that you want to find Him, but you cannot believe, and have asked Him to show you how, you can set to work to do His will. For through the doing what He would like to have you do a part of Himself will be revealed. Now, will you go to Him and tell Him all about it, to-night, and begin to try to find Him? Will you?"

Philip had drawn his hat low over his eyes, and stood looking off to the crimsoning sky. The sun had sunk low as they talked, and the air was growing chill. Margaret, in her intentness, did not know how grateful she was for the warmth of the little scarlet jacket. She waited silently and prayed while Philip thought.

At last he turned to her, and held out his hand with a grave smile.

"I will try," he said.

"With all your heart?" asked Margaret, as she laid her little white hand in his.

"With all my heart," he said reverently, as he looked into her eyes and pressed the hand he held.

Margaret let him know by the quick pressure of her hand-clasp how glad she was.

"And I shall be praying, too," she said softly.

Philip's heart quickened. It seemed to him like a holy tryst.

The young man picked up the idle tools, and they started toward the house, walking slowly through the twilight. They did not say much more. They were thinking of what had been said and promised. It was enough to walk quietly together thus and know what had passed. Stephen was not in sight. He must have gone to the house some time before.

But, when they came in and were ready to sit down to supper, he had not come yet, and Philip went out to call him.

Margaret listened to his shouts, strong, deep, full, with a note of earnest purpose in them. They grew more distant, and she thought he must have gone back to the lot where they were that afternoon to see what was keeping Stephen. She waited a long time by the door, and they did not come, and then she went in to search out the book she wanted to read to them that evening. Marna was keeping supper hot in the kitchen.

Suddenly there came a sound of rapid horse-hoofs down the road. She rushed to the door, and looked out. Down against the western sky, which still kept a faint blush from the sunset, now gone on its way to conquer other days, she saw a rider, hatless, galloping, etched for a moment against the sky. Then he was gone.

A sudden fear filled her heart. She put her hand to her throat, and rushed to the kitchen.

"Marna," she cried insistently, "did my brother come to the house before we did?"

The old woman shook her head.

"Brother rode off fast 'fore dark," she said doggedly, as if she did not wish to tell, but had to.

"Marna," said the girl, catching the old woman's arm in a grasp that must have been painful, "you talked about brothers drinking. I want you to tell me true if you know anything about it. Does my brother go where they drink?"

The old woman shut her lips, and a stubborn look came into her eye. She did not reply.

"Quick! Tell me at once," said Margaret, stamping her foot in her excitement. "Do they both drink? Is that why Stephen and Philip go away so suddenly sometimes? Do they both drink?"

"No!" said the old woman quickly. "Not both drink. One all right. Pretty good man. He take care. Bring other home. Heap good man."

"Which one, Marna?"

"Big man, heap good," answered Marna.

"And my brother drinks?" demanded Margaret, the sad truth hers now. "Answer me."

The old woman hung her head and nodded. It was as if she felt responsible.

Margaret had let fall the arm she held so tight and was standing still for one brief minute with her hand upon her heart, too frightened to cry out, too bewildered even to frame a prayer; but her heart was waiting before God to know what she should do. Then swift as thought she turned, and, snatching up her little scarlet jacket as she ran, fled toward the barn.

The old woman looked up to try to say something comforting, and saw her vanish through the open door. She hobbled after her, some faint idea of protection coming to her withered senses. She found her in the barn with white, set face, struggling with the buckles of the saddle-girth. The two empty stalls beside the one remaining horse had made good her fears.

It was the poor old horse that had been left, for Philip needed the best in his chase through the night. Margaret had never ridden this horse, but she did not stop to think of that.

"Buckle this!" she commanded, as Marna came wondering into the barn, and she held the lantern that Philip had left lighted to find his own saddle.

"Missie no go out 'lone," pleaded Marna after she had done the bidding of the stern little voice. "Missie get lost. Big man find brother. Bring home. Missie stay with Marna."

"I must go," said Margaret quietly in tones of awful purpose. She swung herself into the saddle without stopping to think, as she usually did, how she was ever to get up to that great height. And she was doing it alone now.

"Now had me the lantern!" she commanded, and Marna obeyed, her hand trembling. Tears from the long-dried fountains of her soul were running down her cheeks.

The old horse seemed to catch her spirit, and started off snorting as if he felt battle in the air. Some instinct carried him after the others who had sped along that road but a few minutes before. Or perhaps he had been that way before so many times that he could think of only one direction to take as he flew along.

Margaret held her seat firmly, grasping the lantern and the bridle with one hand, and tried to think and pray as the night wind, wondering, peered into her face, then turned and gently crept with her, protectingly, as if it thought she needed guarding.

Chapter 13

Margaret had forgotten all her fears of former rides, lest the horse should stumble or take fright, lest the saddle should slip or she be thrown. Even the dark had lost its terror.

Somewhere near here the road cut away sharply at its outer edge, and went down to a great depth. She might be even now close upon it, and any moment the horse's feet slip over the precipice. But her heart trembled not. The Father was watching. She must go to find her brother.

Just why it was strongly borne in upon her that she must go herself, and not wait for Philip to find Stephen, perhaps Margaret could not have told. It may have been a wish to see for herself just what was Stephen's danger. Possibly, too, it was fear for Philip. Were Marna's words true? "The big man no drink." O, what comfort if she might be sure of that! What a tower of strength would Philip then become!

Riding, and praying, and trusting to God, she was carried safely through the dangers of a short cut that Philip, knowing and fearing, had avoided, and she galloped into the main road only a moment after Philip had passed the spot.

The moon stood out like a silver thread hung low and useless against the horizon. It made but little difference in the darkness.

Margaret felt anxious to catch up with Philip if possible, or at least get within sight of him. It would not do to catch him too soon, or he would send her back; and that she could not bear. So she pushed on and after a short time could hear the sound of his horse and catch fitful glimpses of a dark form riding hard.

By and by she came out upon a bridge across a gully deep as darkness; how deep she could not see as she peered down for one awful glimpse, and then closed her eyes, and dared not look again. It was too late to turn back, for the way was scarcely wide enough for that, and the bridge swayed horribly with the horse upon it.

She held her breath as if that would make her weight the lighter, and dared not think until she felt the horse's feet touch solid ground. Then behind her came a snap, as sharp as if some giant tree had parted, and something, a bit of timber from the rail, perhaps, fell far and long below.

If the bridge had been one foot longer, or the horse had been going a little slower, horse and rider might have been lying down below in that sea of dark trees. The lantern slipped from her trembling hand, and fell crashing in the road; but the horse flew on, frightened, perhaps, by the danger he must have felt, following habit, too, in these long, wild rides to a certain goal he knew, and had travelled toward many a time before the new third horse came to be used in his stead.

But Philip had not crossed the crazy bridge that had been for some time now discarded, and indeed was supposed to be blocked by logs across its entrance. Either the old horse had jumped the logs in the dark, or some one had dragged them away to use somewhere else.

Philip, further down the road, had crossed by the new bridge, and had not known of the rider rushing along through dangers so profound.

He heard the crashing of the falling rail, and the sound of flying hoofs a moment later. He checked his horse, wondering who could be riding behind him. For a moment the possibility that Stephen had not got ahead of him, after all, but had tried to blind him by going another way, passed through his mind; but he looked back and saw only the darkness, and heard the steady thud of the horse's feet. It was not like the gait of Stephen's horse. He pushed on; but occasionally he halted once more, pursued by the feeling that he ought to wait till that rider came up with him.

Then from out the darkness twinkled the lights of the village below him. In a few minutes he would be at his journey's end. He could see the flare of the saloon lights now, and almost hear the tinkle of the glasses and the sliding of the wooden chairs upon the wooden floor. He paused once more, for the other horse was very near now. It would do no harm to wait a second.

Then from out the night he heard his name called once, in a wild, frightened cry, like a sob, as of some one whose breath was almost gone,

"Philip!"

He stopped and waited as the horse came swiftly toward him, something white taking shape upon its back, till he saw the girl, her face white like her dress, her hair all loosened by her ride, unheld by any hat.

One word he spoke.

"Margaret!"

He had never used her name before in speaking to her. He did not know he used it now. But she did, even in her fright; and it seemed to give her courage and renewed strength.

"Don't stop; keep on!" she cried as her horse almost swept by him and he was forced to start his own horse again to keep alongside of her. "Don't lose a minute's time. I know all about it now. Let's hurry!"

"But, Margaret, you must not go!" he cried, putting out his hand to catch the bridle. "Why did you come? And how? It cannot be you crossed the broken bridge."

"It broke just after we got across, I think," she shuddered. "But do not think about it now. I am here. I cannot go back alone, and you must not turn back with me. Let us hurry on to save Stephen."

"But you cannot go down there. It is not safe for a woman."

"I am going, Philip. I am going to save my brother. And God is with us. There is no danger." In some way she managed to impart her eagerness to the old horse, and before Philip knew what she was doing she flew down the road far ahead of him.

It of course took but a moment for him to catch her again; but their gait was too rapid now to admit of talking, and the lights of the saloon were straight ahead. The horses knew their goal, and were making for it with all their might.

They stopped by the open window, from which coarse laughter was issuing into the night, foul with words and thick with oaths. Margaret raised her eyes, and saw what she had come to seek, her brother Stephen, standing gayly by the bar, a glass of something just raised to his smiling lips.

Stopping not to think of her unbound hair or the rough men staring all about, she slid from the horse, cast the bridle from her, and ran to the open door, from which a wide shaft of light was lying on the darkness of the pathway.

Like a heavenly Nemesis she appeared before their astonished gaze, and some who had already drunk deep that night thought she was the angel of the Lord sent to strike them dead.

She stood there in her limp white drapery, with long golden hair and outstretched arms, and only the vivid scarlet of the little jacket gleaming here and there like a flame among the glory of her hair.

She rushed to her brother, and dashed the glass from his hand even as he held it to his lips; then, turning to the roomful, she looked at them with one long, mournful, pitying, condemning glance. There were the Sabbath class to a man, standing before her. They were not drunk, for most of them could stand a good deal of liquor.

She said not one word to them, but just searched each face with a quick, heartrending glance, then turned, and drew her brother away.

Philip had tried to stop her as she flew from her horse to the open door; but she vanished from his hand like a thing of the air, and now he stood behind her ready to protect or help, even with his life. But she needed no help. Like darkness before the light they fell at her coming; and no one, not even Banks, raised a word or a laugh at her expense.

Even Stephen yielded unwillingly, and followed her from the room. Out into the night she led him, silently to Philip, with none to hinder or scoff. It was as if a messenger from God had walked into that saloon and plucked Stephen away, searching each soul that stood there with one glance of flame.

The little cavalcade started out into the night; and as the sound of their going died away from the silent throng inside the lighted room, each man drew apart from the rest, moving noiselessly out into the darkness, and went his way by himself. The saloon was utterly deserted except by one or two old topers too sodden with drink to understand. The barkeeper cursed the girl who had thus descended and stopped business for that evening. But he soon put up his shutters and turned out his lights.

All silently the three rode, and the tired horses moved slowly.

Stephen went ahead with bowed head, whether in anger or in shame they could not tell. Margaret and Philip rode abreast. Not a word they spoke as they went through the dark. Once Philip turned and looked at the frail girl by his side, her white face and gown lighting up the darkness. He thought she was shivering, and he silently took off his own coat, and buttoned it around her. She tried to protest by a lifted hand; but he would not be denied, and she smiled wanly, and let him fasten it around her. By common consent their communication was wordless. Stephen was close in front.

When they came out on the road near where Philip had first heard Margaret's call, he reached out, took her cold, white hand that lay limp on the saddle-cloth, and held it in his warm, strong one all the rest of the ride. Again she let him have his way, and took comfort in the reassuring pressure.

When they reached home, she did not burst into tears and hang about Stephen's neck, begging, pleading, and reproaching. She was too wise for that, and her trouble much too deep.

She made him lie down on the couch by the fire. She brought some strong coffee that Marna had ready, and an inviting supper, and tried to make him eat. But, when she bent over him to ask whether he would sit up, she saw that upon his face there were tears that he had turned away to hide. Then she stooped and kissed him; and, kneeling there beside him with her face near to his, she prayed. "O Jesus Christ, save my dear brother!"

She kissed him again, and drew a little table close with the supper upon it, leaving him to eat it when he would, while she prepared something for herself and Philip.

Unreproached by any words, Stephen went to his room a little later and laid him down, more miserable than he had ever been in the whole of his gay, reckless life. Thoughts that till now had been too grave to be admitted to his mind entered and had their way. Searching questions he had never asked himself were poured upon him. Through them all he heard, and could not keep from hearing, his sister's voice on the other side of the thin board partition as she prayed and pleaded for her brother's salvation.

All night long he wrestled with the two spirits that were at war over him; the spirit of the demon that cried for drink, aroused by the few drops that had but wet his lips ere the glass was dashed from them; and the spirit of God's Holy One who strove to have him for eternity.

He sat dejectedly beside the fire the next morning after breakfast. His young face showed the wear of the night in haggard lines. He looked up as Margaret came over to him, and smiled wearily.

"I'm not worth it," he said. "You'd better give me up."

Margaret came and sat down beside him.

"I will never give you up, Stephen, until you are safe," she said.

He reached out and took her hand.

"You are a good sister," he said. That was all, but she felt that hereafter he would not be against any effort she made in his behalf.

It seemed as if he could not let her out of his sight the next few days; if she left the room, he followed her, and when he closed his eyes he saw a vision of his sister in white with burnished golden hair like some sweet angel of mercy come to save.

When the Sabbath came, Margaret doubted whether she would have any class but Stephen and Philip. Her heart was heavy over them all. More than she knew had she hoped that they were being led near to Christ. Now all her hopes were gone. Of what use was it to pray and preach and sing to men like this? Men who could stand about and watch quietly or help on the degradation of one of themselves. She had been reading deep lessons of the morals of that country ever since she came, but not until that night in the saloon had she realized how little she had to build upon with any of them. She even looked at Philip doubtfully sometimes. How could he be different from the rest, since he was one of them?

Philip had not presumed upon the intimacy of that night's wild ride. He was the same quiet, respectful gentleman, only with this difference: there was a promise between them; and, when he looked at her, his eyes always seemed to let her know he had not forgotten it.

But contrary to her expectations the entire company of men trooped in at the regular hour, and seated themselves, perhaps with a little more ostentation than usual.

Margaret welcomed them gravely. She was not sure of them, even though they had come. Marna had been telling her just before dinner about a circus, and a painted lady who was to dance in the saloon that afternoon.

"Men no come to-day," she had said. "If come, no stay late. Go see dance-woman."

Margaret's heart had sunk. Of what use was it for her to try to help these men if they were going straight to perdition as soon as she was through?

Margaret's fingers trembled as she played, and she had chosen minor melodies with dirge-like, wailing movements. The singing even was solemn and dragged, for the men only growled instead of letting out their usual voices.

They turned to the lesson, and Margaret read the text; but then she pushed the Bible from her and lifted troubled eyes to them, eyes in which tears were not a stranger. There was helpless despair in her attitude.

"You came here because I asked you to help me start a Sunday school, but I am afraid I have done you more harm that good," she said. The tragedy of it all was in her voice.

"You have been studying for a good many weeks now about Jesus Christ. I have told you how He loves you, and wants you, and how He took the trouble to leave his Home and come down here to suffer that you might be saved from sin, and come home to live with Him. It hasn't seemed to make a bit of difference. You have listened just to humor me, but you haven't done a thing to please Him, my dearest Friend, for whom I did it all. You have kept right on in your wrong ways. You have gone to places that you knew He would not like. You are planning, some of you, perhaps, to go to a wicked place this afternoon when we are through with the lesson. I have been showing you the right way, and you have chosen the wrong. It would be better for you that you did not know the right than, knowing it, that you should not take it. I have made a great mistake. I have shown you the loveliness of Christ, and you have treated it with indifference."

Her lips quivered, and she turned away to hide the tears that came. The nights of anxiety and the days of excitement were telling on her nerves. She could not for the moment control her sadness. She put up both hands, and covered her face.

The silence was profound.

Then up rose Bennett in his might, he of the white eyelashes and the red hair. His face was mantled with blushes, but there was a true ring to his voice.

"My lady," he said, — it was the way they spoke of her with a deferential inflection that made it something different from the ordinary way of saying that, — "we're pretty rough, I know, and you can't say anything too bad about us, perhaps; but we ain't that bad that we're ungrateful, I know. We promised to stick by this thing, and we're a-going to do it. I don't know just what it is you want, and I don't think the other fellows sense it; but, if you just speak up, we're with you. If it's the drinking you mean, we'll shut up that saloon if you say so, though it'll be a dry spot fer some of us without it. And, if it's that there dancing-woman, if a single feller goes out of this room with intentions of visiting her scene of action, he goes with a bullet in him."

Bennett paused, and held his deadly weapon gleaming before him, covering the whole room with it. Banks started back in terror, and then recovered himself and laughed nervously; but the other men faced Bennett steadily, and their silence lent consent. It was evidently understood so by

Bennett, for he put the revolver back in his hip pocket, and resumed the unusual labor of his speech.

"As fer treating any One with indifference, we ain't meant to. It's just our way. We've listened respectful like to what you said about Him, and ain't questioned but what it's all so. But we ain't just up to this Sunday-school act, and don't know what to do. If you'd just say plain what 'tis you want, we might be able to please."

Margaret turned her eyes all bright with tears to the young man, and said with earnestness:

"I want you to be like Him, Mr. Bennett, to live like Him, to love Him, to grow to look like Him. That is what He wants. That is why He sent the message to you."

Bennett stood abashed at the awful disparity between the One spoken of and himself. He looked at her helplessly.

"I'll be gashed if I know what you mean," he replied with fervor; "but, if you'll make it all out easy fer us, we'll try."

It was late that night before she sent them away, for she had prolonged the lesson and the singing, and then had read them a tender story, full of the tragedy, the love, and the salvation of life.

They rolled forth their closing song with their magnificent voices as if they meant it. The words were,

"Just as I am, without one plea,
But that Thy blood was shed for me,
And that Thou bidst me come to Thee,
O Lamb of God, I come, I come."

They were all there yet. Not one of them had stolen away to the revelries in the village. If Banks had entertained thoughts of doing so, he had not dared.

She had asked them to sing the words as a prayer if they could, and each man sang with his eyes on his book, and a strange new look of startled purpose was dawning in some faces.

Then they went out into the starlight silently, but first each man paused and shook hands with Margaret as she stood by the door. They had never done this before. They would not have dared to touch her lily hand unless she gave it them now.

The hand-clasps were awkward, some of them, but each one was a kind of pledge of new fealty to her.

Last of all came Byron, his bold eyes dropped. He did not know whether she would touch his hand or not. He stood hesitating before her. It was something new for him to be embarrassed.

"Will you take my Christ for yours?" she said, looking up and comprehending.

"If I know how," he answered brokenly.

Then out came her eager hand, sealing the promise with a warm grasp of friendliness, and Byron walked out of that door, a new sense of honor dawning in his breast.

She turned back to the room, her face bright with feeling. Stephen stood behind her, and, bending as if he had come for that, kissed her on the forehead, and went quickly into his room, shutting the door behind him.

Then Margaret stood alone with Philip.

Chapter 14

"Had I the grace to win the grace
Of maiden living all above,
 My soul would trample down the base
That she might have a man to love.

"A grace I had no grace to win
Knocks now at my half-opened door;
Ah! Lord of glory, come Thou in;
Thy grace divine is all, and more!"
— George Macdonald

"I have been thinking," said Philip, a strange new light in his eyes, as he turned toward her from the firelight into which he had been looking, "of what value are unbeliefs? They do not change facts. I will throw away mine. I will take your Christ. If there is no Christ, I shall lose nothing. If there is, I shall have gained all. Margaret, I take your Jesus to-night to be my Saviour."

He said it solemnly, as one utters a vow for eternity; and the girl stood looking up at him, the radiance in her face reflected in his own.

When he had gone to his room that night, he closed the door and knelt down. A strange gladness was in his heart. He found that he did not shrink from praying, but longed to register his vow, to begin his new life.

"O Christ!" he murmured, reaching out longing arms as if to grope for and find the desire of his heart, "O Christ! Come to me! Show me! Let me know Thou art here. Let me never go back to doubting. I will give Thee all myself, though it is worth but little. Only come to me! Jesus! Jesus! I take Thee as my Saviour!"

It was a different prayer from what he might have prayed if he had not know Margaret. Even if his will and desire had been stirred to praying at all without her influence, he would not have used such language, he would not have spoken to Jesus, the Christ, if he had not heard Margaret's simple, earnest talks of Him every Sunday. He would naturally have spoken to God more distantly, his praying would have been less insistent, and perhaps he would not so soon have received the blessing.

Some one has said that prayer is the throwing of the arms of the soul about the neck of God.

Philip had laid his soul before the Christ, and all tenderly, as if the great arms of God had folded about him, there came to his soul a sense of the presence of Jesus.

"How sweet the name of Jesus sounds in a believer's ear!" they had sung once in the Sunday class, and Philip had curled his lip quietly, in his corner behind the piano, over the sentiment. How could it be possible that the name of One who has never been seen could be dear, no matter how much one believed?

But now in the new, sweet dawn of his own second birth he suddenly knew that the name "Jesus" was sweet to him. How it had come about, he could not explain. He said it over and over, gently at first, for he feared the sweetness might depart, and then more confidently, as his soul rang with the joy of it. It was true, after all, and one could feel Jesus' presence just as Margaret had said.

With a sense of great peace upon him he lay down at last to rest, but before he closed his eyes in sleep he murmured,

"I thank Thee for sending — Margaret!" and he spoke the name lingeringly and reverently.

They did not say much to each other, Philip and Margaret, about the wonderful change that had come into Philip's heart; but there was a secret understanding between them that made their eyes look glad when they met across the room, and Margaret's heart sang a little song of triumph as she went about her work. It was not for several days that Philip dared to tell her he was beginning to get the answer to his prayer that she had promised, and how he knew that now what she had said was true.

The days went by in much the same way that the preceding ones had gone, save that both Margaret and Philip exercised a more vigorous watchfulness over Stephen. The evenings were spent in delightful readings, and Margaret invented all sorts of little things she wanted made, which the young men could work at while she read.

Margaret was getting to be a good rider since her adventure by night. It seemed to have freed her from all fear, and constantly the three rode about the country together, enjoying the clear, crisp days as the winter hastened on.

It was about this time that there came to that region a young minister, who had broken down in his first charge, and who had come out to the West to fight nervous prostration on a cattle-ranch. He was an earnest young fellow with no foolish notions, and he had not been long at his new home before he had made friends of the men with whom he was constantly thrown. He had a desire to do them good in some way, though it must be confessed he saw little hope for any such thing. He did not feel well enough to preach, even if there had been any encouragement for starting religious services on

Sunday. There seemed to be no church within possible reach, and he pondered much as he rode, and laughed, and learned, of the rough men who gave him no easy lessons, how to rub off the "tenderfoot" looks and ways.

At last, one day he questioned a man from his own ranch. Was there no service of any kind held in the whole of that region? Did they not know of even a Sunday school? Surely there were some Christian people.

The man whom he happened to question was Banks.

Now Banks had been growing exceedingly unpopular among the members of the select Sunday class which met with Margaret Halstead, because he did not take kindly to the extreme principles she taught, nor yield up his rights in the matter of drinking and gambling as some of the others were discussing the possibility of doing. He had made one or two attempts to raise an opposition to the power of the fair young priestess, but they had not been successful. He felt his loss of prestige, and with a half-idea of revenge by getting the minister on his side, and running him in opposition to the young teacher, he began to tell him about the Sunday school.

Banks had a gift of imitation, and a vein of what he supposed was humor. He used them both in this case, and the result was not to the advantage of the Sunday school. However, the young theologue was not altogether without some insight into character. He did not take all that Banks told him as strictly true; and, when the fellow wound up by offering to take him around to the school the next Sunday, he decided to accept the invitation. It would at least give him a chance to study the men and see what influence was able to hold them. It also held out the only opening for a religious service that the neighborhood afforded.

"But you must wear your outfit things, or the boys'll get on to you bein' a preacher, an' make it hot fer ye," said Banks. "They won't have any snobs around. The teacher might think you'd come to break up the meeting, and Earle might take a notion to put you out the back door."

The minister wondered what kind of a strange Sunday school this might be to which he was to be taken; but he quietly accepted the advice, and the next Sunday just as the opening hymn was being sung—Banks had timed his coming well, when all would be occupied and there would be none to dispute the appearance of the newcomer—they walked into the room and sat down.

The minister looked about him in wonder on the beauty and refinement everywhere visible, but his eyes were held at once by the loveliness of the girl who, dressed in soft white, presided over this motley gathering. His eyes went from the hard faces of the men to her pure profile, in wonder, again and again.

There was an ease and mark of the world about the minister, even in his cowboy garb, that Philip noted at once. He drew his brows together in almost his old frown of displeasure as he watched him covertly, jealous of the looks the minister cast at Margaret, jealous of his easy way of smiling and accepting the book that Banks handed him open to the place. It was not till the name "Jesus," repeated several times in a chorus that was being sung, reached Philip's heart, and felt for that vibrating chord that was learning to thrill with joy over the name of his Master, that he realized what an ugly feeling toward this utter stranger had sprung up within him all unbidden. He tried to down it, and looked about for some hospitality to offer the visitor, but in spite of himself he felt dismay at the presence of this man. He was different from the other fellows, and Margaret would see it at once.

Fortunately for Margaret she had no time to look the stranger over closely until after the lesson was done; else she might have been disconcerted. She had long ago overcome her fear of the men she taught every Sabbath, through her intense desire to lead them to the Saviour; but, had she known that her audience that afternoon contained a full-fledged minister fresh from a long theological training, she would have trembled and halted, and perhaps have had no message to deliver that day.

She went through it all as usual, the solemn, silent waiting, and the simple, earnest prayer; and the young minister felt that there were things he had yet to learn about preaching which might not be learned in any theological seminary.

She found him out as soon as he spoke to her, however, which was at the close of the lesson and while they were passing the usual cups of delicious tea and the cakes. She knew him for one of her own world, and welcomed him pleasantly.

Now the minister was small and slight. In contrast with Philip and Stephen and the others he looked insignificant to Margaret's eyes, newly grown accustomed to this giant build of men. So, when he asked permission to come to the class sometimes, she did not feel the trepidation that she would have felt before she came out here. He positively declined to teach. He said his physician had forbidden anything of the sort, and he thanked her warmly for all the help she had given him that afternoon. She found afterwards that he had left her with the impression that he needed help, too. He did not seem to have the same idea about a personal friendship with Jesus Christ that had grown so dear to her.

She felt strengthened, however, at the thought of another Christian to help in the work, and began at once to plan how she would ask him to explain deep points in the lessons that she might in turn explain them to the class. He seemed a bright, interesting young man. Margaret was glad he had come. He was from near her own home, also, and knew many of her intimate friends. That made him doubly interesting.

As the winter went on, the minister began to drop in upon them at sunset, occasionally, to spend the evening. Stephen had taken a fancy to him, and encouraged his coming. Margaret rejoiced at this, and made the minister more welcome because Stephen liked him.

During the long evenings they would read and talk and have music, much as when they were alone.

The minister naturally gravitated to a seat beside Margaret. It was his hand that turned the music for her when she played, and his voice that joined in the duets they sang, for he was something of a musician as well as theologian.

He was also a good reader, and often took the book from Margaret, and read while she rested or busied her hands with a bit of embroidery.

Occasionally the entire Sunday class would be invited for an evening of reading and song. At such times the minister proved to be an admirable helper always ready with some witty saying or a good recitation. He had the power of whistling in imitation of different birds, and would whistle wild, sweet tunes to a running accompaniment on the piano.

He was not altogether unpopular among the men. He had the sense to keep any extra self-esteem he might have brought out West well locked away in his breast, carrying about with him always a hearty friendliness. The men could not help liking him, and Margaret more and more turned to him for advice and looked for his help in planning for her different gatherings. But when he was present Philip was always silent and gloomy.

Three times during that winter did Stephen grow restless and slip away. Twice his faithful guardians came galloping after him when he was scarcely out of sight of the house, and took him on a long ride that ended only late at night, when they all were worn out; but they brought him safely back, sober. The third time he met Bennett on his way, who immediately suspected and shadowed him till he made sure, whereupon he laid strong hands upon Stephen, and insisted on riding home with him.

Margaret had hoped and prayed. She had even ventured to talk with Stephen at dusk sometimes, when he would come in and throw himself down upon the couch by the fire. He always listened, but he said very little. Not much hope had she ever received from him that he was paying heed to her earnest pleading to come to Jesus Christ and be a new man.

And the winter wore away into the spring.

Chapter 15

"All I could never be,
All, men ignored in me,
This, I was worth to God."
— Robert Browning

It was one day in early summer that the minister and Stephen set out on a long ride. They were to return in time for supper, and Margaret had planned a pleasant evening for them all. "The boys," as the Sunday class were now called, were all coming.

She stood watching them ride away into the pleasant afternoon light, and wondered whether the minister would improve his opportunity to say a word to Stephen. She felt very sad about her brother. He did not seem to get any further toward eternal life.

Philip was to have gone with the riding party; but a message in the morning had called him in another direction to attend to some business, and he would not return till evening.

Margaret watched the two riders out of sight, and then went in to finish her plans for the evening. There were one or two little things she wanted to do for an unusual attraction. She was always thinking of new things to win these men into another world than the one they lived in every day.

The two riders went to a distant ranch famed for its superior cattle. They passed spots of marvellous beauty on the way, and stopped to look and wonder; and the minister did improve his opportunity to speak a few earnest words to Stephen, as Margaret had hoped he would do.

Stephen answered sadly, half wistfully, but would not commit himself. He did not repel the words, and seemed to like his companion even better that he had dared to speak.

They spent some time going about the ranch, and late in the afternoon turned their horses homeward.

They had gone about half-way back when a messenger overtook them to beg the minister to return. A whisper had gone around the place that one of the visitors was a minister. The mother of one of the men was lying very ill, not likely to live, and she begged that he would return to pray with her. The message, scrawled feebly, was so pitiful that no one, least of all the kind-hearted young minister, could refuse.

Stephen insisted upon going back with him, but this Mr. Owen would not allow. He said that Stephen must go home and tell his sister the circumstances. He would come as soon as possible. The messenger offered a fresh horse and an escort for returning, and the minister said he would be with them before the evening was over. It would not do for Stephen to go with him, as his sister would wait supper and it would spoil all their plans.

It was a disappointment to the young man, and a deep one. All day as he rode through the brilliant air his heart had been rejoicing over the thought of the evening. He had formed a little plan during the past week, that to-night he would ask Margaret to ride with him some day soon. Then he could have her all to himself, and perhaps—that was as far as he let his thoughts go in the presence of others. He liked to be by himself when he thought of Margaret.

Many miles away there rode another man, thinking of Margaret, too, and of the minister, sometimes letting his heart rejoice over the smile the girl had given him and the little wave of her white hand in farewell as he rode away that morning, sometimes feeling the heavy gloom of foreboding as a vision of the delicate, spiritual face of the minister rose before him. For Philip had long known that he loved Margaret better than his own life. Now and then he lifted his eyes up to the clear blue overhead, and called from his heart to his Father, and her Father, not praying, not asking for anything for himself, for he did not dare do that, but just to assure himself that there was a heavenly Father who belonged to them both, who loved them both, and would do well. More than this he did not venture to think.

Stephen sat in his saddle, watching his friend out of sight on the road they had just come together. He felt a strong impulse even yet to turn and follow him. Something told him it would be better. Something whispered that here was his safety. He half called to them as they disappeared around a knoll; and then, remembering that Margaret would be watching anxiously for them, and determining for once to show he was a man and could be trusted, he reluctantly started his horse on alone.

But the devil came also.

The devil had not had so good a chance at Stephen for nearly a year. He had been watching his opportunity, and had almost given up this soul that was once so firmly in his clutches. But now he came swiftly, and attended him with all his old arts and many more beside. He whispered:

"You'd better ride around by the town, and go through, and then you can tell Margaret how strong you are."

That was the first thought. Ride through town, and not go into the saloon, nor stop once to talk to any one! He would enjoy knowing that he could do that. He might even try to be the Christian Margaret and the minister wanted him to be if he could do that once. He would not be so ashamed. He half decided he would do it, and turned it over in his mind, that mind so easily influenced by his own imagination that to think of going through town was almost as much of a temptation as going. He could see how the saloon-keeper would stand at the door and look, and wonder, and perhaps call. He could smell the odor of the familiar room as it was wafted out into the road from the swinging blind door.

Something wild seized him with the thought of that odor. A spirit that would not be downed. He forgot that he had intended to ride safely through town to astonish and please his sister by his strength. He forgot his half-desire to be a Christian. He forgot the words the minister had spoken, which indeed had taken deep hold upon his wavering nature. He forgot everything save that one fiendish thirst for strong drink, and he set the spurs cruelly into his faithful horse, and rode like mad, his breath coming in great, hot waves through his lungs. His eyes grew blood-shot, and all the devils in the service of the arch-fiend flew to urge him on. There were miles yet to be covered, but that was nothing. He was alone and unsuspected. He had time to get there and get all he wanted. All he wanted! For once no one could stop him, for no one would know until the minister came back, and that might not be to-night.

He turned upon a road that would not lead past home, and galloped on. It was the road his sister had taken in her wild night ride after him and Philip.

It was quite dusk when he neared the bridge that she had crossed in safety and but just escaped with her life. He knew the bridge had long been disused. He knew that it was considered extremely unsafe. He did not know of the great supporting timber that had parted and fallen into the ravine below on the night Margaret had crossed. But he knew enough about it to make him feel even in his most daring moods, heretofore, that he would rather not try to cross it.

But something stronger than reason was urging him to-night. This bridge would lead to a crossroad where he would not be in danger of meeting any of the fellows coming up to Margaret's gathering. The fellows had of late been a sort of self-constituted watch-guard. He could not shake them off. They had kept him many a time from himself. He would escape them all to-night. The fever in his blood had taken fire through all his veins. A blind purpose took possession of his reason.

With sudden quick jerk of the bridle he turned his trembling horse, and put him at the bridge, nor would he let him lessen his gait. He half knew in his wild folly that his safety lay in getting over quickly, if safety there was. And so under full gallop the panting horse flew at the bridge in the fast-gathering darkness.

It wavered and cracked, and wavered long, and then suddenly, too late, the horse drew back upon his haunches with a frightened snort almost human in its anguish, and poised a moment in mid-air! The bridge did not reach across the chasm! One whole section had fallen! The last support was tottering in decay!

One awful second Stephen realized his position, and saw in vivid panorama the follies of his life and the sins of his heart. Saw, and cried out in one wild cry to God, in acknowledgment and late submission. The cry rang through the upper air, down into the dark ravine; then all was blackness of unconsciousness to Stephen as bridge, horse, and rider fell crashing below!

The supper had stood waiting for some time when Philip came. Margaret was growing restless, and was glad to see him. His face was anxious when he heard that the riders had not returned, though he tried to laugh it off and say the minister was not used to long rides. Perhaps it had been too much for him, and they had had to stop to rest; but in another half-hour Mr. Owen, his horse all covered with froth, rode gayly up to the door, and dismounted.

He made his apologies, explained his lateness, and then looked around for Stephen.

"Isn't he here yet?" he asked in surprise.

But there was more than surprise in the faces of the other two. There was trouble. Philip excused himself immediately, and went toward the barn. His own horse was weary with the long, hard day. He must take the other horse. He saddled it, and quickly led it out into the darkness; but at the door stood Margaret, her face white and drawn, a steady purpose in her eyes. Philip could see it shining through the starlight like another star. She had followed him to the barn, intending to ride with him after Stephen.

He dropped the horse's bridle, and came over to her. Taking both her cold little hands in his strong ones, he looked down into her face.

"Margaret," he said, and there was deep tenderness in his tone. "I know what you would do, but you must not. You must promise me you will stay here and pray. You cannot go out into the night this way. There is no need, and I will not let you. I will not go myself until you promise."

She caught her breath in a half-sob, and dropped her face miserably upon his hands that held hers so firmly.

He drew her to him in the shadow of the great, dark barn, and, bending over her, kissed reverently the silken coils of hair upon her head. "Margaret, I love you; will you do this for me? Will you promise to stay at home and pray?"

He was half frightened afterward that he had dared to speak to her so, but she did not shrink away. Instead, she stood very still, and held her breath for a moment, and then answered low and sweet,

"Yes, Philip!"

He longed to take her in his arms, but he dared not. He gave her hands one long, tender clasp, and sprang into his saddle; but Margaret's white face looked up now, and she ran a step or two beside the horse. She clasped her hands in pleading.

"You will be careful, Philip—for yourself," she said brokenly, and his heart leaped with joy as he promised. Yet, after all, he told himself it might be only a sisterly care.

She watched him ride away through the dark, her hand at her throat to still the wild, sweet, fluttering thing of joy that had come to thrill her soul. And for the minute she half forgot her fears for Stephen in love and fear for Philip. She stood still several minutes, and let the memory of his kiss flow over her and cover her with its glory and its joy. Then she went swiftly in, and tried to entertain the minister, who was wondering and rejoicing that he had her to himself for a little while. Poor soul, he did not know her thoughts were far out down the dark road, following a rider through the night.

As Philip rode along, he could not believe that he had really dared to tell Margaret that he loved her. It seemed too strange and wonderful to be true that she had not repulsed him when he kissed her. As the tumult in his heart quieted a little to let him think, he told himself that perhaps she was excited about Stephen, and had needed comfort. She had not realized what his words of love had meant. It might be she only took his meaning as a kind and brotherly feeling. If that were so, he would never take an advantage of her. That moment they had spent together should be a sacred thing between them. He would rejoice always in that kiss and that chance to hold her dear white hands.

But wild and sweet through such thoughts thrilled the joy of loving her and the song of hope in his heart. For something every now and then made him sure that she loved him, marvellous as it might seem.

So he rode down through the dark into town, and, finding no trace of Stephen nor any one who had seen him, turned his horse back to the house to see whether he had come; anxious now and grave, canvassing every possible way to turn next for the finding of Stephen. Then he remembered and began to pray for guidance and help.

Stephen's wild cry had reached the ears of two men travelling along the upper road above the ravine with a wagon. They stopped, listened, and heard the crashing timbers and fall of horse and man.

Instinct taught them what the accident must be, and they went to find out who it was that had fallen to a death so sudden. They carried a lantern; for the night was dark, and one was old, and the road they had to go was treacherous in some places. So now, when they could see only the blackness of horror below, they climbed down another way, leaving their horse tied above, and found the place where Stephen lay.

The horse was dead, and lay quite motionless with all his four faithful legs broken and a great beam of rotten timber across one temple, where it struck and mercifully ended his life.

But Stephen lay a little further off, flung, partly by the struggles of his horse, perhaps, or it may have been by some wild leap of his own in the moment of falling. He was stretched upon a grassy place, the kindest that the old ravine could offer, and lay unscratched apparently, the damp gold waves of hair lying loose upon his forehead, his hands flung out as if he were asleep. He was profoundly unconscious of the majesty in which he lay.

The men held the lantern to his face, and one muttered with a great oath:

"Steve Halstead! Drunk again!"

They tore his shirt open, and felt for his heart, but could not tell whether he was dead or living. Finally they carried him with great difficulty up a sloping, circuitous path, and put him in the wagon.

Bennett and Byron and two or three others had just arrived when they brought him in. Margaret turned away in sick horror. She had never seen her brother drunk. She could not bear to look now. They motioned her from the door, and laid him upon his own bed; but something in his face made Byron stoop down. There was no breath of liquor upon him. They listened with shocked faces as the two who had found him told their story. Then Byron flung himself upon his horse, and galloped off into the night for the doctor, while the others worked in desperation to bring him to consciousness, with the door closed against his sister.

It was Bennett who told Margaret that her brother had had a fall on the way home, and that he had not been to the village at all, but was found on his way there. Her face lighted at that. She understood his meaning. She was glad Stephen had not been drinking. They sent the minister to stay with her; and she was wide-eyed and brave, and would talk but little, looking anxiously through the open front door.

There came a sound of horses presently, and she rushed out into the night. Mr. Owen thought she was looking for the doctor, and let her go, thinking it might be well for her to have something to do, even if it were nothing but to watch for the doctor, who could not possibly have come so soon.

It was Philip who had come.

She ran out to him, and looked anxiously through the dark.

"O Philip, is it you? And are you safe?"

And Philip's heart warmed with hope.

"They have brought him home, Philip. He had fallen through the bridge. I was afraid you had fallen, too. I do not know how badly he is hurt; but, Philip, he had not been drinking!"

There was a ring of triumph in her last words, as if it could not be all bad, whatever might be coming. Then together they went into the house.

"She is a wonderful girl, isn't she?" said the minister to Philip in subdued tones a little later, as he watched her go quietly about getting a cup of tea for Philip. "It seems so strange that I should have had to come away out here to find her, when our native towns were but twenty miles apart." In his voice was a tone of possession and pride, and Philip's heart sank as he listened.

Chapter 16

The doctor came by and by, and was able to bring back the spirit into the form that had lain so still and deathlike. Stephen opened his eyes, and looked about him with a bewildered gaze as of one who had expected a different scene. He looked first at his sister, who had come into the room with the doctor, and then he smiled.

"I didn't get there, though, Margaret," he murmured. "God stopped me on the way. It was the only way He could save me."

He closed his eyes, and they thought he had fainted again; but he opened them with his old, careless, mischievous smile, and looked around upon the boys, his eyes lingering lovingly on Philip's face.

"I've been a coward, boys," he said, "and I've tried to get away from Him all the time; but still He kept drawing me, and you all helped. And now He's going to take me to Himself. There won't be any more drinks up there, and maybe I can begin over again."

The words were faint, and the doctor bent over him and administered a stimulant.

He made a thorough examination, and told them that Stephen was hurt internally and could not live long. They thought he was not conscious; but he opened his eyes, and smiled at them.

"It's all right, doctor. It's better so," he said feebly. "But can't you give me something to strengthen me up for a few hours? I've got something I want to say to the boys."

The doctor turned away to rub his hand across his eyes; and the men moved, choking, away from the bed, and went to the windows or slipped into the other room.

"I'll try!" said the doctor huskily. "If you'll lie quiet and rest a little, you may live through the night."

Stephen obediently took the medicine, and lay quiet for a few minutes; but as soon as the artificial strength came to him he began to talk. The gay, reckless tongue that had been the life of so many gatherings had but a little while longer to speak.

It was Philip who came to him first, and tried to quiet him with that strong personality that had so often saved him from himself.

But Stephen's mind was abnormally active. He seemed to think of things he had neglected all his life. He spoke of this and that he would like to have Philip do for him, and he talked tenderly of his sister.

"You'll look after her, Philip?" he asked anxiously. "You know she'll have no one now when I'm gone. She will be sorry. You like her, don't you?"

Philip's eyes filled with tears, and his strong chin quivered.

"I love her, Stephen, with all my soul," he said with choking voice. "I will care for her as far as she will let me care. I will make her my wife if she will consent."

"Consent?" said Stephen, his voice rising and his old petulant manner coming back to him, as ever when his will was crossed in the slightest. "Consent! Of course she will! Why shouldn't she? No one could help admiring you, Phil. Why can't you be married right away, before I go? I'd like to see it. I'd like to give you my blessing."

He looked up eagerly into Philip's face.

Philip almost groaned.

"Why can't you, Phil?" he urged again.

"I have not asked her yet," said Philip. "She may not love me at all. Sometimes I think she loves the minister."

"Then ask her now," said Stephen, and he called in the high, thin voice of those who are almost done with life, "Margaret!"

She heard his cry through the slight partitions, and came at once.

Stephen had almost exhausted his breath with his eagerness, and lay panting, looking up first at Philip wistfully, then at his sister.

"Phil — has something — to tell you," he gasped, and then swallowed the spoonful Philip gave him from the glass the doctor had left, and closed his eyes.

Philip scarcely dared to look at Margaret. It seemed almost a desecration in this hour of death to speak of what meant life and joy to him.

"I have been telling Stephen of my love for you," he said, trying to control the tremble in his voice. "I have been saying I would like to make you my wife. I would not dare intrude this upon you now, but Stephen longs to know how you feel about it."

Philip had come near her, and they both stood close to Stephen's side. There was an undertone of pity for her in Philip's voice as he spoke, and a slight touch of formality in his words because of the presence of a third person, that made it seem like a contract in writing. But Margaret remembered his impassioned tones a little while before in the shadow of the night, and did not doubt his deep love for her.

With the tears brimming her eyes she looked up to Philip, and tried to smile. Her lips were trembling with emotion, but she said simply,

"I love you, Philip!" and put her hands out to his.

Then Stephen's great brown hand, so weak now, came groping out to them and clasped them both, and the two with one consent knelt down beside his bed.

"Be married now, while I am here," he whispered. "I can leave you better so." He looked pleadingly at them.

Margaret caught her breath with a sob, and Philip put his arm tenderly about her.

"Can you bear to—dear?" he asked.

She was still a minute with drooping face and downcast eyes, and then she whispered softly,

"Yes."

Philip stooped and kissed her forehead reverently, and Stephen smiled his old joyous smile. For a minute the shadow of death that was beginning to hover over his face was chased away.

"Where are the boys?" he asked. "I want the boys and the minister. I'll tell them. No, it won't be too hard. I'd like to. Go and get ready."

They came trooping in, the great, rough men who loved him, and who had tried so hard to ruin him and save him both. The minister came behind them, and the doctor hurried in and felt Stephen's pulse. But he did not notice the doctor. He was all eagerness.

"Boys, we're going to have a wedding!" he said in a cheery, weak voice. They thought his mind was wandering, and looked sorrowfully at one another.

"That's all right, boys," he said as he saw they did not understand. "It's sure enough. I want you to carry me into the other room for the ceremony. No, don't say they can't, Doc. I'll stay alive long enough to say all I need to say. I must go out there where we've had so many good times. I'd rather die out there. Take me out, boys; we've no time to waste. Philip and Margaret are out there waiting, and the minister will marry them."

His old impatience was using up his strength fast. The doctor looked grave, but said in a low tone:

"Take him out. It cannot make much difference."

They gathered up the mattress tenderly, the clumsy fellows, and carried it out to a cot that was placed across in front of the fireplace. Almost they thought he was gone when they laid him down; but he rallied wonderfully, and, smiling, whispered,

"Go on."

Philip and Margaret, quiet and white, stood together, hand in hand, in front of the mass of summer blossoms that Margaret had arranged a few hours before for the expected evening gathering. It was just where she had sat to teach their first Sunday class, and she was all in white as then. There was a glorified light in her eyes that defied the sadness even of death. Stephen wondered as he looked at her whether she was looking up to and speaking with the unseen presence of her Christ.

The room was beautiful, and only Stephen as he lay with partly closed eyes and watched them, half impatient for the ceremony to be over, remembered the bare old room filled with the odor of lamp-smoke and bacon into which they had brought his sister on the night of her arrival. And in his heart he thanked God for her coming.

The minister with stricken look and trembling voice performed the ceremony. It was hard for life to take away his love just as death was stealing a good friend. He had begun his portion of sorrow, and would learn his lesson; but it was bitter at the start.

There in the "chill before the dawning, between the night and morning," while the angel of Death delayed a little, to watch, they were married. The night was black around the little house, and the stars kept watch above.

As soon as it was over and the short prayer ended, Stephen made a movement as if to rise, and then, remembering, dropped his head again.

"Boys, I can't stay long," he said eagerly. "I only stayed for the wedding," and he smiled in his old, reckless way. Then, growing sober, with an honest ring to his voice that sometimes came in his speech so winningly, he said:

"There's something I want you to do, boys. You can if you only will. I want you to promise me before I go. I want you to build a church here, and get the minister to run it. You can do it well enough if you don't go to the saloon. It's the saloon, boys, and the gambling, that has taken all our money, and made us into such beasts. It was the saloon that ruined me. You all know that. You all know how I came here and bought this place, and then drank it all up and everything else I had, and would have gone to the devil at once if it hadn't been for Philip coming out and buying back the place, and keeping me half-way straight."

His breath was growing short. His sentences became more broken.

"You all know what my sister's done for me," he went on. "God bless her. But even she couldn't save me. The devil had too tight a hold. I'm sorry I didn't do as she wanted me to, and take Jesus Christ — it might have done some good — but now it's too late — He'll just have to take me. I guess He'll do it. I've made a clean breast of it — but it's been a wasted life. Don't wait any longer, boys. I've thought if there'd been a church here when I came — and a minister — who lived right up to what he said — it might not have been so with me. Now, boys, will you build the church?"

They had turned away to hide the tears that were coursing down their bronzed faces; but they went solemnly, one at a time, and took his cold hand in a strong grasp, and made the promise in hoarse, broken murmurs.

"That's all right, then, boys. I know you'll do it," said Stephen; "and, boys," with almost a twinkle of the old mischief in his eyes, "I want them to put me on the hill here under the big tree, and mark the place so you'll remember your promise. I'll maybe be able to help a little that way by reminding, and so make up for all I've wasted."

He was still a minute. His voice kept its strength wonderfully.

"Sing, boys," he said, opening his eyes. "Sing all the old songs. It will make me feel more at home where I'm going to hear your voices on the way."

They looked helplessly at one another. They did not know what to sing.

"Sing 'Jesus, Saviour, pilot me,' boys," he said. "I didn't live for Him, but maybe I can die with Him."

Trembling the great voices started, like some grand organ that has lost its player, and creaks on feebly at the touch of sorrow with a broken heart.

When they were through, he said:

"Sing 'Safe home in port.' I always liked that. And, boys, sing it as if you were glad. Sing it as you always do."

Then they mastered themselves and sang:

> "Safe home, safe home, in port!
> Rent cordage, shattered deck,
> Torn sails, provisions short,
> And only not a wreck:
> But, O, the joy upon the shore,
> To tell the voyage perils o'er!"

They were singing as they used to sing it in those first bright Sundays, now. Something of the spirit of the triumph in the song had caught them.

> "No more the foe can harm!
> No more the leaguered camp,
> And cry of night alarm,
> And need of ready lamp;
> And yet how nearly had he failed,
> How nearly had the foe prevailed!"

"That's right, boys! That's me! It's all true," called out Stephen to them. They could see the shadow deepening about his eyes now.

Their voices grew softer with tenderness, but they sang on. They would sing him right grandly into heaven if that was what he wanted, even if it broke their hearts. Their voices should not fail him while he could listen.

> "The exile is at home!
> Oh, nights and days of tears!"

Stephen pressed Margaret's hand that lay in his, at these words, and she tenderly kissed him.

> "Oh, longings not to roam!
> Oh, sins and doubts and fears!
> What matters now grief's darkest day
> When God has wiped all tears away?"

It was the minister who started other hymns, words that he had heard them sing in their gatherings. They needed no books, nor could they have looked at them with their tear-blinded eyes, if they had them.

Stephen was sinking fast. He did not talk any more, nor look at them. Once he opened his eyes, and, looking at Margaret, murmured, "Dear sister!"

He had lain so still for a long time that they thought he had ceased breathing, when he suddenly opened his eyes, and with a strength born of his flight into another world raised himself from the pillow, calling in a loud, clear voice:

"Did you call, father? Yes, sir, I'm coming!"

Then he fell back dead.

Was it some memory of his boyhood that came to him at last, or did he hear his heavenly Father's voice?

It was the minister that started to sing,

> "Safe in the arms of Jesus,
> Safe on His gentle breast;"

and with choking sobs that did not need to be suppressed the men joined in the song that Stephen loved. Just then the sun shot up behind the hills, and laid a touch of glory on the gold of Stephen's hair.

"He is safe home in Port," said the minister. "Let us pray."

They knelt about him in their grief, and heard him pray for them, and then went out and left Philip and Margaret with their sorrow and their joy.

They went out to a new world wherein were vows to be kept and a goal to be attained, and each man was resolved to do his best to keep the sacred trust that Stephen had left to them.

They went about among Stephen's friends, and gathered up a goodly sum. They brought it to Margaret on the day of the funeral service, and told her it was for the church, and that it should be built at once. Margaret, smiling through her tears, thanked God, and knew her prayers were being answered.

They laid him in the place he had spoken of under the great tree that crowned the hill, and to mark it they put a stone whereon were engraved Stephen's name, the date, and the simple words,

"SAFE HOME."

Beside the grave up rose the little church, its spire pointing heavenward, its doors stretched wide to save both day and night, its bell calling over the lonely country at set times of worship, and over the door, cut into the stone, the words,

"STEPHEN HALSTEAD MEMORIAL."

The minister has found his church; and Stephen's life, though gathered safe home, is going on in the memory of those he is helping.

Lone Point

Chapter 1

Rachel Hammond sat by the open window with her Bible on her knee. The muslin curtains did not blow with the breeze, for there was no breeze that hot morning in June. The air seemed breathless. Rachel had put her pretty room in order, finished all her little morning duties, and now had sat down for a quiet minute with her Bible before she began the day.

Her sister Maria, two years older, sat in the adjoining room, her door open for all possible circulation of air. Indeed the door between the sisters' rooms was scarcely ever shut by day or by night. But Maria was trimming a hat instead of reading her Bible. Not that Maria did not read her Bible, for she did, but she never had a set, quiet time for doing it as Rachel had.

The hat was white sailor and had been very stylish and consequently very expensive earlier in the season, but now the mass of people were supplied with millinery for the summer, and poorer people were enabled by the great reduction in prices to indulge their taste for pretty things. It went very much against the grain with Maria Hammond to have to wait until late for the pretty summer things she wanted, and even then to be obliged to buy with careful hand and long-hoarded savings, for until recently she had been used to buying when and what she pleased since she could remember. Maria had taken more bitterly her father's change of fortune than any of the other members of the family. The others had looked on the bright side of things and cheerfully told each other how good it was that matters were no worse; that the father had not fallen ill physically under the heavy burden that had been placed upon him by the fraud of a trusted partner; that the dear beautiful home where the three children had been born was saved to them, with a little—a very little, it is true, but still a little—with which to keep things going; and best of all, that all the creditors had been fully paid. But Maria could only see the dark side. From a rich man, who was able to do what he pleased, and who intended soon to build a home lovelier even than their present one, and who could afford to place his daughters in the best society, her father had become a poor man. Thus to her the present home had lost even the charms which it had possessed before she looked forward to the finer one.

This present home was by no means an undesirable one. It was located on a quiet, pleasant street where the neighbors were staid and old-fashioned, people of fine old families. It was built of stone in a comfortable manner, with ample room and broad piazzas, vines peeping in the windows in summer, and lawn enough about it to give the feeling of plenty of room.

It was in the plainest end of a fashionable suburb, but it was not fashionable. The house had none of the modern twists and turns which art and fashion have decreed shall adorn the modern handsome dwelling, and for this reason Maria despised it and pitied herself for having to live in it. A look of discontent had settled down upon her pretty white forehead which was gradually but surely changing her expression permanently.

"Oh, dear!" sighed Maria, as she jerked a loop of white ribbon into place behind the many cheap white wings she was arranging on her hat. "What's the use of fussing and fixing up things to wear after all? There won't be a place to wear them except church, and all the people we know or care about will be out of town by another month. One might as well wear one's old duds after all."

Rachel looked up from her Bible, through the open door where she could see her sister at work.

"Oh, yes, there will be plenty of places. Don't be so disheartened, dear," she answered brightly. "How pretty that hat will be, 'Ri! It looks just like you."

"Does it, indeed?" responded the elder sister. "Then my face must be badly snarled up, for this ribbon is. I can't get the right twist to it any way I put it. I do wish I could afford to take it down to Haskins' and have it trimmed by our old milliner. It is awfully vexatious to have to do everything one's self or else go without. But I'd be willing to do it myself if we could only go out of town for a little while, Ray; it's so horribly plebeian to stay in the city all the year round. Everybody else is going."

"You forget, 'Ri, we don't live in the city, we live in the suburbs, and plenty of people stay all summer in the suburbs. Some people prefer to take their trips away from home in the winter, you know. Look at the Adamses and Monteiths, they don't go away at all, and even Mrs. Burbank told me the other day that they didn't care to take any vacation, they enjoyed their home in the summer so much."

"Oh, yes, I should think they would. They have a park surrounding them, a great, cool house with plenty of servants, all the guests they want, and are up on a high hill besides, with plenty of shade about. Besides, it's nonsense for them to talk about not going away. They are hardly at home two weeks in succession all the year around. Mrs. Burbank and Tilly spend a week at a time at Atlantic City every time they sneeze or have a headache, and Mr. and Mrs. Burbank took a trip to California last winter, while Tom and his aunt went to Florida. When they don't run up to New York or out to Pittsburgh for a few days they go up to that sanitarium in the mountains for their health for a month or take a trip to Bermuda. I don't know that I should care either about going away in the summer if I only knew I could go whenever I pleased, and what is more, knew that everybody else knew it. I tell you, Ray, the hardest thing to bear is to feel that folks are saying we can't go anywhere now, and pitying us! I just can't stand it," and Maria threw her half-finished hat on the bed beside her and lay back on one of the snowy pillows in a discouraged attitude.

Rachel by long experience with her sister knew that it was of no use to argue with her, so she tried to cheer her as best she could, sighing a little regretfully as she closed her Bible and came into her sister's room. She had been reading the verse, "For me to live is Christ," and she wondered wistfully if she would ever know what that meant, and wished that Maria felt more of the spirit of it, so that her life would not seem so hard to her.

"If you want to go away so much perhaps we might go to the same place Marvie Parker told me about yesterday," said Rachel, seating herself on the foot of Maria's bed and resting her chin thoughtfully in her hand.

"No, thanks!" said Maria promptly and decidedly. "I don't think I should care for any place where Marvie Parker goes. I don't see what you find in that girl to attract you, Ray. She is the dowdiest thing I've seen in a long time. Her father is nothing but a clerk in his brother-in-law's store. There are plenty of nice girls for you to go with without choosing her for a friend."

"But she is nice, 'Ri," said the younger sister, her eyes flashing bright in her eagerness to defend her friend. "You don't know her or you wouldn't talk that way. She is very bright and has read and studied far more than either of us. The whole family are very bright. I never enjoyed myself more in my life than I did the evening I spent with them last week. She has a brother just home from college who is as full of life as can be, and Marvie is the sweetest girl I know, next to you."

"She may be sweet enough," answered Maria, ignoring the earnest compliment, "but she is not of the same social standing with you, and it is a great deal wiser and pleasanter not to try to upset the world and drag people out of their spheres." This with an air and expression of long experience with the world.

"Well, I think you might wait until you have known them before you judge them; but listen. Let me tell you where they are going. It sounds very interesting. The place is an island right between the bay and the ocean, not very wide either, so you get the view of both. Marvie says it is beautiful there, and the sunsets are go gorgeous. It is a real, old-time beach such as you read about, with no boardwalks and no merry-go-rounds, and everybody does as he pleases, and lots of bathing and boating and fishing and sailing. I think it would be delightful. Marvie says there are cottages down there for seventy-five dollars for the season, just think of that! They are not fine, of course, but are real comfortable, with big rooms, and lots of corners and shelves and places to fix up. I think I should like it immensely."

"Now Rachel Weldon Hammond, what in the world do you mean?" said Maria, sitting upright on the bed and looking at her. "Seventy-five dollars for the season! The very idea of our living in a cottage that costs only seventy-five dollars for the season! You must be crazy. Why the cottage the Johnses lived in last year at Atlantic City was twelve hundred, and even the Pattersons paid a thousand. I think you are nothing but a child, in spite of your seventeen years."

Just then a servant came to announce that a young lady was in the parlor to see Miss Ray, and Rachel with a bright spot on each cheek went down to find her friend Marvie.

It was not until dinner that evening that the subject was renewed. Maria had spent the afternoon in town hunting among the bargain tables and had come home thoroughly tired. There is something in a disappointing day of shopping which particularly exasperates some people's nerves. Every subject that came to Maria's mind seemed to be productive of discomfort. At last something was said about Rachel's morning caller. Then Maria burst out:

"Was that Marvie Parker here again? I think she is rather running things into the ground. Mamma, do you know what kind of a girl is getting an influence over Rachel? I think the friendship ought to be stopped. She isn't in our set at all, and Rachel will feel most uncomfortable in a year or two if she makes a special friend of a girl like that, whom she can't invite nor go with, of course, when she gets old enough to care about things."

"What is the matter with Miss Parker?" questioned Mr. Hammond, turning his sad gray eyes to his elder daughter's face. "It does not seem to be a good reason for objecting to her merely because she is not in your set. If she isn't in, bring her in; that is, if the set is worth her coming. If it isn't, it might be a good thing for Rachel to have a few friends outside it, in case of an emergency. Miss Parker ought to be a good girl. Her father is a fine man, and I used to know her mother years ago when we were children. The girl ought to be well brought up. What is the matter with her, aside from that senseless notion?"

Maria's face grew red. She did not like to have her father against her, neither did she feel fully prepared to face his keen eyes or his searching questions. She was on the point of reminding him that she and Rachel were no longer in a position to say who should or should not belong in their set, and that their own footing there might at any time grow insecure, but she remembered just in time to save herself this disgrace and her father the pain of such a remark. Instead she flew at once to some defense of her own statements.

"She may be a good girl, papa, I presume she is," she replied; "but you will surely acknowledge that she is putting queer notions into Ray's head.

Why this morning she actually confided to me that she would enjoy going to some out-of-the-way place, on an almost desert island, where the Parkers are going to seek solitude for the summer, and live in a shanty at seventy-five dollars for the season. Just think of it! I don't know where she thought even the seventy-five dollars was to come from, with the railroad fares and all, but she would really like us all to go. Did you ever hear of such an idea!"

Rachel's fair face had grown rosy red during the conversation.

She was an exceedingly sensitive girl, and shrank from being the center of observation, even in her own family, and now as the glance of father, mother, and brother were turned upon her, she could scarcely keep the excited tears from rushing into her eyes. But she tried to smile in answer to her father's encouraging look as he asked for an explanation.

"Why, papa, I didn't really say I wanted to do it," said Rachel, her cheeks flushing redder, "I only said I thought it would be real nice. And of course I'm perfectly happy where I am. But if we were to do it I suppose we'd have to in the same way that the Parkers do. They rent their house here, and they get two hundred and fifty dollars for the season for it from some people who have to stay in town on account of business all summer and have to be at their store at seven o'clock, so they couldn't get in from far away from the city in time. Marvie said her father knew a lot of men who wanted just such homes as ours for the summer, where they could bring their families out of the rows of brick houses. I thought maybe there would be come one who might want our house that way, and it ought to bring more that the Parkers', because it is larger and has more ground and is on a nicer street. But I didn't really mean ever to say anything about it, for 'Ri seemed to think it was all so dreadful that I didn't mention the renting of our house."

Rachel dropped her burning face from the exclamations which she knew would follow.

"Rent our house!" said Maria aghast. "Whatever can you be thinking about? Are you crazy? I guess we have not quite come to that state of disgrace!"

"My dear child!" exclaimed the mother, not so much in horror as astonishment at the new thought". How could we have people using our carpets and our dishes?" There came a little distressed pucker between her eyes, showing that the idea was not an impossibility to her after all and she was really considering it.

"And what did you propose to do with father and me, Ray?" asked her brother Winthrop, who was a little older than Maria and in business with this father, struggling to bring back the name and fame which the former firm had lost through the treachery of one of its members. "You know we are obliged to be in town at a set hour every day, as well as some other folks!"

Rachel's cheeks flushed anew at the implication that she, the quietest member of the household, had taken the family affairs into consideration and assumed to make the plans, but she answered shyly:

"I hadn't thought it all out, but Mr. Parker and his son go in to town every day. Marvie said there was a train leaving the island early enough to get here before nine, I think, and there are special season tickets for business men, so it doesn't cost much, and the store closes early during the summer anyway, doesn't it? But I didn't mean to plan. I am happy where I am. I wouldn't have said a word, only 'Ri was worrying because we had to stay in town all summer, and I thought maybe mother would enjoy the coolness by the shore."

"She is nothing but an absurd child! " exclaimed her sister. "Papa, surely you are not going to encourage her in such plebeian notions. I'm sure I'd rather die respectably than go away for the summer in such a disgraceful manner." And she sat back in her chair with a sneer.

"My daughter," said Mr. Hammond, looking straight at Maria, "I am ashamed if a child of mine has come to the place where she can say such a thing as that. You do not mean it. And as for this 'notion,' as you are pleased to term it, it is nothing new to me. I have long thought that I could save a good deal and make matters mend in our pecuniary affairs much more quickly if I could rent this house. Indeed, I had an offer last week of four hundred dollars for this place, stable and all, from now till the first of October. The reason I declined the offer was not on account of any such frivolous and unworthy motives as you have expressed, but simply because I knew of no cheaper place where my family could be comfortable while the house was earning the four hundred dollars."

"I should think not!" put in Maria with red, excited face. It meant a great deal to her, this question of fashion, and what her little world of "they" would think and say. It meant all that she now cared for in life, though she would not have believed it if she had been told that this was true of her. But her father went on in his calm tone:

"Now if the Parkers have found a place for seventy-five dollars where they can be comfortable, I should think we might do so as well. The Parkers are respectable people and used to having the necessaries of life, at least, if not all of the luxuries. I should think it might be worth the looking into at least. Don't you think so, mother?"

And the wife, with a troubled look at her eldest daughter's face, and a sigh of longing for the cool air of the ocean, assented that she thought they ought to make inquiries, at least.

Maria, with tears of chagrin in her eyes, suddenly left the table, and Rachel, whose tender heart was sorely distressed at having been the cause of the trouble to her sister, went soon to her own room, where for once she found the connecting door between her room and her sister's closed, and upon softly turning the knob a few minutes later she discovered it was also locked. This was something that had not happened since the two girls were very little and first had rooms to themselves, and Rachel could not keep the tears back. She betook herself to her Bible for comfort and through blinding tears she found it, and resolved to try to make Maria happy that summer no matter what happened, seashore or home, heat or cool breezes, pleasure or disagreeableness. And so she slept.

Chapter 2

Maria Hammond was a girl of very determined nature. When she liked or wanted a thing she liked or wanted it intensely, and bent all her energies to get it. What she disliked she was equally persistent in opposing; and when it happened, as it often did in her life, that her plans and desires were frustrated, it took a great struggle of will before she could give up and yield to the inevitable. Even then, should the least chance occur, she would try for her own way again. She insisted that it was not her own way, however, which she desired, but merely to have things right about her, and as they ought to be; and that if the way were another's and it seemed right to her, she would be just as eager to have it as though it had been her own. With such sophistry did she excuse herself to herself and to others for her persistency and headstrong, stubborn willfulness, and because of a discontented nature, which was always desiring the unattainable, she was constantly in trouble.

When she went to her room after her stormy speeches at the dinner table the tears of anger, defeat, chagrin, and disappointment swelled into her throat and eyes. Locking her door, she threw herself on her bed in a torrent of weeping. It is true she had attained the years when young ladies are supposed not to weep violently, unless for some great grief of life, and she would not for the world have had any one, even a member of her own family, see her thus; but her nature was so uncontrolled that when it burst out upon her in this way she could but give way to it. Moreover, in her eyes very little things often seemed important, and thus it came about that what to another might simply be an annoyance to her became a great and overwhelming grief. It was, as it were, her very life that was in the balance. For what else was life to her but the good opinion of the world? And so Maria lay upon her bed crying for a long time. It was not merely what had occurred at the dinner table which caused her trouble, nor even the prospect of spending the summer in a most unfashionable retreat, though that seemed to her mind very unlikely, even after what had been said by father and mother, "For surely," thought she, "their reason will see that it would be dreadful, simply dreadful"; but it seemed to her a sort of climax of all the disappointments which had come since her father had lost his money. In consequence, she mourned and cried and pitied herself, and perhaps pitied the rest of the family a little with what heart she had left after her own need was lavishly supplied. By and by she grew more calm, and then there came to her a shadow of her religion to question why it could not help her in this trying time, for she had a religion, this stormy-natured girl, in spite of all her will and her fear of what "they" would say. And with the thought of her religion came the reflection of all she had meant to do to help in the church work during the summer, of the class of delightfully bad little boys she had promised to take in the Sunday-school; of the young people's meeting she had promised to lead; and of the tennis picnic in the park she was planning for those same young people, which was to close in the dusk of evening with a short prayer meeting under the trees, and which she hoped would do much good. Then she told herself it could not be that she was to be removed to an out-of-the-way place where there would be no possible opportunity for anything of the kind when she had planned to do so much. Thus she magnified her own projected goodness until she seemed a very martyr.

Now such a nature as Maria's is not one which long remains under a cloud. She began to persuade herself by and by that things could not possibly be as bad as they seemed about to be, and to silence her own uncomfortable conscience, which was beginning to reproach her keenly for the way in which she had spoken to her father and sister. She resolved with a large sigh of conscious martyrdom to go to her father the next morning and tell him she was resigned to being a hermit if it would conduce to his financial comfort. Having thus resolved, and being comforted by the thought that if she pursued such a course her father would by no means be likely to accept her sacrifice, she went to sleep.

Meantime the father and mother had been holding a consultation. Money matters had been coming to a crisis during the last few weeks. Business was very dull at the store. Mr. Hammond hoped if he could tide affairs over until fall that he might be able to weather the gale. He now felt that a serious talk with his wife was necessary, though she was such a frail little woman that he always spared her all he could because she took every burden at twice its weight, and went about with her face sad and anxious. The result of this talk, however, was that Mr. Hammond took his breakfast a half-hour earlier than usual in order that he might stop in and speak to his friend Mr. Parker on his way to the office. And so it was that Maria did not get an opportunity to speak to her father until evening.

It was just as the dinner bell rang through the house, and Maria, hastening down the stairs that she might speak to her father as he entered the dining room, heard her mother's voice speaking to him as she passed the door of the library. She spoke with an anxious sigh: "Yes, it would be very nice and just the thing. I would do it in a minute if it only were not for the girls' sake. I hate to do it when they are so opposed."

And her father's weary tones answered: "It is Maria that is opposed, not both of them, remember, and things are as they are. Maria may come to worse trouble if we do not do this."

"Yes," said the mother sadly; "but Maria is the oldest, you know, and just at the age when everything of this sort makes so much difference to her. It might hurt her future life, my dear."

"Nonsense!" said her father rather sharply, although he felt the truth of what his wife was saying, keenly enough. "If Maria's future is to be hurt by the fact that her father rented his home to good, respectable people for a few months, and went to a quiet, unfashionable place to stay during that time, I think it had better be hurt. It seems to 'me that friends who are affected by such things are not worth the having." But he sighed again as he came down the stairs, his face wearing a careworn expression.

Maria's heart beat fast and the tears came into her eyes. She had not realized that she was making her loved father so much trouble. Her impulsive nature at once forgot all about any personal sacrifices, and rushing up to her father, she drew him into the door of the sitting room they were passing, and throwing her arms about his neck, begged him to forgive her for all she had said, and not to mind her in the least in anything he wished to do, that she would try to be as helpful as she could.

And so it came about after all that it was through Maria that the Hammond home was rented to a family who would pay well for four months' use of it, and the Hammonds themselves migrated to the seashore. It must not be supposed that Maria was changed all in a moment. She had many evenings of weeping over the inevitable, but the memory of her father's weary face and her mother's anxious tones was sufficient to keep her from demurring any further to the family plans, and it was only to her sister Rachel and her brother Winthrop that she permitted herself to grumble. Winthrop had long ago said that his sisters were well named: Rachel was like a ray of bright sunlight everywhere, always, cheery, never cross, while Maria, or 'Ri, as they all called her, "always took things awry and kept a wry face much of the time."

"I say 'Ri, do let up a little, can't you?" said her brother one day when Maria had finished one of her sarcastic speeches about their summer outing. "It's too late now to give up, so you'd better make the best of it. Where's the Christian fortitude I hear most church-members talk so much about? Can't you summon up a little bit to help you through this vale of tears? I'm sure you've taken every grain of pleasure out of this summer that it might possibly have contained for Rachel and me, so do be satisfied, for you surely can't wish father and mother to suffer."

This somewhat caustic speech from her usually good-natured brother sent Maria to her room weeping. The days had been very hard for her even before this. She had endured, in imagination, the heavy trial of coming home to find her room treasures spoiled by ruthless alien hands. She had pleaded that certain necessary articles — necessary to the thorough furnishing of the house — be put away under lock and key, but had been made to understand that this could not be. She suffered a great deal while clearing out her bureau drawers and closet and all her little private "cubby-holes," realizing how in a few days these places would be filled with some other girl's belongings, and she felt that when she returned she never could feel the same toward the home-corners again after strangers had called them their own. She had also been obliged to help in packing cushions and cretonne draperies that could be well spared from the home, with curtains, pictures, screens, and a few such things as were considered essential to make the summer cottage, to which they were going, habitable.

This had also gone much against the grain. To think of having to spend one's summer amid things that were merely fit to put in a bedroom! It was humiliating. If they were to have a cottage, why couldn't they at least have it look comfortable, cheery, and furnished with taste? Maria was the artist of the family, and so had been called upon to select the draperies they should take, but when her mother found that Maria's choice would be to carry silk-chenille portières and satin embroidered sofa pillows and a plush hand-painted screen, she was obliged to do the selecting herself, or quietly put it into Rachel's hands, for Rachel had been down to the little beach cottage. Her friend, Marvie Parker, had invited her for over a Sunday, and her father thought this would be a good opportunity for some member of the family to judge of the fitness of the cottage for their abode. It is true Rachel had hitherto been considered the child of the family, but her judgment was usually good, and her father and mother felt her to be a much more unprejudiced judge than her sister would have been, for Rachel would tell not only the best but also the worst, which Maria would not have seen at all, had she desired to go as much as her sister did. So Rachel had accepted the invitation, much to the chagrin of Maria, who told her that if she did this she would open the way to the Parkers to be entirely too intimate with them for the summer, a thing she, for one, did not intend to countenance. But Rachel, having the consent of father and mother, went and enjoyed her two days immensely, coming home with glowing accounts of all the pleasures in store for them, as well as an accurate description of the cottages for rent. They were rough, she admitted; not finished inside except for a high facing of heavy manilla paper. The ceilings were high, reaching indeed to the peak of the roof, and thus giving the rooms a lofty appearance. She felt sure that Maria could make of the parlor or sitting room, or whatever they chose to call it, a perfect summer bower, and the rooms, though few, were all large, indeed quite spacious for a place so cheap. It was all on one floor, with a wide piazza for hammocks and a view of sea and bay. But when Maria — a slight interest awakened for the moment — began to select silk and velour portières, Rachel laughed and then looked troubled. She saw endless difficulties in making her sister understand.

"They will look incongruous, 'Ri," she said. "You ought to have gone in my place and then you would know just what to take, for you always know how to make things fit; but really I should think some of that pretty printed burlap we bought to make cozy-corner cushions for our bedrooms would be just the thing."

"If I had gone," said Maria severely, "I should probably have brought back such an account as would have made the family understand it was no fit place for us to live in. However, you seem to be having everything your own way this time and I suppose we will take what curtains you say. I wish with all my heart we were not compelled to spend the summer entirely in a burlap atmosphere. I didn't suppose things would be quite so rough."

And so had Maria gone on, fighting every step of the way, contesting every inch of the plans that were made, until all who asked her to help were glad to see her go away and leave them to finish alone.

Poor Maria! Don't be too hard upon her. Her heart was very heavy during these days. She discovered a day or two before they flitted to the shore that the place selected was but a mile from a fashionable summer resort of which she had often heard as being at the very height of refined and aristocratic summer haunts. She also discovered to her dismay that the De Veres, of the West End of the city, who were very wealthy and literary and cultured, had taken a cottage there. Now Maria had met the Misses De Vere and their brother some three or four times at various social functions, and she felt that their acquaintance would be worth cultivating. But she knew she should shrink into herself with shame if they discovered her whereabouts and came to see the kind of place in which she was summering. She had really taken quite a liking to those young people, and it was hard for her to think of them as looking down upon her. Why she did not feel that people who would look down upon her because of the house in which she lived were not worth her caring for, is hardly explainable, unless it was because she knew that she should look down upon any one similarly placed, and so judged them by herself. She had listened to a bit of talk between George Parker, Marvie's brother, and her sister Rachel, wherein he described some of the cottages at Lone Point and told how the Spray View people laughed at them and called them "Lone Point Barracks," and all sorts of funny names. Maria's spirit writhed within her as she pictured to herself Roland De Vere driving by their cottage some day and laughing with other strangers about their home. The blood crimsoned her whole face, and she resolved that by no word of hers should the De Veres find out where she was to spend her summer, even though she missed many a pleasant invitation thereby.

One more experience Maria had to complete her wretchedness before they left for Lone Point. She had been with her sister on some last errands prior to their departure from civilization for a time, and just before they took the car for home, stopped at the public library to secure a store of books for summer reading. It was while they were waiting at the desk for their cards to be marked, that Roland De Vere, with his arms full of books, stepped up to them and touched his hat. Maria introduced her sister, of course, and the three walked out together.

"By the way, where do you spend your summer this year?" asked the young man as they paused at the corner to wait for a car.

Maria's cheeks grew rosy. She never could keep her face from telling tales which she would rather were untold, but she caught at her presence of mind and answered:

"Papa is talking of the seashore somewhere," rather vaguely, and then looked eagerly to see if the car were not coming.

But Rachel, not noticing her sister's vague response and not understanding in the least its intention, turned in her eager, girlish way and said:

"Why, yes, we're going quite near to where you will be, if I have heard aright. Are you not going to Spray View? Your sister told a friend of ours. I hoped I might meet your sisters this summer. I have heard so much about them, and Maria is quite in love with both of them. Our place is only a mile from there, Lone Point; do you know it?"

Maria's face was crimson now. She motioned violently to the car which was still half a block away, and telling her sister the car was ready, never even turned her eyes to see what Mr. De Vere was thinking. She had so often rehearsed in her mind how under such circumstances his face would grow astonished, and he would utter a very expressive "Oh!" and turn away, that her imaginings became a reality to her, of which the true scene which followed was not able to efface the impression. So with a vexation and embarrassment that amounted almost to an agony she stepped out into the street with the other waiting passengers, thinking to prevent all further conversation.

This, however, Mr. De Vere did not notice. He was entirely taken up with talking to Rachel. His face lighted with pleasure and he said: "Know it? I should think I did. It is a delightful little place. I had a good friend there last year. I hope we shall see each other often. You go to-morrow, you say? How pleasant! We go the first of next week, and sooner if mother can get ready. Good-afternoon, Miss Rachel; Miss Hammond, good-afternoon. I am glad there is a prospect of our seeing one another often this summer."

He touched his hat; they stepped on the car and were soon speeding away. The car was crowded and the two girls had difficulty at first in finding seats, but as they neared the suburbs the passengers grew fewer, and Maria found opportunity to seat herself beside Rachel, who in blissful unconsciousness of her sister's state of mind had been letting her eyes dance and her heart rejoice in the innocent pleasures in store in the possibilities of the summer. Maria had been bottled up for nearly twenty minutes and the vials of her wrath had not cooled during the process. She always showed her feelings to their full extent in her face, so Rachel had a sudden and unpleasant awakening from her girlish dreams.

"Rachel Hammond!" said Maria, trying to lower her excited voice so none of their fellow-passengers could hear, "I should think you might learn to keep your mouth shut occasionally. I never introduce you to one of my friends but I regret it bitterly at once. It seems as if you might be old enough now to know how to behave."

Poor Rachel! Her sensitive face flushed and she roused herself at once to remember what terrible breach of etiquette she had been guilty of, but could think of nothing. She dreaded one of Maria's tirades beyond almost any experience that came into her life, and was constantly studying to avoid them, and perhaps as a consequence she was the one who had to receive the larger number of them.

"What did I do, 'Ri?" she faltered, and if Maria had not been too angry she would have been touched by the pitiful quiver of the pretty, sensitive lips, and the grieved, troubled look of Rachel's large eyes.

"What did you do, indeed! You little tattle-tale! You need not tell me you don't know, for you did it just to annoy me, you know you did, or else from some high and mighty notion that you would rebuke me for not telling everything I knew. You will have to learn that it isn't necessary to tell all you know in this world in order to avoid telling a falsehood. Why was it necessary for you to explain fully to that elegant Mr. De Vere in what a humiliating state we were to spend our summer? I should think things were being made uncomfortable enough for me already without that being added. I shall simply die of shame if they come over to that horrid little place and find us rusticating in a cowshed. I think you have fully overstepped the mark this time. You have chosen your friends and I have a right to mine. I shall ask papa to let you know hereafter that you are not to interfere with me and my friends."

Maria had grown angrier as she talked. She had kindled her imagination during the silent ride with fancied scenes of meeting between herself and Fannie De Vere at Spray View, until she scarcely could contain herself. Rachel's fair face grew almost white at her sister's words. She tried to explain, but Maria was in no state to be reasonable.

"But, Maria dear," she pleaded, "I didn't dream I was saying anything unpleasant to you."

"Then you must be very blind," snapped Maria. "You certainly must have seen from the way I answered him that I would have bitten out my tongue sooner than have him know."

"But I didn't, 'Ri, indeed; indeed I didn't dream of such a thing! I was only delighted for your sake, for I thought you would have some company, and he seemed so pleased about it."

"Oh, yes, he was pleased!" sneered Maria. "He's too polite to let anything else appear, but he's probably laughing in his sleeve this minute. You needn't worry. We shall not see either him or his lovely sisters at all this summer. As soon as he said he was acquainted with Lone Point I knew what to expect. I heard a man from Spray View talk about Lone Point the other day, and they don't consider the place fit for Spray Viewers to wipe their feet on."

Poor Rachel quivered under her sister's upbraidings, until when they reached home she could bear it no more and went to her room to do an unusual thing for her, have it out with her tears. And then she went to her Heavenly Father with her little bruised heart and found comfort.

Chapter 3

Meantime Roland De Vere was walking down Walnut Street reflectively.

"Strange," he said to himself. "What could have been her reason? Was she ashamed of going to a quiet, unfashionable resort? She was angry with her sister for telling me. I could see that. Her face struck me as being a very intellectual one when I first saw her, and a pretty one too, but I didn't notice that discontented curl to her lips. However, I have never seen her in the daytime before. Gaslight makes a wonderful difference. It is not so good as I thought at first. But that other face is like a flower. The younger sister must be worth cultivating. I did enjoy her frank eagerness. Fannie would like her. I mean to take her over to call as soon as possible after we get to the shore."

How Maria's eyes would have opened in surprise could she have known his true feeling. It is a pity that some inventor could not give us a little instrument for divining occasionally what other really think of us. It would sometimes save a world of worry. But how careful we should then have to be of our own thoughts of others. Perhaps some one greater than Edison will arise one day who will search out the hidden law that governs thoughts and let us look into one another's hearts, and then how much better — or how much worse, alas — we shall be! For surely the kingdom of heaven will be near at hand when men's judgments of one another are kind and loving.

The Hammonds' journey to Lone Point was taken on a Saturday, for then they might have the escort of father and brother and their assistance during the day in unpacking and arranging their belongings for the summer. Maria looked sadly about on familiar objects as she walked toward the nearest station in the early morning. She felt as if she were going out of the world, and that when she returned, if she ever survived the humiliations of the summer, all would be different to her, and she could never be the same girl again.

Rachel, however, had gone ahead with Winthrop. He had seen how her bright spirits were clouded by her sister's gloomy countenance and had made a pretext of some errand to get her with himself. He had in some way found out from Rachel all that her sister had said to her on the street-car the night before, and he was indignant with Maria for being so hard upon the sensitive younger sister. He resolved upon the first opportunity to give her a plain talking-to, and save Rachel from further annoyance of that sort. He managed the seats in the cars so that Rachel should be with him, his father and mother together, and Maria installed with a fresh magazine and a pile of hand-baggage in a third seat. This suited Maria exactly, and as Rachel was in front of all she did not have to think about Maria and her troubles during the journey. Rachel looked a little pale that morning from her unusual vigil of the night before, and Winthrop set himself to make her forget it. He succeeded wonderfully, for soon her face lighted up and her silvery laugh could be heard occasionally, which made Maria look up and frown, to think that any member of the family could make merry on such a journey as this. She felt as if she were attending her own funeral, and the procession would never cease. However the magazine was interesting and she soon forgot herself for a little.

Through pleasant villages of gardens, and then through wastes of sand and scrub they sped, and the time seemed to Rachel short until they wound their way out at last upon the lovely bay and ran for several miles with water on either side and the sea breeze blowing fresh in their faces through the open windows of the car. Rachel and her mother drew in long, life-giving breaths, and even Maria aroused to a sense of relief from the heat and her heart seemed not to be quite so heavy as before, though she did not stop to explain to herself why it was so. Finally they came in sight of Spray View in the distance, its cottages and hotels seeming quite imposing beyond the blue waters of the bay and with the deep green sea as a background; and Maria, when she heard the name of the place, was looking enviously ahead and wishing that that tallest dark green cottage with the trumpet vine in full bloom over its lordly piazza were to be theirs, instead of—when suddenly the train came to a halt and the brakeman called out "Lone Point," and they were all hustled suddenly out upon a bare platform in the sand, and the train sped on toward the towers of fair Spray View a mile ahead.

"What did we get out for?" questioned Maria querulously. "We haven't got there yet. They said that was Spray View ahead there. Isn't the place (scornfully) the other side of it? This isn't any place at all apparently," and she looked about with curling lip on the waste of sand with the cluster of small buildings nearer the beach.

But no one was paying any attention to her, and she was obliged to pick up her umbrella and hand-satchel and follow the rest.

"Here we are, and there it is!" shouted Rachel gleefully, in her excitement clapping her hands and going back to her childhood ways of several years before. "There! that's ours, that green one over there with the white trimmings. And there comes Marvie to meet us, and her brother George. Oh, I'm so glad we're here!" and she flew to meet her friend.

It was all fully as humiliating as Maria expected. To have the "Parker boy," as she designated him—though he was fully as old as young Mr. De Vere—come and meet them, and offer assistance and insist on taking her hand-bag from her; then to be under obligations to the Parkers, whose cottage was next door and who had kindly prepared dinner for the Hammonds and had it served on the table by the time they had their hats off! It was simply unheard-of and dreadful, and Maria had no appetite to choke down the delicate fish and fresh vegetables prepared so nicely. She wished her mother had declined any assistance whatever and would rather have starved until their own servant could prepare some kind of a meal. However, the others of the family did not share her feeling and did ample justice to the dinner.

The afternoon found plenty for even troubled Maria to do and left her no time for thought. The one poor servant whom they had brought down with them and upon whom they depended to make everything move smoothly and bear all the burdens had, it would seem, ideas also about watering places. She went out and took a brief survey of the place, and above all of the terrible ocean, heretofore unseen by her. One swift gaze over the turbulent blue waves, and with a wild look in her eyes she turned and fled. Returning to the cottage where the family had improved her absence to fit up an impromptu partition in the kitchen and so make her a bedroom, she took a hurried invoice of that, exclaimed in dismay over the roughness of things, said "My land!" several times, went out on the porch and took in the narrow stretch of land between ocean and bay, and going in told Mrs. Hammond she must go right back to town by the next train, she "couldn't stand it nohow," that she was "sure that there water would meet and flood the place." Nor could any amount of persuasion on the part of the united and dismayed family change her firm decision. No, indeed, she would not stay over-night! She would never expect to see the morning light. She did not wish to let the sun go down and darkness settle upon her with that awful ocean roaring and surging back and forth so near her. What mattered it to her that the Hammonds had paid her fare down from the city, had indeed bought her a return ticket? What cared she for losing her place? Fear had taken hold upon her, and her frenzied soul cared but to flee; and flee she did on the two-o'clock train.

Then the family sat down in dismay to consider what they should do next. Rachel was cheery. She had been to the beach and it had filled her with exhilaration. She was ready for anything, and to call it fun, even if it meant washing dishes and peeling potatoes. They all looked fearfully at Maria. She had made her gloom felt so severely all day that each one dreaded the effect of this last blow upon her.

Then up rose Maria with a martyr-like resignation. She had not been to the beach, she did not wish to go. One spot on this deserted island was just the same to her as another. As she was condemned to stay here, what mattered it where she stayed or how she was employed during that time? If one must have a disagreeable time, why not have it just as disagreeable as possible, and so get greater credit for one's endurance? (This, however, not audibly.) She would do the work. She was perfectly capable of doing as much as that good-for-nothing girl had been. If she wasn't, she would learn. She could at least save a few more cents from the girl's wages to add to the family treasury and so increase the vast sum which they were to make during this summer of humiliation. Their downfall was complete; why not accept it and go to the bottom gracefully? They had to live in a hovel; of course they must do their own work; it was no more than she had expected.

Now Maria did not say all this; instead her sentences were very short, her words were few, but by tone and manner more than by words, she contrived to convey her meaning to the family and made them feel it to the heart's core. The father's face took on a gray look, and the mother's grew old and careworn. Rachel's brightness faded. It seemed as though Maria would manage to dampen the spirits of them all.

But Winthrop was determined that this first day should not be spoiled. Without an instant's hesitation he took Maria's proposal up, not in its spirit, but in its words.

"Why certainly, why shouldn't we? Mother, we can all help. I can't do much all day, but I fancy I can make it up evenings. I'll see that the wood is cut and the coal handy, and make the fire in the morning, and get the ice in the refrigerator, and go errands. There'll be plenty of time for errands before breakfast and train time if I get up a little earlier. And Sundays I'll agree to wash all the dishes three times a day to make up for what I can't do on week days. I can wash dishes beautifully. It will seem like old times when I was a little chap and 'Ri was a baby and mother had no girl, and I helped wipe dishes. Mother, don't you remember? I used to be as proud of the shining white dishes as if I had been a girl, prouder I fancy. Then I can go errands over to Spray View evenings after supper. We don't need to live high, anyway, and there can't be much housework to do in such a small house."

"Of course we can do the work," echoed Rachel eagerly. "I'm sure both Maria and I have had cooking lessons; and besides, here is mother, who knows how to do everything in the world, and can direct us in anything we have forgotten or never learned. I think it will be delightful fun. I'm all ready for it. Come on and let us wash those dinner dishes right away, Winthrop, and then there'll be more room in which to get to rights." And so saying, she ran humming out of the room followed by her brother, and the two had a gay time clattering the dishes.

Maria, with scornful dignity befitting the occasion, followed them, and was soon engaged in stirring up some mysterious concoction for supper and starting some bread for the morrow, as it was found there was no bakery nearer than the neighboring town, and all were too busy to go there for anything.

It was perhaps a half-hour later when all were deep in work; the girls with their sleeves rolled up and hastily improvised kitchen costumes snatched from the open boxes and trunks, Mr. and Mrs. Hammond unpacking and sorting out the most immediate necessities, and Winthrop in his shirt sleeves with a large checked apron tied about his waist and a wiping towel over his arm engaged in mopping dry a thick white-ware soup plate — he was whistling a merry tune and calling out comical sentences to his sisters between times — when a light rig drew up in front of the door and some one got out and came up the steps, but no one in the house heard.

"I say, 'Ri!" called out the diligent brother in a cheery tone, "don't look quite so cross or that bread'll be too sour to eat. It'll be 'rye' bread. See?"

Just then came a distinct knock on the open door, and the irrepressible brother disappeared through the calico portière which belonged to the house and separated the dining room from the parlor, to answer the knock, supposing the intruder to be a butcher or a baker or a candlestick maker, and caring little as to his appearance. Was he not on a lark and on a desert island where he knew not a soul? Besides, his was a spirit that did not feel degraded by a gingham apron and a dish towel.

He had hardly, however, bargained for the immaculate apparition that stood before the door trying to keep a smile from playing politely round his well-shaped, merry lips.

"I beg your pardon; I hope I'm not intruding," said the young man on the porch, with a graceful touch of his hat, "but is not this Mr. Hammond's..."

"Shanty? Certainly," finished Winthrop with a low bow and mock solemnity. "Walk right in. Things aren't quite ship-shape, yet; but I think we can find you a chair."

Winthrop Hammond was not to be embarrassed by any strange gentleman in fashionable driving costume. He dusted off a chair with a flourish, using the dish towel as a duster. Rachel, with a merry face, appeared in the doorway, one cheek well dabbed with flour and her arms dripping with soapsuds. Her dark hair, a trifle rough and loose about her face, had curled itself into little rings, and her cheeks were flushed with excitement and work. She heard Winthrop's gay talk, and never doubted he was making fun for their benefit with some grocer boy or fish man. The young man at the door with a laugh entered into the occasion and stepped willingly into the room, then catching sight of Rachel in the doorway, he came forward with easy grace.

"Good-afternoon, Miss Rachel," he said. "Welcome to the shore. Have you just arrived? You didn't expect to find me here ahead of you, did you?

But you see mother sent me on ahead to attend to some arrangements and make everything ready for them on Monday. Up to your eyes in work, aren't you? Is this your brother? I thought so. Glad to meet you, Mr. Hammond. Having a jolly time, aren't you? I envy you. I'd like nothing better than to pitch in and help. Haven't you something for me to do? Come, now, I've got a horse here and can run all the errands you want. Do put me to work. I've got my own garden all weeded and not a thing to do till the folks come Monday. I'm lonesome, and should enjoy it. Is your sister here?"

"She's in the kitchen making bread," laughed Rachel, entering into the spirit of their guest's speech. "Maria!" she called, and started laughing to find her sister; but Maria had listened to the voice at the door in dismay and had fled.

Chapter 4

Into the midst of the turmoil of work and settling came the calm of the
Sabbath. There was a little church near by, and at the appointed hour they
could see the neighbors in simple dress wending their way thereto. Rachel,
having completed her morning work and helped all she could in the
preparation of dinner, announced her intention of going to church, but the
others were too weary, and even Mrs. Hammond thought it as well to wait
until the next week to begin their acquaintance with the place. However,
Winthrop took up his hat and followed his sister down the steps, when she
came out a few minutes later arrayed in dark serge skirt, clean shirt waist,
and sailor hat.

"For pity's sake! Rachel Hammond! You're surely not going to church
in a strange place in that rig?" called the horrified Maria as she caught sight
of her sister going out the door. "You haven't any gloves, either. I do think
you have taken leave of your senses. You might have a little sense of decency
left, at least."

But Rachel, happily, was out of hearing and went serenely on her way,
drinking in the salt air and the Sabbath quiet as she walked.

Maria, looking after her, wondered how her sister could be so happy,
half envied her her sweet, happy nature, and then went by herself to shed
some tears of discontent. They had not been able to make her listen to any
account of the visitor of the day before. She had kept in hiding during his
short stay and disappeared as suddenly again when he returned with some
packages which Rachel had laughingly sent him after. Maria did not
approve of taking Mr. De Vere into their family at this stage of events and
letting him see all the ins and outs of the rude cottage and the makeshifts
of the family life. She wanted to receive her guests in the right way or not
at all, and so she had left herself severely out of yesterday's affair. Her soul
writhed within her at the thought of the laughing account Mr. De Vere
would give his stately mother and elegant sisters of his visit to Lone Point.
She resolved to keep away from their sight as much as possible, and
wondered why it had been considered necessary to add this humiliation to
her list of troubles for the summer. After her little cry she went to the
kitchen, where her martyr spirit bore her up grimly, while she made the rest
of the family uncomfortable with the elaborate dishes she prepared, and of
which she tasted but little herself. She did not intend to make them all
unhappy, but she was not averse to their knowing how extremely uncomfortable they had succeeded in making her and how well she was bearing

herself under the circumstances. She continued this conduct during the week, even carrying it so far as refusing to go to the beach, when she could have gone as well as not. She declared she had no wish to meet the people of the place; they were a common lot, anyway, she could tell that from their appearance on Sabbath, and as for the sea, she never cared much for it. There were none of the usual enjoyments of seaside life here to make this place endurable, and she would rather stay at home and let others who could enjoy things go to the beach. And so she stayed in the cottage and cooked, and arranged the cheap draperies into graceful fashionings, not taking pleasure and pride in her pretty work as she might have done at another time, but urged to it from fierce necessity. If there were danger that the De Veres might call at any time she would at least make things as presentable as possible that they might not see an utterly barren place, though she firmly resolved to always absent herself and be unfindable when they did call. Thus she wrought, and the room grew truly beautiful in spite of the rebellious spirit of its artist. She asked little help from any one, but her brother and sister were both watching to be of assistance and supplied the needful help without being asked. In one corner of the parlor there grew up a cosy-corner or divan of vast dimensions, composed on one side of the woven-wire cot on which Winthrop slept, and on the other of the packing-box in which the curtains and tin dishes had traveled. This was upholstered deftly in dark blue burlap bearing a wreath and crest design, and the whole was united by a deep valance around the sides. In the corner were many cushions, some only filled with straw or excelsior from the packing, others being the pillows used for Winthrop's bed at night and stuffed during the day into calico and chintz covers of gay design. Two or three were genuine eiderdown with embroidered denim covers, and the effect was not only lovely but luxurious. Maria manipulated pretty screens out of cheap torn paper ones, and one corner was curtained off in a most novel way with a heavy bamboo pole Winthrop found on the beach, and curtains of green and brown figured burlap hanging in fold from it. Behind this no one would have suspected Winthrop's washstand and a few hooks on which he hung some of his clothes. It seemed terribly low to Maria that some one had to sleep in the parlor, but as there was no help for it, there being but two other sleeping rooms in the house, she disguised the fact as prettily as possible. Crêpe paper lampshades and a quaint little bookcase of odd shape and original workmanship, which knew its origin in a shoe box and an old peach crate, also gave touches to the room, which when done was pronounced to be a perfect gem of beauty, comfort, and coziness by the entire family.

"Isn't this beautiful! What a transformation!" exclaimed Roland De Vere, as he entered the room the next week to announce that his family were coming over to call as soon as the Hammond girls were willing to receive them.

"I declare I never saw such a change. Who is the fairy that has waved her wand so effectually?" he asked, and looked at the sweet-faced Rachel, who immediately disclaimed any part in the work and gave it all to Maria. Meanwhile Maria continued invisible to all callers. Mr. De Vere did not notice this fact so much, however, as he would have done had he been less well pleased with the company of her brother and sister. They began planning numerous excursions and moonlight sails, in which she was always included, but in the preparation of which she did not figure. She felt very much cut at heart at the way things were going and blamed it all on the others, not seeing that it was her own doing. She persisted more than ever in her purpose of isolating herself. She would not even go to the beach, though the others entreated her and invented various ways of trying to get her there. He headstrong, stubborn will had set itself up against all their pleadings and she would not be coaxed by anything or any one, so at last they gave it up. Maria arranged her hair in the most unbecoming way possible, took on hard, drawn-down lines about her mouth, significant of her martyrdom, and went about in an old work apron most of the time. Rachel grieved over it as much as she had time for amid the merry round of delight that was open to her. She found a great deal of joy in wandering over the beautiful beach in search of shells with her friend Marvie Parker and Marvie's brother George, who proved to be fully as bright and interesting a companion as she had prophesied, though he was a busy student and had little time, even that summer vacation, for a frolic. She enjoyed her brother Winthrop's merry talk in the evenings, and rejoiced in going to the seven-o'clock city train to meet him and their father every evening. She looked upon the delight of a visit from Maria's friend, as she called Roland De Vere, as some great treat which did not belong to her, but by special privilege she was permitted to share with the others. The summer seemed to be unfolding before her with a beautiful promise.

She sat one evening just at sunset in her room. She could look out on the beautiful bay in the distance and see the softly rippling waters calming down for the glassy effect of sunset. The white sails here and there were speeding homeward. In a few minutes the evening train would slip silently along by the water and she would run down to meet her father and brother. Supper was nearly ready. The bisque of clams was perfect. That had been her work and she was proud of it. Maria was busy with some one of her special concoctions and seemed to desire the kitchen to herself, and Rachel had been glad to slip away for this little silent minute to rest and think and pray. Since they had been doing their own work she seemed to find so little uninterrupted time for her Bible and thought that she was glad to find it anywhere. The mornings were now so full of work, and as soon as the work was done Marvie Parker was sure to run in and claim Rachel for some scheme. To be sure it was not yet a week they had been by the sea, and yet it seemed to Rachel that things had settled down into a routine. She thought sadly of it, for Maria, her dear sister, seemed left out of everything. She would not have anything to do with the Parkers, and she seemed fully as loth to have to do with her own friends, the De Veres.

Rachel wondered what it meant and if there was anything she could do, if perhaps she was to blame in some way for having suggested this summer scheme. But no, when she thought of her mother's face taking on a glow of health from the life-giving breezes, and of her father, whose face had dropped its load of anxious care, and who seemed to be really enjoying life once more, she could not feel that she had done wrong; for surely it had turned out to be the best for all of them. No, it was clearly not her fault and she must not mourn over it as such. The next question came: What could she do for Maria? for she was ever one who was looking out to be her brother's keeper. She took up her Bible, from habit perhaps, for her own heart could not answer the questions that multiplied upon her. She felt it fully laid upon her to do something for her sister; but what could it be? Coaxing would not do, sacrifice would avail nothing, and neither would pity; she had tried them all. They merely seemed to irritate the loved one. The Bible opened of itself as it often did, to the sweet old call, "Come unto me, all ye that labor and are heavy laden, and I will give you rest. Take my yoke upon you, and learn of me; for I am meek and lowly in heart; and ye shall find rest unto your souls." Rachel had marked those verses when she was but a little girl with her new pen and some bright red ink. She had turned to them many, many times since, at first because they were familiar words and seemed like old friends on account of the red lines about them, and afterward because they had comforted her and had grown dear for their own sakes.

It was not strange that she opened to them now, and as she read them mechanically, though reverently, she did not linger there, for at first thought their message seemed more for her sister than herself, and she sighed as she half turned the leaf and wished that Maria could find rest, so that her life would be all peace and a joy that she could reflect everywhere. Then suddenly a thought stopped her hand as it slowly turned the leaf. Wait! Was not that message for her after all? She was burdened with the gloom of her sister. Might she not find rest from that as well as from some burden of her own? The dear Lord surely would not have her carry that burden. He would show her if she "came to him" what it was, if aught, she could do, to help lift the cloud that was over Maria, and she could come to Jesus and find rest and strength, so that even the burden of her sister's attitude would not disturb her calm, for it would be his calm. She turned the leaves slowly to another verse also marked and which had been her help many a time before. "Ye have not chosen me, but I have chosen you, and ordained you, that ye should go and bring forth fruit, and that your fruit should remain, that whatsoever ye shall ask of the Father in my name he may give it you." Then it was not her business to look after the fruit. She was to do his work because he had chosen her. She would do whatever he put into her hands to do, and meanwhile she had forgotten that whatsoever she would ask of the Father he would do it for her, and she might trust him to do it in his own good way and time. She would trust him with this dear sister. And so she knelt and poured out all her heart, full of worry, that had been so anxiously filling from day to day with the many little petty irritations that had arisen in kitchen and parlor and all over the house, and which she had tried to bear patiently but which had worn on her sweet spirit till now and then sharp words had escaped her. She told her Heavenly Father all and then asked for her dear sister's happiness as the greatest joy that could come. After that she smoothed her hair and rushed out into the kitchen with her heart full of love for Maria and trust for the answer to her prayer, and putting her arms impetuously around her warm and weary sister's neck gave her a great big hug and whispered softly: "'Ri, dear, forgive me. I've been awfully cross and teased you a great deal to do what you don't want to, and I have not helped you half enough. Will you forgive me? I'm sorry."

Now Maria was frying fish and was just in the act of turning over a large beautiful piece so that its perfections should remain unmarred. Besides, she was very warm and the stove had been acting abominably all the afternoon, and the brownness of the fish was only due to repeated shakings and coaxings on Maria's part with kindlings and bits of paper. Maria's hair was coming down, or was so nearly so that any movement on her part was precarious. Also she had burned her wrist and the pain was quite severe, aggravated as it was by the heat of the stove. Therefore Rachel's eager hug was scarcely pleasant just then, and Rachel's willingness to confess her fault, when she herself, the greater offender, was very unwilling to do so, irritated Maria more than words can tell. Perhaps she was not so much to blame, poor child, for she certainly was having a very uncomfortable time, largely her own fault though it was. She had just received a letter from one of her dear friends describing in detail the delights she was enjoying in a popular hotel in a lovely mountain resort. It was no wonder perhaps that her tone was ungracious.

"For pity's sake, do get out of my way, Rachel!" she said crossly. Don't you see what you're doing? You'll make me break that lovely piece of fish. I do wish you would ever be considerate. I'd much rather you'd show your sorrow by your actions than your words. Words are cheap."

With that Maria jerked the fish over and pushed the tea kettle and two or three pans around on the stove with such a nervous clatter that there was no chance for any more words even if Rachel had chosen to speak them, and Rachel, with the tears brimming over in her eyes, went her way to the train, full of sorrow that she had made another mistake. "I never seem to know what to do or say to please her," she said to herself. "I'm sure if she had spoken crossly to me and had asked me for forgive her I should have been so happy and forgotten it all, but it only seemed to make her feel crosser with me." Then Rachel remembered that it was not her work to look after results, and that she had taken her burden to her Heavenly Father and given it to him to carry. She must not pick it up again and bear it away with her; it was hers no longer. So she cast it all aside and hurried toward the station with a lighter heart.

Chapter 5

Maria stood on the piazza later that evening. The sunset glow was fading over the bay. The supper dishes were all washed and put away. There was nothing more to be done in the kitchen that night. She was at liberty to watch the pearl-colored sail that floated lazily on the pink and gray waters. Winthrop and Rachel had gone over to the pavilion directly after supper with Marvie Parker and her brother. They had not thought it worth while to ask Maria to join them to-night. Indeed, Rachel had hinted to her brother that perhaps it would be better to say nothing of their purpose to Maria, as everything of the kind seemed only to make her feel badly, and so for the first time since they had been at the seaside, they had gone off without coaxing her to go with them. Although Maria had declined these invitations quite curtly every time, she nevertheless felt cut by the omission to-night. Tears filled her eyes and blurred the pearl-colored sail as she thought how easily they could get along without her. Heretofore she had been the life of the family, the center of every excursion, the witty talker, the graceful leader in all. Now Rachel, her younger sister, hardly grown up as yet, seemed to have taken her place. She was not then so indispensable as she had thought. Even her father and mother had strolled away, arm in arm, like a pair of lovers, pointing out a bright star overhead or calling one another's attention to a sail in the distance. Maria felt very lonely.

Things had proved a great deal worse even than she had feared. She had supposed that after the family saw how uncomfortable things were going to be they would set about to right them in some way. They would perhaps go over to Spray View and take some sort of a respectable cottage where they could live in some decent style, as she phrased it to herself; there would be some enjoyment in that, and perhaps they would try to get another servant, though she herself would be willing to help in the kitchen and get along with a very poor one, if they might so save enough to be able to live in what seemed a respectable manner and, what was more important to her, would seem so to her friends. Then she would gladly welcome the De Veres and enjoy whatever they could offer her in the way of pleasure. Now, however, all was different. The family seemed entirely indifferent to their surroundings. They were actually happy. As she thought over it she realized that she could not remember to have ever seen her father and mother so thoroughly enjoying themselves before. She wondered that they did not see how unhappy she was. Oh, if she could but go away to that mountain resort where her friend Nellie Mayhew was having such a delightful time! To be sure she couldn't hope to share in everything because she could not buy the clothes in which to go to many of the entertainments and social affairs participated in by her friend, but she told herself that if she could but get there, be in that great hotel, one of its guests, she would trust herself but that with a very few dollars she could construct a wardrobe that would make her look well enough to vie with the others. But what was there here? She cast her eye about. Nothing but views and air! She curled her lip. And a father and mother and sister and brother who were too absorbed in their own pleasures to think of her or know that she was at home moping alone after a long day of hard work in the kitchen.

Now at that very minute father and mother, as they pointed out the stars and the sails, were discussing whether or not they could possibly manage to scrape together money enough to send Maria to the mountains in the style she wished to go. The mother, strange to say, was the one who objected this time.

"No, Richard," said she, "I cannot help feeling, even if we felt it right to afford it, that it would not be best. Maria is young yet, and while I think she is perfectly to be trusted to behave herself and take care of herself in every way, I am not sure but it is much the best thing for her to have the discipline of this summer. Already she had shown traits of character which I did not dream that she possessed. It has grieved me to the heart to see it. She has behaved in an utterly selfish and inconsiderate manner. You do not see it all day long as I do. She works, oh, works like a slave, harder than she ever worked before. I shall put a stop to that overwork pretty soon, for it is utterly unnecessary, a great part of it; but she is unlovely to me and to her sister, and as disagreeable as she knows how to be. I have been meditating how to go about it to have a talk with her, but it seemed best to wait a little while and study her present mood. Sometimes I am afraid she never has understood what it means to be a true Christian, she is so utterly rebellious at her lot."

And then in tender tones the father tried to excuse her and pity her, and so they talked and walked much farther and longer than they had expected to do, and the evening wore on while Maria sat alone, until from very weariness of herself and her own thoughts she was forced to go to bed.

It was the very next day that Maria was at last driven to the beach. It was Saturday. Winthrop had remained at the shore as his father felt he would not be needed that day at the store. The dinner being out of the way, and Maria's dress being soiled beyond hope of further use until it was washed, she retired to her room to make a severe but crisp toilet. If she could have found anything ugly to put on she would have done so, but fortunately for her nearly everything she possessed was tasteful and pretty, and the ugly things brought along for rainy weather or hard usage she had entirely used up for that week, therefore she was obliged to betake herself to a dainty sheer dimity, clear blue and white. The belt and collar of this dress were light blue ribbons with fluttering bows. Maria tried to fit on a linen collar and go without a belt, but the effect was so incongruous that she finally gave in to her own innate sense of beauty and put on the blue ribbons. Then her hair did not seem to harmonize with the costume, and by this time her sense of fitness had been sufficiently aroused to make her loosen her hair and coil it in the old way which was so becoming. Altogether she was quite like the familiar Maria when she was ready to leave the room. As she passed the window to pick up a novel that she had been reading, her eye caught sight of a double surrey, drawn by handsome horses, just turning the corner by their cottage. There were three ladies and a young man in the carriage and the elder lady was leveling a lorgnette at the unpretentious little dwelling. That lorgnette made up Maria's mind. That carriage contained the De Veres — mother, daughters, and son. They had come then, at the son's instance, to patronize the Hammonds. Maria, for one, did not intend to be investigated through a lorgnette. Her soul boiled at thought of it. Quick as a flash she caught up her book and a white parasol belonging to Rachel lying on the bed and flew out of the back door, straight across the sand lot to the next street and in line with the house so that she could not be seen from the carriage, which was now standing in front, and then turned and went swiftly to the most unfrequented portion of the broad beach she could find; there she established herself behind her parasol and a fortification of sand, and gave her mind to the reading of her book, assured that no unwelcome visitor could find her here.

Meanwhile Rachel, as she opened the door all smiles and played the gracious lady to the elegant Mrs. De Vere, remembered with satisfaction, not for her own sake but for Maria's, that she had caught a glimpse of Maria's blue dimity on the bed as she had passed the door, and that by this time she must be arrayed in it, for of course Maria would be obliged to come out of her shell now. But lo, when the anxious mother, who felt that Maria would need an extra word from her in order to make her put aside her new and foolish notions, came in search of her elder daughter, she could find her nowhere, and Rachel, being sent in search, though she looked in all Maria's former places of retreat, could find no trace of her. Much puzzled, Rachel returned to enjoy the call and forget all about her sister's disappearance.

Perhaps the De Veres thought it strange that Maria was absent from the house, especially as they knew from their brother and son that she had always been absent when he had called; but if they did so think they were far too well-bred to let any one know it. They were not nearly so overpowering in grandeur of manner as Maria had anticipated. Mrs. Hammond was quite charmed with the gracious and cordial friendliness of Mrs. De Vere, and a mutual liking seemed at once to draw the two elder ladies together. Meantime the young people planned innumerable pleasures in company, and the time flew by and the call was prolonged far beyond the usual length prescribed by fashion. In a most unceremonious manner, and one that would have shocked poor Maria beyond believing had she been present, the three De Veres followed Rachel through the sand and gayly fell upon George and Marvie Parker with a demand that they join their moonlight sail planned for the coming week. How it had come about Rachel could hardly understand, but they had found out she had friends in the Parkers and had delicately suggested the invitation and then proposed that they go at once and give it. Rachel wondered as they went whether Maria would blame her for it, and if she would make trouble about the Parkers going with them, and finally resolved to say nothing about it to her sister, letting things come about as they would.

Meanwhile Maria, clothed daintily, as was her habit to be, and having attained her purpose of getting away from her visitors unseen and un-suspected, felt much more at peace with the world than she had done for many a day. She settled herself without the usual hard could upon her brow to really enjoy her book. So much are clothes of value that the subtle consciousness of being well-dressed has often power to lift one for the time at least above a seeming fret of circumstance or sordidness of surroundings.

Now had Rachel Hammond been consulted as to the answering of her earnest prayers for her sister, she would have said that the most unpromis-ing thing that could happen for Maria was to have her run away from the De Veres and spend the entire afternoon by herself in a lonely part of the beach, reading a highly-wrought novel wherein the heroine suffered impos-sible things and was crowned with untold rewards for her pains. Rachel would have said that a pleasant afternoon in the company of pleasant people, planning a delightful excursion, forgetting things that might have been, and learning to be interested in things that are and are to be, would have been the best thing for her sister. But God knew better. He was leading this child of his through a narrow, thorny path, it is true, but through the only straight road that would take her home. She sat there and read, and as she had not visited the beach before and knew little the peculiarities of wind and tide, she did as most newcomers do, settled herself by the edge of the surf, as near as seemed safe and pleasant, that she might watch the water. Then after a good look she forthwith forgot to watch the water in the tide of the fortunes of her heroine. The ocean's tide at that time was going out, but almost at its turn. It receded a little and a little, and Maria read on, and by and by it did not recede, and then it gained a little and a little, until it crept nearer and nearer to the seat upon the sand and the straying blue ribbon that fluttered out from the white silk parasol. Now a larger wave came and almost stretched its lip of foam to kiss the foam of white lace on the blue dimity ruffles; then it went back again for a while to gather force, and now another came and did just touch the dainty ruffle and dampen it, but still the wearer read on oblivious to recession or approach. She had turned herself sidewise to keep the ocean glare from her page and did not notice. Moreover, the heroine was just on the point of being rescued from a desert island on which she had been cast with a noble hero who loved her, by an ignoble lover who had come in search of her. The situation was a thrilling one and Maria had no eyes for aught but the story. Neither did she see a young man who was sauntering leisurely down the beach toward her from the direction of the lighthouse, a mile or two away.

The Rev. Howard Fairfield, in the most unclerical dress he could find in his very unclerical wardrobe, had been visiting the Point Rock lighthouse, and joking with its keeper, entering with zest into all the stories the old man told of his wild life as a young sailor, himself posing as a young man who understood and enjoyed all such escapades. Now he was walking slowly along the beach and, wholly unconscious of any inconsistency or incongruity, was engaged in weaving the wonders which he had just seen and heard of God's providence and man's skill into a fine illustration that should well set off the conclusion of the address, both eloquent and learned, which he was preparing for the first sermon he should preach after his vacation was ended. He was a very young man for the important charge he occupied, and he had chosen this simple, quiet summer resort as a suitable place for him to spend his vacation, with the idea that the absolute quiet if not loneliness of it would conduce to the rest and study which he meant to alternate so judiciously, and thus send him back to his city church thoroughly fortified in health and with a store of material for sermons for the winter's campaign.

He was not an unspiritual minister, neither was he ashamed of his calling; but in college and seminary he had acquired some "advanced" notions concerning the doffing of clerical clothes and the "clerical manner" which, while they might be good in a degree, had been carried by him to their utmost extremity. He delighted, on going to a place, to keep the people from finding out that he was a minister. Indeed, he carried this so far that he would sometimes allow himself to be taken for almost anything else rather than let others know his true character or profession. He had a fancy that he could do a great deal more good in this way, by entering into other people's lives and sympathies and not letting them feel that the good he did was because it was his business to do so. Perhaps there was truth in this, the great drawback being that he spent so much time in entering into people's sympathies and lives that he frequently forgot or found it awkward to do the good that might have resulted from the influence he had gained thereby. Sometimes too, others felt that he allowed the line between right and wrong to be glossed over a trifle in this "entering-in" business. He called it "being all things to all men." However that may be, he was a student, an eloquent preacher, somewhat conceited because of the extraordinary praise he had received during his short pastorate, and very much opinionated, but nevertheless very much in earnest. He considered himself very spiritual indeed, and in his heart longed to be all that his Lord would have him be. In person he was handsome, with a scholarly air, graceful in manner, a little distant but exceedingly attractive to most people, especially when he chose to be so. Rachel Hammond, had she known him, would have considered him the most unlikely person to help her sister Maria that could be found, and yet he was coming toward her on the beach and the waves were creeping toward her on the sand, and the Lord was ordering it all. For the winds and the waves obey his will, even in so seemingly slight an affair as this.

The young man had advanced quite near to Maria and without particularly noticing her, except to realize that his favorite combination of light blue and white was lying over there on the sand making a pretty picture against the background of sky and sea. As he drew nearer he saw it was a young woman with a shapely hand that held a book, and he wondered, because he was a student of human nature, what sort of a young woman she was, reading thus alone so close beside the sea, and what was the book which so absorbed her that she did not mark the approach of the hungry waves. He thought he must warn her if she did not look up before the next wave, and lingered a little to see if she stirred. Then, before he could think further, there came one of those unexpectedly large waves which take people, and almost themselves it seems, by surprise, and rush and tumble in mad glee far beyond any predecessor. It not only touched and soaked the crisp ruffles of the dimity, but it merrily dashed into the young lady's lap, wetting her feet and book and sending her flying back from the spot in alarm. And then it calmly seized the white silk parasol which was a treasured present from a rich uncle to Rachel, and boasted a solid gold handle, and hurled it out in its retreating arms, a toy upon the billows. Maria, finding herself on solid ground and seeing her sister's precious parasol tossed on the water, made another dash to catch it on the crest of the next wave, but the water was again too quick for her and it floated out, this time a little farther, where the breakers tossed the delicate thing so rudely that Maria despaired for its frail structure. At this juncture the young man standing by took two strides in the saucy waters and brought the wet and dripping thing to Maria with as much dignity as he could command considering the wet and flapping condition of his white duck trousers.

It was certainly an embarrassing situation for both young people, but the Reverend Howard Fairfield rather enjoyed carrying off trying situations in a graceful manner, and he certainly did himself justice in this instance, to the admiration of the young woman concerned.

"Oh, not at all, let me carry it home for you," he said, as she reached her hand for the sunshade. "Your cottage is near by, is it not? Nothing is very far away from anything else in this place, is it?" Here he stopped to pick up her book, actuated more perhaps by a curiosity to know its name than anything else. "No, no, let me carry it. You will have enough to do to walk in this sand with your wet gown. I am going this way, you know, and it's no trouble whatever."

And so Maria, much against her will, walked the length of the beach to her home with a stranger, a young man, her dress wet and bedraggled, her borrowed parasol and book carried by him, and his own costume rather the worse for water. It was altogether too dramatic for Maria's liking to appear at home in this condition after the lofty way in which she had been acting. She knew her brother would never cease teasing her. She was trying to plan some way of retreat, or getting rid of the stranger who was chatting pleasant nothings to which she need not reply except by monosyllables, when lifting her eyes she saw her sister, accompanied by the Misses De Vere, their brother, and Miss Parker, coming toward them. There was no escape. They were on the point of meeting. It was horrible! Maria caught her breath, and then she heard her sister's exclamation and knew there was no hope but to turn and face the situation.

Chapter 6

It turned out that Howard Fairfield was an old college friend of Roland De Vere, and the two young men met with great delight and gayety. Introductions followed all around, and Maria's chagrin was covered by this ceremony, until she had time to recover herself and smile an apologetic retreat, leaving the minister to make explanations. The merry little party, however, followed her, Rachel, who had hurried on with her sister, was kind and eager to help, solicitous lest she might catch cold, and plied her with questions as to how it happened. The others came more slowly to the cottage and chatted a little till Rachel and Maria, who had hastily replaced the dimity skirt by one of black serge, again appeared. Then the De Veres said they really must be going home, and drove away with promises for the next day and many merry words about the moonlight excursion. The minister lingered a little after the departure of the carriage, politely saying he hoped no harm had been done Miss Hammond by her unexpected sea bath; thanked her for his part in the affair which had resulted in so pleasant a meeting with his old friends; and bowed himself away to the hotel, leaving a good impression behind him.

As he walked he reflected:

"Two very pretty girls. I had not bargained for friends this summer. Perhaps it may interfere with my plans for hard study; but, after all, why shouldn't I take a little recreation? I can't enjoy ladies' society at home, because if I look at one young woman more than another, I feel as though all the gossips of both sexes were proclaiming marriage banns from the housetops for us; but I don't believe it is good for a man to be forever with men alone. One forgets how to treat one's sister after a while. It was a pleasant interruption to the monotony of the place to meet De Vere. I always liked him in college. Well, things are turning out better than I had expected. I don't know but that I shall stay the month out, after all. At any rate, I won't give up my room yet until I have time to decide."

Then he went in to prepare for supper.

The afternoon's experience had done this for Maria: she was drawn out of her shell at last and by necessity pledged to go on the moonlight excursion. She reluctantly gave up her role of martyr little by little, and by Sabbath evening was sufficiently herself to go to church. It really would be more bearable than this continual staying in the house, which was beginning to wear on her patience. Besides, her brief glimpse of young, merry company the day before had made her restless for more.

There was no settled minister at Lone Point. The church itself had been built by the donations of visitors, who had spent their energies one summer in raising the money and making as pretty a little house of worship as could be desired for the chance sojourner by the sea. Some of those who lived for a large part of the year in the place took it upon themselves to keep the services going all the summer. Occasionally there were ministers visiting over Sunday who preached, to the great delight of the little audiences; but during the rest of the time, earnest workers from city churches, who were not taking a vacation from their religion as well as from their other work, took turns in either reading a sermon or making a short talk to the little company gathered there, and the songs of praise swelled forth from worshiping hearts as truly thankful as if they had been feeding on the bread of life dealt out by regularly ordained hands. These services were divided among several men, who were always willing to do with their might what their hands found to do. Rev. Howard Fairfield, in spite of his experiences of the day before in finding old friends, had succeeded in keeping his incognito so thoroughly that no one dreamed of asking him to preach, for which he was in his heart truly thankful, since he really needed the rest. He had perhaps, though, a little of the natural feeling of a man who was fresh from the ecclesiastical atmosphere of the seminary, a slight doubt as to the genuineness of Sabbath services conducted by a man who not only had not been through a seminary course, but who was not even college bred. It amounted almost to a feeling of sacrilege, as though they were "playing church" as children do, to have the laymen handle sacred phrases and forms. Young theologues are apt to feel at first more anxious for the orthodoxy of the worship than for its spirituality, though if you asked them, they might tell you it could not be truly spiritual unless it was thoroughly orthodox. Mr. Fairfield sat through the morning address, given by a white-haired brother who had served his church for full fifty years, and was amply competent, by reason of his wide Christian experience, to have ministered even to the needs of a theological student. His face wore a look of gentle toleration, which scarcely masked the critical impatience he was feeling all the while. He told himself that an hour spent at home with his Bible would have been more profitable. But by reason of the command of his Lord, which he reverenced, not to "forget the assembling of yourselves together," he went again in the evening.

Now in the evening the service was led by a younger man who had spent some time in a training school for Christian workers, and who, though thoroughly versed in the Bible, was yet not so thoroughly trained in the English language. He did not attempt a sermon. The service was largely composed of song. His own part in it was two or three gentle, earnest talks interspersed with illustrations, carrying home to the heart the true meaning of as many Bible verses, whose practical teachings were linked together into a single, fully developed theme. There was singing between each of these talks. They seemed to scarcely belong together, and yet when the hour was passed, the thoughtful soul went forth with something to carry into daily life to help in making ready for heaven.

The service was short. No one need complain that he grew weary. They issued forth into the bright moonlight from the cheery little chapel, some with kindly greetings, some with earnest words or merry ones upon their lips. The minister, quite as a matter of course, walked along beside the two young ladies he had met the day before, and they chatted pleasantly as they walked. He stopped a moment on their piazza to watch the moonlight on the bay, and they began talking, for want of any other topic of common interest, about the place, the people, the church, and the day itself with its services.

"I supposed, of course, we should hear you preach this evening, Mr. Fairfield," said Maria pleasantly. She was regaining her good-humor and quite liked the young man. She had never had a ministerial friend. It was something new and interesting.

"Oh, no indeed," said the minister laughingly. "I took good care no one should know that I was anything other than the most ordinary of idle young men on a pleasure trip. I don't want to preach. It isn't fair when one is off on a vacation. It isn't fair to my people, either, you know. They expect me to rest and not use up my strength on some other church when they are sending me away to recruit it. You don't know how a minister feels when he gets away from his work. I have a clerical friend who said last year, when he started off on his vacation, 'No more preaching, no more praying, no more reading of the Bible, for six whole weeks,' with a sigh of relief. I wouldn't go quite so far as that myself," laughingly; "but at the same time it is a relief to get away from all reminders of work when one goes off to rest."

Maria laughed gayly at the story. She thought the young minister very clever. There was a prospect of something enlivening, after all, in this desolate place. But Rachel glanced up quickly. "Did he really say that?" she said with a troubled look in her eyes; "a minister of Jesus Christ?"

There was something embarrassing in the anxious expression of those clear eyes that made Mr. Fairfield, for the first time since he had told that story, reflect that it was not altogether the feeling for a minister of Jesus Christ to have, even if the expressing of the thought had been merely in fun. He was a trifle vexed with himself for having told the story and began excusing his friend, and finally mildly condemning him. But there was an uncomfortable consciousness of something, the minister did not exactly know what, which he was certain he would have to face out with his own conscience after he got by himself.

"Well," said Maria, hastening to cover what she considered to be an impoliteness on her sister's part, "I suppose it's all very well for the poor ministers who have to work all the time, but I must say I don't enjoy hearing a man who doesn't know how to conduct a service. Did you ever see such a hash as that meeting to-night? Upon my word, I began to wonder if they wouldn't ask us all to get up and recite some little verses or stories next." She ended in a bubble of laughter over her own fun. She was in the habit of saying bright, daring things and of having them laughed at. The young minister was no exception. He laughed. He was tired of loneliness and her laugh rested him.

"Well," he said, "that man did very well for a layman. I fancy he got some of his thoughts out of some one of Moody's books, or something like that, but really that first bit of a talk he gave us on what we live for was not so bad. I never heard that story about the old sea captain before. It did sound odd when he kept repeating 'When I'm at the North Pole I live sperm whale, when I'm at the South Pole I live sperm whale.' It was well expressed too, and a good illustration. I suppose some of those old fishermen would say for them to live was fishing. I know a man in the city whose entire life is for money, just like the man he was speaking of to-night. It really was a good thought to bring before those young people."

"But," said Maria laughing again, "did you hear him say 'opportoonity'?" She brought out the broad "oo" in exact imitation of the tone in which it had been uttered so earnestly a few minutes before. But her laugh was interrupted by Rachel.

"Mr. Fairfield," said she, lifting those clear, thoughtful eyes of hers with the moonlight shining into her pure face, "do you suppose that it is possible for any one — that is, for young people — well, say for — me, to be able to say with perfect truth, 'For me to live is Christ'?"

The minister felt once more that strange embarrassment, mingled this time with a desire to answer the question aright and a feeling of inability to do so. His pastorate had been a short one, his experience was small, and there had not come to him many times in this earnest way an inquirer who seemed to be searching for the light. It is true, in a theological sense, the question was easy enough to answer; but he knew by the look on Rachel's face that she meant more than an ordinary question asked out of curiosity. She really wanted to know in order that she might if possible use the knowledge.

He searched his mind and his catechism for a suitable reply, but none would come. At last with his usual tone of positiveness, which carried weight with so many who questioned him, he replied: "Why, yes, surely; why not? If you are a Christian, you certainly can say that."

"No," said Rachel, shaking her head in a thoughtful, troubled way, "I can't. I have been thinking about it ever since Mr. Brown told that story about the sperm whale. My life isn't 'sperm whale,' but I am afraid I would have to say if I answered truthfully, for me to live is having my own way, having a good time, and having everything go just as I planned it. I'm afraid I put that above Christ. I certainly must, or I would be happy with whatever Christ gives me, if for me to live were Christ."

Maria listening was surprised. She had thought uncomfortably that evening during the meeting that for herself to live was to have her own way, but she would never have laid that charge at her gentle sister Rachel's door. Rachel, who was always willing to give up when others insisted on having their own way! But Maria did not like to have the conversation drift into so solemn a theme, and she hailed the coming of her brother upon the porch with relief.

"Mr. Fairfield," she interrupted just here, "you have not met my brother yet."

During the introduction that followed, Rachel slipped away. She felt that she wanted to be quiet and think. Perhaps sometimes she could find that minister alone for a few minutes and he would have some help for her; ministers all knew how to help, and he was young and she would not be afraid to ask him, unless—unless he should be like that other dreadful minister, who had said that awful thing about not wanting to read the Bible or pray for six whole weeks. She shuddered as she thought of it again, and her literal soul was greatly disturbed that a minister should be so like the rest of the world. But just now she wanted her Bible to answer her, and she went softly in and lighting her little shaded lamp went to her Rock for help.

Mr. Fairfield did not remain long that evening. It was Sunday, and he did not as a rule make calls on the Sabbath, unless it were an errand of necessity or mercy. He looked about for Rachel as he left, and was both troubled and relieved to find her gone—troubled, because he felt in some indistinct way that he had not done his duty; relieved, because "what business had duty to follow him around on his vacation?"

After all, the little girl's question had been true enough. How many people were there in the world who really could say that? Could he himself? Was it Christ for him to live, or was it fine sermons, a good name, a large church roll? Did he think most when he preached of whether he was speaking to the hearts of men and leading them to see Jesus, or was he looking after the praise of men? Was he not sometimes looking about to see if there were a committee from that big Chicago church sitting in some dim corner of the room and wondering what they thought of that rounded sentence? Could it be possible that for him to live was getting to be whether he would in a few years receive a call to a better church with a larger salary and a greater name?

He wandered down by the sea in the deep moonlight where he could be alone with his conscience and his God. As he walked to his retired musing place he said to himself: "How strange it is that that man, who is evidently not a highly educated man, can with his few words so touch a heart that it will ask itself such questions as that girl asked me to-night! Did any one ever go home from one of my sermons and ask himself such searching questions as that, I wonder? There it is again. I am looking out to see what other people think of me and my words. No, not all that either. Perhaps I'm looking out now to see what God thinks of me. I must find that out to-night."

Chapter 7

Does Satan also walk sometimes beside the sea? Perhaps he saw the trend of this young man's thoughts, and hoped to turn them aside. Perhaps he feared too much the searching questions that would surely come to this thoughtful heart, which if once awakened to itself and its possibilities would be a dangerous enemy to the powers of darkness and of this world. Or it may be that what happened next was just another link in God's wonderful chain of influence that was to draw this disciple nearer to himself.

"Ho! I say! Stop a minute!" shouted a voice, that at last made itself heard above the roar of the waves, sufficiently at least to attract the attention of the preoccupied man.

The voice proved to belong to a fellow-boarder at the hotel. "Is that you, Mr. Fairfield?" called the man, hurrying along the sand almost out of breath with his efforts; "I wasn't sure in this uncertain moonlight. There's a telegram down at the hotel for you and they've been hunting all over creation for you. They went to church but found it closed. The boy came over from Spray View with it and he is almost frantic to get back and seems to consider it a part of his duty not to surrender the message till the right man turns up, though a number of us offered to pay the requisite fifty cents, the ridiculous price they charge to bring a message over to this forsaken spot."

The minister thanked his informant, turned hurriedly and retraced his steps along the beach to the hotel, wondering meanwhile if aught had befallen his mother or sister far away on a foreign trip, or if some member of his church was lying very ill, or perhaps dead.

Telegrams may mean so much or so little, they always set one's heart beating faster till he has them safely read.

It proved to be only a notice of a special business meeting of importance to himself and his church, to which he was called home early the next day to accommodate a member of the church committee who was himself called suddenly away and wished some matters attended to before he left. The minister stood on the moonlit piazza a moment after he read it, and crushed the yellow paper irritably between his fingers. It did not suit him to rush back to the city in the heat just now. He had expected that meeting to be deferred until the first week in September. It annoyed him too, to have such a message as this sent on Sabbath evening. He did not stop to analyze why, except to think that it might have waited, or have been sent the night before. A feeling came over him of how utterly it lacked harmony with the day's quiet resting and his evening's high thoughts. So much was he disturbed in mind that he did not again go back to his musings by the sea. His line of thought as well as his walk was broken off. The hour was late. He must take a very early train in the morning. He must prepare his mind for the business in town which awaited him, and there were a few preparations he must make for his hurried journey. So he went reluctantly up to his room, wondering vaguely whether he would ever get back to the time and place to have that talk out with himself alone by the ocean and resolving that he would take the first opportunity for it. He remembered the moonlight sail planned for that week, and new friends he had found and the old ones he had discovered to be near by, and resolved to leave his baggage here in this secluded place beside the sea and return on the evening train or by the next day if possible, rather than pack up and move on to some new place as he had half resolved to do three days before. Somehow there seemed to be a new charm to the place now that he had found friends, even though what he had wished to get away from was all social obligations. He was interested in the family who had such a pleasant little cottage around by the bay. He believed he would like to talk further with that bright, intellectual older sister, and perhaps even hear more of the flower-faced younger sister's searching, innocent questions. He felt that they were not bad training for him in many ways.

Mr. Fairfield was scarcely seated in the uptown car the next morning on his arrival in the city when he became aware that two bright eyes were watching an opportunity for their owner to claim his attention, and looking up, he beheld across the car a young lady who was one of his parishioners. She greeted him with gushing frankness. There was always a good-natured openness about Miss Lou Marlow. Everybody called her Miss Lou, except those who went a little further and called her "Lou." She was hail-fellow-well-met with every one, as intimate on the first day of acquaintance as she bade fair to be in ten years from that time, a large, pretty girl, with good spirits to overflowing, and a laugh and joke for every one. The minister always felt as if he had come in contact with a splash of brilliant sunlight unrelieved by any softening shadows when he met her, and yet she affected no one unpleasantly; there was too much true good-nature and native humor about her. Still, one always looked with her to have their faults or virtues hauled out and laughed over with jolly, ruthless hand, and for this reason the minister rather dreaded a tête-à-tête with Miss Lou. He particularly shrank from one in a street car, as Miss Lou's voice, like her taste in dress, was not altogether subdued, but she had moved to one side and made room for him beside her on the seat, and her movement was unmistakable. Besides, she plainly showed that she had something good to tell and would scarcely be deterred from it by so small a circumstance as having to talk across a car aisle. The minister changed his seat, but as he did so put on his most dignified air in order to check as much as possible a too exuberant manner, should such appear.

"Oh, Mr. Fairfield, when did you come back? Why I'm so astonished," began Miss Lou volubly. "Really this is quite a coincidence. I had the strangest dream about you last night, and it was so real and vivid, and now to think I should meet you when I thought you were far away! It really looks as though there must have been something meant by it," and she giggled uncontrollably.

Mr. Fairfield looked nervously about the car to see if there were others of his acquaintance present, and his informant went on between her gurgles of laughter.

"Oh, it was too funny!"

"Yes?" said the minister helplessly. He hoped it was nothing connected with selecting a wife for him or anything of that sort, but he greatly feared from the young lady's tone it might be some silly dream linking him with some one of his congregation. That it would be something embarrassing he felt sure. He waited helplessly, hoping he would be given the grace to keep from looking too red and angry if it were, and prepared a hearty unfelt laugh to bring forth at need to cover her telling.

"Why, I dreamed I was riding in a car down this very street, and it was summer just as it is now, and you were away, at least we all supposed you were away, on your vacation, and suddenly you came into the car and spoke to me, and you told me that you had been called home to attend a funeral." Here Miss Lou uttered another spasmodic giggle. "And I asked you who it was and you said it was that little Lillie Hartley,-don't you know, — the carpenter's little girl who sings in the children's Sunday-school exercises so sweetly. You told me when the funeral was to take place and asked me to come and sing, and I said I would. Well, I went to the house at the hour, and we sat there, and sat there, and you didn't come, and it got awful late and still you hadn't come, and they had to go way out to Mt. Laurel to bury, so they got awfully worried, and finally they sent after you, and the girl where you board said you were in your study, — that is, she hadn't seen you come out, — and they went up to the study and found the door locked on the inside. The girl said that was the way you always had it when you were studying hard, and they called and knocked and got no answer, so at last they burst in the door and found you sitting there dead by your desk with your book of funeral prayers, or whatever you call it, beside you, with the page open to the children's burial service, and everything looking as if you were just ready to go out, and you dead! There was an awful time just beginning, but I woke up and didn't see the end. But wasn't it too funny that you should come in the car just now? Oh! here's my street; I must get off. I hope you haven't come home to any funeral. Good-bye; wasn't it funny?" and the loud-voiced young woman swung herself off the car, having completed her last two or three sentences as she moved hastily toward the door, and ended with a loud giggle in which the minister felt somewhat called upon to join, at least with a sickly smile. Then he sat back with a scowl of annoyance on his face. Of all disagreeable things to happen, this seemed among the most disagreeable just now. Not that he cared about the dream, of course not. He was neither superstitious nor nervous, but it grated on his fine sensibilities to have the solemn and ridiculous mixed in this way. He could scarcely brush it aside and forget his unpleasant entrance into the city. He bought a morning paper and tried to bury his mind in that, but he felt irritated even when he reached the house he called home, and went to his rooms for any letters or papers that might have gathered during his two weeks' absence, which had not been forwarded.

It was almost time for him to go out again to meet the board of trustees, when the house servant tapped at his door.

"Please, Mr. Fairfield," she said, "there's a man downstairs as has been here yesterday to see you, and when he found you wasn't here he come back again this morning to get your address, and I told him you had come back unexpected, and he's most awful anxious to see you."

"You don't know who it is, Jane? He didn't send up his card?" said the minister, anxiously consulting his watch. "I have an engagement in five minutes. I can't spare much time."

"No, sir," said Jane deprecatingly, "I don't; but he's a plain-lookin' body, and if you're busy I'll just tell him to come back again when you can see him."

"Oh, no, I'll go down," he said, gathering up his hat and some papers he wished to carry with him to the meeting.

It struck a chill to the minister's heart when he reached the hall to see plain, honest Mr. Hartley standing there, heavy-eyed, his whole figure dropping with unmistakable sorrow.

"Mr. Fairfield," he said, the tears beginning to start to his eyes, "I'm so glad you're here. I made certain you'd come when you heard; but I didn't have the face to trouble you so far; but the wife she did want you and say she couldn't have Lillie buried without her minister she loved so much, and it's to be to-morrow afternoon. And could you get somebody to sing? The wife, she wanted 'Safe in the Arms of Jesus,' same as Lillie sung herself last Children's Day in the church."

There was something very strange about it all. The minister thought of it after the man had gone, tarrying until he had to hasten not to be late to his meeting. The broken-hearted father had had so much to say about his little girl and how she loved her minister and how ready she had been to go to heaven! He laughed a mirthless laugh as he walked down the street in the hot sunshine and told himself that if he were a superstitious man this would be a good chance for him to run away. He held his head high and rather gloried in the fact that he was not superstitious, but in spite of it all he could not get away from Miss Lou's dream and the strange coincidence of the death of the child. He wiped the perspiration from his brow and longed for the cooling sea breeze he had left behind, half wishing he had told the father he could not stay and suggested a brother minister for the funeral. Then his heart accused him sorely as he remembered how the father's face had lighted up when he saw him coming down the stairs. He knew in his heart he never could have done such a thing, and was glad with his better nature that he was here and able to be at least of so much comfort to the stricken parents.

It was strange too, after the day's business was over and he had time to think about the funeral and remember the father's request for a singer, that the only singer to be found in the city who could possibly be at leisure at the hour of the funeral was Miss Lou Marlow. He knew she would come, and that her voice was rich and sweet, though not so highly cultivated as some others. He knew that her generous nature would be willing to do anything in her power for the sorrowful family, and that she often went to funerals to sing, and people liked her singing then because she sang with so much sympathy in her voice. There were good things about Miss Lou, and her pastor knew it. Nevertheless he searched far and thoroughly before he made up his mind that there was no one else to ask. He told himself it was not in the least for his own sake he did this, but merely because he shrank from what she might say in her blunt way, and the giggles with which she would intersperse it, whatever it was. He sent a message by Jane at last with the request of the father and mother, leaving himself out entirely. He did not care to have Miss Lou see any more likeness to her dream than was necessary.

Then he shut himself into his study, and as he turned the key, he remembered Miss Lou's words vividly, how they had come and knocked and called with no answer, and how they had burst in the door and found him dead. Nevertheless, he locked the door as usual and sat down in the study chair, as was his custom, beside his desk and tried to think. A strong feeling of destiny laid hold upon his mind. He felt as if he were living out something that had been laid down for him to do. He felt as if he could not help it, but must go on living it out to the end, even to dying. He could not shake it off. He had heard of people dying with less cause than this, just dying because they thought the time had come. He didn't feel afraid that he should, but in spite of him, he began to wonder what he would do, what he would like to do before he died, and to realize if it all should prove to be true, what a short time he had in which to prepare! There were papers to be put in shape, if he knew he was going. There were messages to leave; there was his mother and sister and his church. How could he leave his church? His work was not completed. He had not carried out his plans; he had not won the souls he hoped, intended. There were those young men who sat in the back seat by the door and whispered sometimes and never listened. Something ought to have been done for them. He had in times past thought seriously of applying for a policeman. Now it seemed as if he might have won them some other way. Was it forever too late?

There was — why, there were all his people, as they started up one by one! He might have brought comfort to one and a word of warning to another; and what had his preaching been, now that he faced the thought of its being over forever? True he had spent hours of labor and study upon his sermons; but while the sentences were finished and perfect as to grammar and rhetoric, and sometimes even eloquent, would that stand before God? And then he looked upon himself. Was his soul ready to meet his Master? Had he not been living selfishly, serving the Master as second and himself as first, living a self-life, gratifying his desire for the intellectual, filling his soul with ambitions for a high calling on earth rather than one in heaven? Then the souls he had been set to keep! What of them? While he had supplied them with the flowers of his oratory, or sought to, had they starved for lack of a little of the plain bread of life? He was searching his own heart and accusing himself now as he never had done before. He seemed to realize all that was about him, to know that the time was near for the funeral, that he must prepare, and yet he could not turn his thoughts to anything else. Once he reached out his hand for the book of forms and funeral services, and opened it, finding, as if by necessity, the little child's funeral service, but he could not read the words. He could only think that he must set his own heart right. If some one had stepped to the door just then and asked him the questions, "Are you afraid you are going to die in a few minutes? Are you nervous about this dream and the strange coincidence?" he would have answered almost wonderingly; "No, certainly not. I am not afraid to die. I know that these strange coincidences cannot hasten or delay the day of my death one second. I know that all is just as it was with me before I heard of these things. But in some way I have suddenly realized what it would be to leave this world and my work — my unfinished work — with these few moments' notice. I know that it is not impossible that I may die at any moment. If not now, it may come, *will* come, at some equally unexpected moment, and I feel that I am not ready — not so ready as I *would* be."

That was the undercurrent of his reasoning as he sat in the study chair, his face buried in his hands, and thought. And now he heard footsteps below, and it reminded him again that the time of the funeral was near, perhaps was almost come. In a few minutes, if he did not hasten, some one would actually come to his door to see why he had not come, or to say the carriage had been waiting and the people were wondering where he was.

Down upon his knees he dropped and spent those last few minutes in prayer, such prayer as he had never known before. Out of the far depths of his soul rose a mighty cry for forgiveness for his past, a great longing for the Saviour to come into his heart and cast out the self in him. Yet, as he knelt, the room was still as death. Not one audible syllable did he utter. It was perhaps such preparation as he had never made before for any of his public duties of the ministry. And when a few minutes later Jane did tap at the door to say the carriage had come, he rose from his knees, his face shining with a holy light of something deeper than he understood, and found that he had forgotten the curious dream and had not watched to see if he should die at all, but had been getting ready to live. He took the little book of services and went to the funeral, feeling utterly unprepared, and yet, strangely enough, not worried about it. He knew that preparation was worth all he had felt it to be, but that there were times also when God took that out of his messengers' hands and made them look at him for a while, and then supplied the words. And the words were supplied now. Verse after verse of comfort from God's holy word, with now and then a comment of tender explanation, were all he essayed; but surely the Lord himself guided his selections, made as he rode along in the carriage, for the broken hearts were comforted and the sorely wounded spirits bound up, and many other hearts not so sore wounded, but there from sympathy, were touched, and made to feel how near and sure and grave a thing is death, and the life to come.

As the clear, rich voice of Miss Lou broke the stillness of the room that followed the minister's prayer, in the tender old refrain of "Safe in the arms of Jesus," the minister, listening, remembered the dream, and bowed his head in thankfulness that he was yet alive with a hope before him of better living and better work, Christ living in him, the hope of glory, and no longer the hope of the glory of his own intellectual powers.

Chapter 8

It was night, and along the coast the wind raged wildly. The ocean fairly thundered its waves against the stolid black sands. The sky was of black velvet, slashed here and there with vivid flashes of lightning. Above the roar of the waves and the voice of the wind came the distant roll of the thunder as it muttered its approach.

In the cottages the dwellers nestled closer in their beds at thought of the comfort about them which seemed all the more delicious as they slept, indistinctly aware of a storm without. Mrs. Hammond gave a sigh as she turned over on her pillow, a sigh of relief that now there would be rain water in the cistern again and they would not be obliged to scrimp and save water on account of having to carry it so far, from the hotel well. It was a little thing to give comfort, perhaps, but she felt that lack of water had been one thing which had made Maria's life so hard the last few days, and the mother was troubled on Maria's account. Now it seemed as if things might be a little easier, and Maria was getting in with pleasant young friends, and perhaps their summer would be a happy one after all. It was such a comfort that this pleasant little house had been procurable, so cheap that they need not feel they were extravagant in taking this vacation. Then she slept soundly again, aware that the storm was almost ready to break, and glad of the refreshing sound thereof.

The great raindrops came at last and pattered rapidly down on the high roof, sounding almost like tumblers full, they were so large, and soon the rain fairly poured down. Rachel was awakened by the cold wet touch of a great drop falling plump upon her cheek. It startled her at first and she could not make out what it was, but before she was fully awake it was followed by another, and they fell at regular intervals. Rachel remembered having read somewhere about criminals who were sentenced to be executed by a peculiar method, the falling of a drop of water at regular intervals upon the person from a great height, for a certain set length of time. She had wondered at the time how this method could possibly cause death, as she knew it did, the long-continued strain upon the nervous system of even so little an annoyance as this, being awful to endure. She lay still, trying to see how it would seem, so interested for a few minutes that she hardly realized that her pillow was growing quite wet. Then she heard movements in her mother's room—her father and mother conversing in low tones, a match struck—the pushing of furniture about. She realized the roof was leaking in there as well. She could hear drops falling out in the room on the floor, and now a new one that sounded on the dressing bureau. Suddenly her sister Maria started up in bed with an angry exclamation that "there was water falling on her head." It all struck Rachel as exceedingly funny. Somehow such things always showed on the humorous side to Rachel, quiet and sober as she usually was. This was one thing which often irritated Maria very greatly, this having Rachel laugh at a trying time. Rachel always said it was better to laugh than to cry or be cross, and she must do something, and Maria replied that she had a "hystericky nature." She should control her feelings. Then Maria would proceed to control hers by being cross. But Rachel always forgot about hysterics and laughed, a pure, mirthful laugh.

It gurgled forth now, sweet and amused, as she hurriedly got out of bed and brought her sun umbrella, raising it over their heads as she got in again. It was very funny to camp out in real picnic style and have to go to bed under an umbrella. She enjoyed it.

Maria lay down again angrily.

"Rachel Hammond, I do wish you would grow up and learn not to giggle when anything happens. I'm sure I don't see anything funny in being leaked on when you are fast asleep."

That was the beginning. Before many minutes had elapsed the movements of furniture in the next room together with the conversation back and forth and the various excursions for waterproofs and awning cloths with which to protect the beds from the constantly increasing drops, had thoroughly awakened Maria and roused her temper to a pitch quite beyond endurance. She found fault with the house, and the landlord, and said it was what might have been expected of the cottage at the ridiculous price they paid for it. Then when the family had hushed into silence she began at her sister, in a low whisper:

"Rachel, I think you really ought to try to realize that you are grown up in years if you are not in mind yet. I meant to speak to you about a thing you did Sunday night that made me so ashamed I didn't know what to do; but I haven't had a chance to talk to you about it; you manage to keep yourself so busy away from us except just when you are helping with the work, that I never have any chance to see my sister any more," this in an injured tone. "I'm sure I hope the Parkers appreciate your society. Perhaps you manage to make yourself more agreeable there than here. But at any rate, please confine yourself to being polite when you are with me and my friends, whatever you do when you are with yours."

"What in the world have I done now, Maria?" asked Rachel in a troubled voice. She really wanted to please her sister, though she found it much harder work than usual these days.

"Done!" said Maria growing irritated at the remembrance of her discomfiture two days before. "Why, you've acted like a perfect little prig, and almost insulted a minister. What in the world did you think Mr. Fairfield would think of you, Sunday night, turning around and as much as contradicting what he said? It didn't make it the least bit more polite that you put it in the form of a question. He is bright enough to see through that. Who are you to set up to rebuke a minister, anyway? You might as well try to find fault with the Bible."

"Why, 'Ri, I didn't rebuke him. I only asked him a question that honestly puzzled me. What do you mean? I never intended—"

"Nonsense!" said Maria sharply. "You were rude and you know it. If a man doesn't seem to come up to your standard you immediately set about telling him so. You will simply get yourself set down as an insufferable little prig for your trouble if you keep on in that way. I was surprised that Mr. Fairfield didn't tell you that you were a child who didn't know what you were talking about. For my part, I hope I shall not be called upon to endure another such insult to a caller of mine; if I am, you may be sure I shall call mother to come and take you in. It is the only fit rebuke for such actions. You talk religion too much, anyway. It isn't ladylike to stick it in every one's face. A minister hears enough of it in his profession without being called upon to talk about it in his social life. Religion is much better acted than talked, I think. I should hope you would take that to heart. If you attempt any of that sort of talk with the De Veres you will find you won't be tolerated in their society very long. I'm sure I'm ashamed of you. Now do go to sleep if you can. I don't want to talk any more," and Maria turned over with a twitch and pretended to go to sleep herself.

But for Rachel sleep was effectually routed. She lay there thinking. The tears chased each other down her cheeks. It hurt her so to have her sister talk to her in this way. She felt as if she ought to make some protest, but what could she say that would help matters? Her protests always seemed to anger her sister more. Was Maria right after all, and did the minister feel in the way she had said he would about the questions she had asked? If so, was she all wrong in her way of feeling about things? Of course a minister must be right, for he had spent his life in getting ready to preach Christ's gospel, and had given up all to that work. He ought to be consecrated if any one was. But surely he ought also to be one to whom any one could go with a question about Christian living.

Then she remembered Roland De Vere and how differently he had talked about religion, just the few words he had happened to speak on the subject. Somehow she felt that Maria was mistaken about Mr. De Vere at least, and she wished that he would talk to Maria and perhaps he would be able to influence her. Perhaps this minister would know how to help Maria by and by. Ministers' lives ought to be an influence on those around them, without any words, as Maria had said. She would pray for that. Meantime, was there not some little thing she could do for her Master? She felt that her life was so full of pleasure this summer, that without some definite, special work to do, she would be apt to grow selfish. She had tried to help Maria, but all help seemed only to irritate her. Perhaps it was wrong in her to set up to help an older sister. She would just pray and try to keep her tongue from doing aught to make her sister trouble. Her tongue did seem to be a very unruly member. So she closed her eyes and prayed to be shown what to do, and then, like a tired child, threw off her burden and went to sleep.

In justice to Maria be it said that she had been feeling deeply chagrined that Mr. Fairfield had neither called nor come upon the beach when they were there, nor in any way appeared since to claim his acquaintance with them, which he had seemed eager to do on Sabbath evening. It puzzled Maria greatly, for while she cared nothing about the man in particular, still she was deeply sensitive to the opinion of any one, either stranger or friend, whose manner and appearance seemed to make his judgment of value in her eyes. She feared that he had set them down as a family of fanatics, and that the whole fault lay with Rachel's babyish way of talking religion, as if it were an every-day matter.

Having nothing else to do, she brooded over the matter until it appeared very large to her. She felt that the minister was intentionally slighting them, and that now as he had found his friends at Spray View, he wished to show them that he had only been polite to Maria on account of the very awkward accident which had thrown them together on Saturday. Maria's imagination was so vivid, that as the days went by—which, by the way, continued to be rainy, the clouds pouring down water in a very deluge at times—she began to think that the end of all pleasant times had come even as they had just begun. Of course there was no moonlight excursion.

Maria stood on the piazza one afternoon, toward the end of the dreary week, gazing discontentedly at the desolate landscape. The mist of fine rain was still falling, when it was not varied by terrific showers. A stiff breeze was blowing, first from one direction and then from another, as if in fitful mood, uncertain what to do. Off at her right Maria could see the banks of sand piled high, looking almost like cliffs in places, with their low undergrowth of huckleberry and wild sage and laurel, the only growth which the island seemed to afford, for there was not a tree in sight. Now and again the waves of the ocean would dash so high that the spray would be carried up in clouds above these sand banks. There was one break in the banks, just at the end of what was supposed to be their street or "avenue," in the parlance of the place, where one could gaze far out over the wild, turbulent ocean in its dull gray and brown tones, with a seething touch of vivid green here and there and froth of maddened yellow-white. It all looked so cold and wild and awful.

Maria turned from it, shuddering; on her left there stretched the steel-colored bay, once so bright and gay, reflecting tints like an opal, now an almost interminable stretch of mist and desolation. The long reaches of waste sand, and heavy, wet-headed, salt marsh grass, bending with the wind, only added to the dismal character of the scene. The girl walked back and forth on the green piazza, which was wet with the mist, and looked with horror, almost with hatred, at the whole view. Yes, for one can hate even sky and grass and water when one is in the right mood for it. The scene embodied to her the desolation that seemed to have come into her life. It was like that waste of water and sand and dark-leaden sky. There seemed in it no hope of brightness for the future, just as it seemed impossible now, after these days and days of rain, that the sky could ever be bright again or the waves would ever grow soft and lovely and the bay take on its gemlike look. God seemed nowhere to her. She felt a kind of desperation, as if she could not endure another hour of this hateful existence.

It almost frightened her to realize that she felt so. She knew it was wrong. She had been too well brought up not to have been conscious during the days that had passed just how wrong and hateful she had been in her feelings and actions. She began to wonder if she ever had really loved God, or been a Christian, and whether there was anything in it. Wild ideas ran through her brain. Where was God, anyway? Why did he want her to be so unhappy? Had he forgotten her? Over and over in her mind kept going a verse of an old hymn learned in childhood, or rather one line of the verse, she could remember no more. It ran like this, "Has God forgotten to be kind?" She tried to shake it off, but it came again and again. She brushed back the hair that clung wet with the mist to her hot temples and went into the cottage.

Anything was better in this vast desolation alone. She went to the kitchen and in desperation took out her recipe book, to find the most difficult thing she could make for supper. It would at least occupy her hands and her mind. There were books, to be sure, but she felt dissatisfied with them all. She could not interest herself in one of them. A book was all very nice and cozy on a rainy day, when all was cheery indoors and there were visions of bright days in the hopeful future after the rain should be passed, but Maria felt that for her there were no such visions.

The trouble was deeper than these few days at the seashore. It went back to the time when her father lost his money. She was rebellious. She was not willing to give up that money and the position which it carried. Now that it was gone, she felt there was nothing else in the world worth living for. She had been a pretty good Christian, according to her own way of thinking, in those days when things had been prosperous. Why had not God seen that? She could have done much more in the world for him if he had left her life as it was. Now she was no Christian at all, and he must see how he had made a failure of her Christian work by taking away her father's money and her social position. She did not say these things even to herself, in so many words. She would not have dared, because she had been taught to be reverent in her speech, and in a degree this teaching had reached to her thoughts, but she felt them strongly, deeply, fiercely.

And Rachel sat in the other room and apparently read her book, while all the time she had been uneasily watching her sister and quietly praying for her. Oh, why was it that this her great, longing prayer for the beloved sister could not be answered? Had she not prayed earnestly enough? Or must she be willing to pray longer? What was the matter? God had promised to give what the believing heart should ask for. She laid down her book and went into the bedroom, carefully fastening the curtain behind her against interruptions. She would kneel down now and pray again for Maria. But though she knelt and prayed fervently, she felt no sudden sense of answer such as she had heard other people talk about, and when she listened, she could hear Maria rattle the pans and kettles as fiercely as ever in the kitchen. There was no sign as yet in her of any spiritual change. Rachel's was a sweet nature, struggling for light, and she was not being guided by human help perhaps as much as would have been good for her. She believed everything intensely and at once, and wanted to see a vindication of her belief, like many another eager, impatient one, but she was willing to be led. She took her little Bible. It had aided her many times in perplexity. She turned to it now from habit and read one of her favorite psalms. "Delight thyself also in the Lord, and he shall give thee the desires of thine heart."

She had read that verse over without thinking about it, when a thought seemed to arrest her attention. Was it possible that God had sent her that very promise now? Did he want her to delight herself in him first before he gave her what she had been asking? Perhaps that was true and she had not made him her chief delight. She slowly closed the book and went out again to the sitting room and her story, but though she held the book before her eyes, she was not reading. She was going over her life and thinking how she might make the Lord her chief delight, and how she had not done it. It was a revelation to her of herself, for had she been asked a little time before reading that verse, she would have said that Christ and his life-work were her chief delights; but now she saw that she had made other things chief and Christ's work only a part — a very small part — of the pleasures of her life. She saw that there was something which needed a radical change in her whole soul, so that Christ would be in her pleasures, the source and center of everything, instead of a mere outside pleased observer, as she felt she had been wont to regard him heretofore.

Meantime, she remembered that there were peaches to be peeled for supper. She disliked this work intensely, and was not always prompt to remember that it belonged to her; but to-night she arose with alacrity, saying to herself, "He wants me to peel those peaches; I will try to remember I am doing it for Him and then perhaps I can take delight in it." And she succeeded so well in what so few succeed at all that presently she was singing a happy little song:

> "There is sunshine in my soul to-day,
> More glorious and more bright,
> For Jesus —"

"For pity's sake," snapped Maria, "do select something more appropriate, if you *must* sing. It doesn't look as if there would ever be any sunshine any more anywhere."

And for once Rachel was enabled to laugh and make a pleasant reply and then go on with her singing, instead of closing her mouth and letting the tears steal up to her eyes at the sharp words, as she usually did. And so supper was prepared in much more peace than usual.

Chapter 9

The sun shone out at last bright and clear as though he had never thought of anything else. The bay, blue in the distance, sparkled in the sunrays like a wondrous sapphire set in emeralds. White-winged sailboats, like great birds, floated lazily across the glassy surface, carried hither and thither by the light winds, in the very joy of life and motion. As one gazed westward toward the bay, not a sign could be seen of the gloom that had shrouded the landscape for days. Turning toward the sea, radiant with brilliant coloring, bordered by a shining garment of newly washed sand, the late rage of the elements was more apparent, for the sea, slower in rousing to terrible wrath, is more reluctant to cease from its anger, and long after nature smiles, pours thunderous billows upon the unresisting shore.

Had Howard Fairfield been there, his whole day would have been passed at the very edge of the surge, gazing far out to sea over the majestic spectacle, still more striking by reason of the contrast it presented to the calm sky overhead, until his soul had been filled with the wonder of the scene. But much to his own disappointment, a series of unimportant details still held him in the city. It was Saturday. Rachel sat on the piazza peeling peaches. Her father had brought from the city the night before a quantity of fine fruit, for in their island home all such luxuries had to be imported. In the salt-laden atmosphere they decayed rapidly, and to Rachel therefore had been assigned the task of preparing them for preserving and canning. Although this was a task always especially distasteful to her, yet the morning was so bright and beautiful that she caught the spirit of its gladness and sang blithely as she worked.

Moreover, was not her life henceforth to have a new motive, to be filled with a joy not of this world? Jesus was now to be to her a delight, and to her surprise, perhaps, she discovered that that delight shone up at her through the most commonplace tasks. It seemed wonderful. She rejoiced in the brightness of the morning because he had made it bright. Thus she sat thinking her happy thoughts, working with deft fingers at her task, and as she worked, caroled forth a little song.

Maria felt very differently about the change in weather. Of what good was the sunshine when one did not care to go out into it? She had no place to which to go if she did go out; no one for whose companionship she cared, who was likely, as she said to herself, to care enough about hers to seek it. To be sure, there was the beach to visit, mother and sister for company, books and embroidery for occupation, to say nothing of the kaleidoscopic scenery of sea and sky; but these went for nothing with her, having no place in the catalogue of her desires.

A fierce resentment filled her at the mockery of the day's brightness contrasted with the gloom of her own mood. It was plain, now, even to her mind, that she had been taking a sort of grim, self-pitying satisfaction in the melancholy of the weather. It had stood for a distinct grievance, and now she was almost angry that it was taken from her. As her mother passed through the room, she sighed at sight of the discontent that sat now so often on her elder daughter's face. Rachel's song floated in through the open doorway and made her wonder why one daughter should seem to find all the sweetness while the other persisted in drinking only the bitter. It was the more difficult to understand because it had not always been so, for in her younger days Maria had been as sunny as her sister. It was unlike her to cling to her self-conceived wrongs for so long a time, to show to others only the thorny side of her nature.

Could it be that Maria was on the verge of illness, and that here was the hidden reason for her discontent? With this idea stirring in her heart, the mother passed again into the kitchen and urgently begged Maria to resign her place at the stove to her and Rachel for the day and to lie down in her own room. Her advances were met with scorn, and Maria prepared to cook a more elaborate meal than usual, as a proof that there was nothing the matter with her health. The mother, repulsed, went sadly away again to her sewing, on which more than one tear dropped, as she anxiously asked herself what *could* be the matter with Maria. She found herself wishing that that handsome young Mr. De Vere would pay a little less attention to Rachel, who seemed to care nothing about him, and a little more to Maria, who, with the keen intuition of a mother, she feared did; or else that that intellectual-looking minister, who had brought her home that day she got the drenching, would come again — anything to take her child out of herself and infuse a new interest into her life, that she should not brood over her misfortunes so much, and perhaps thus give a permanent bent to her character in the unfortunate direction of melancholy. She had hoped that even the sunshine would cheer her, but it seemed to have rather the opposite effect.

Across a strip of neatly mowed marsh grass, not many rods distant, stood a small unpainted cottage surrounded by a well-kept vegetable garden. The wide piazza, peculiar to the place, ran across its front, and around this, in attempting to cope with the mosquitoes, some one had at one time tacked a blue mosquito bar which now hung tattered, waving in the breeze. This was the home of the Higginses, little and large.

The family was one of many and varied occupations. The father fished a little, and gardened a little, and drove parties of three in his rickety old green spring wagon over to Spray View on errands, at the rate of ten cents per head, or three for a quarter. Rachel, when she heard this, had rejoiced that they might often take the beach drive, it was so cheap; but Maria had curled her lip in such scorn at the idea of driving past the elegant De Vere villa in the old green wagon that Rachel had not mentioned it again. Mrs. Higgins washed for a living, besides sewing and cooking for her large family, carried tomatoes, which she called "tomats," delicious beets, fresh eggs, and chickens, to the few people who lived near enough to purchase them; went into the bay when requested to dig clams, which she sold at a ridiculously low price, and was the delight of all 'curio-loving' people who came in contact with her, by reason of her quaint dialect, a mixture of Irish, German, and Jersey.

There were four grown sons with their wives and children, who lived, some in the same house, some near by, and others came often to visit, on which occasions the eggs, "tomats," and fresh fish were scarce for the time being. There were two young women, daughters, who plodded through the sand every morning at five to reach the Spray View Hotel in time to perform their daily duties there of chamber-maid and nurse-girl, respectively. There was a son who worked on the railroad when the trains ran (which was only during the summer) and fished between times, and last but not least were Katy and John, the two youngest children. They solemnly and silently appeared at the door from time to time, bringing milk or eggs or other things which had been ordered, but fled in dismay if any questions were asked them.

Rachel had found out all this about their neighbors during the first few days of their stay at the shore. She was always interested in every human being that was within her sight. The rest of the family knew of them only as a convenience for the performance of odd jobs and for the supplying of cheap vegetables, fish, and clams. Maria knew them but to despise, because they never by any means happened to have the thing she wanted at the time she ordered it. But Rachel was really and truly interested in watching their movements and realizing that they were human beings, with emotions like herself, in spite of the fact that they were such queer people and seemed to exist and be happy under such very different circumstances from her own, which in contrast with her father's former condition in life she had unconsciously come to regard as none of the best.

In one of Rachel's intervals of song, when she had been on a trip to the kitchen in search of more peaches and another dish, which latter was of course not to be had in this cottage of few conveniences, Rachel heard a burst of song from over the way. I will not say it was music, though it was evidently meant for that. The singer was one of the young women members of the Higgins family. Rachel could see that she was sitting in the wide porch behind a tattered remnant of the blue mosquito netting swinging a much-used hammock, which evidently contained a baby, probably one of the many Higgins grandchildren. Her voice was loud and sharp and clear, with a decided nasal twang. The song was a lullaby improvised for the occasion, but sung in such a tremendously high key as to seem to be intended for the benefit of some baby up in the clouds, or away beyond Spray View.

Rachel broke into a low soft gurgle of laughter and called her mother and Maria to listen, as the loud twang of "Sleep, sleep, sleep, baby, sleep, Hush-a-bye, sleep, hush-a-bye, sleep," rang out above the voice of the majestic waves. The song continued for some time, and Rachel hushed her own singing, partly to listen and partly because the metallic tones grated on her delicate musical susceptibilities. By and by the singer changed her song, while the hammock still rocked violently. The baby was evidently being brought up to be a sailor, for certainly no other vocation would be more suitable after spending one's infant days in such a turbulent cradle.

"There's a land that is fair-rer than da-ay,"

rang out the words distinctly,

"An' by faith we c'n see it a-fa-ar."

All through the verses sang the girl, her lungs apparently as unwearied as when she began, and the energy with which she brought out each word distinctly, making a listener sure that she enjoyed her own music, whatever might be said of others.

She finished one song and went on to another, a gospel song, of date so many years back that Rachel could remember it only as having been familiar with it in her very early girlhood. Her eyes grew dreamy as she thought of various occasions when she had sung these very words which now seemed a little out of date because of the many new jingles which had superseded them in a way. She wondered where this girl had become acquainted with all these songs, that she could sing them from beginning to end. The family, she had heard, had been on the island both summer and winter for several years. She had heard that they never went to church or Sunday-school. Indeed, Sunday seemed to be a sort of merry-making time with them, for there were sure to be several sons with their wives there to spend the day, and Rachel had noticed a case of beer bottles outside the porch once when she went to get some clams to make clam bisque for supper.

Where, then, had this girl gotten her knowledge of religious song? She had words enough of the way of salvation at her tongue's end, to save a whole family, if words could save. It must have been acquired before the family moved to this deserted place. It would be interesting to know where and how. Perhaps she had sometime been an attendant at Sunday-school, or perhaps she had gone to a series of Moody meetings and the songs had grown familiar there. Rachel was a bit given to letting her imagination have free rein, and when she had thought out the possibilities thus far she began to grow intensely interested in the family over the way and to wish to know more. She would talk with that girl the next time she came over with the milk and perhaps find out something.

Meantime, how grand a thing it would be if through those very songs some day the whole family should become Christians. What a nice story that would make. Rachel dropped her peach and looked dreamily off over the bay. She liked to scribble little stories herself, just for her own amusement sometimes. She never showed them to any one. This would be a splendid start for a plot. But how would this marvelous change be brought about? The Spirit of God could do it, of course, but he would be likely to use some earthly instrument. Some one must come who would speak words, or do some helpful thing, or get an influence over them, perhaps some young minister on his vacation, like Mr. Fairfield, or even some young lady, or —

Here Rachel's thoughts came suddenly back to the practical from the imaginary and a soft pink color stole up into her cheek. Why sit and plan a story when, perhaps, there was really an opening for work? She had been asking God for some work for him, maybe her was showing it to her through that loud-voiced singing over there. It was not, at first thought, as attractive work as some she might think of, not nearly so interesting in reality as it would be in a story; but perhaps it was work she could do, at least she could try a little of it. She picked up her peach and began to peel it rapidly again, revolving in her mind whether there really was anything she could do after all. She felt herself shrinking from the undertaking when it was presented to her and she wished she had not thought of it at all, nor listened to the horrible grating singing. How could she do anything, anyway? It would only be another trial for Maria if she should associate herself with any of those despised Higginses. They would be less to her sister's liking than even the Parkers. Then she had never been introduced, and perhaps the girl would resent anything she might do or say as patronizing. Rachel had a horror of seeming to patronize any human being. There was not the least danger that her gentle, loving smile and winning way would ever be mistaken for that, but in her true modesty she did not know this.

Finally she cast aside the thought with this feeling: "If God wishes me to do anything in that way he will show me. Perhaps I am as mistaken about this as I was about trying to help Maria." With an upward turning of her heart she cast the thought at her Saviour's feet. He knew best. If he wished her to do anything he would show her.

By this time the peaches were finished and so was the song from over the way. The baby probably had succumbed at last to the boisterousness of hammock and song. Rachel carried her peaches into the house, washed her hands and came out again with her little work-basket of dainty lace which she was making for the border to a center piece, and two little books, still in the paper wrappings as they had arrived that morning, by messenger, for her from Spray View. The handwriting of her own name in bold, manly characters had told her who was the sender, and Rachel postponed the opening of the package until her work was done that she might the better enjoy what was to be found therein. Perhaps too, there was a shy, sweet pleasure in opening the package by herself, and was it to keep up a show of work that she also carried her basket and lace work out with her, or did she really intend to make lace and not read? Anyway, the morning was charming and it was so nice to have a package to open and her pretty work lying beside her, and nothing to do but enjoy it all. Slowly she untied the knots of the string, tracing meanwhile the graceful, strong letters of her fair name, "Rachel Weldon Hammond."

And then she undid the wrapping and brought the two books to view. She had known they were books, for Roland De Vere had told her he had two books which he wanted her to read, as he felt sure she would enjoy them, and they would perhaps lead her into lines of reading which were new to her. Now she looked curiously to see what they were. One was of a dark red paper cover, but attractive in print, short of paragraph and brief of chapters. It was called "A Castaway." A glance through it told her it was the one he had told her would be of special use to help spend the long Sabbath afternoon, and aid her in her Christian life. She smiled with pleasure in her eyes as she turned the leaves a few minutes, snatching a sentence here and there that seemed to have been written just for her, so perfectly did it fit her circumstances and thoughts, and then she laid it aside. Sabbath reading like this, aside from the Bible, did not often come in her way. She must treasure it for the Sabbath. She would just take a few peeps into it and leave the rest of it for a Sunday treat.

Then she turned to the other book, a daintily bound volume all in pale green and gold. The paper was thick and creamy, the print clear, and the whole appearance of the book exquisite. Rachel loved the feeling and the look of such a book. It was poetry. She opened at random. One poem was styled "Day's Parlor." She read, and it seemed to her that that day had been fashioned in just the way described.

The day came slow till five o'clock,
Then sprang before the hills
Like hindered rubies, or the light
A sudden musket spills.

The purple could not keep the east,
The sunrise shook the fold,
Like breadths of topaz, packed a night,
The lady just unrolled.

The happy winds their timbrels took;
The birds, in docile rows
Arranged themselves around their prince
(The wind is prince of those).

The orchard sparkled like a Jewel,
How mighty 'twas, to stay
A guest in this stupendous place,
The parlor of the day!

Rachel caught her breath and looked up at the bay and the blue, blue sky, drinking in all their loveliness. How those jeweled words had brought out the beauties! She turned a few pages and read again:

She sweeps with many colored brooms,
And leaves the shreds behind;
Oh, housewife in the evening west,
Come back and dust the pond!

You've dropped a purple raveling in,
You dropped an amber thread;
And now you've littered all the east
With dust of emerald!

And still she plies her spotted brooms,
And still the aprons fly,
Till brooms fade softly into stars —
And then I come away.

Ah! Rachel drew her breath again as if she had caught some delicate perfume that was new to her, and she feared to lose a single atom of the delightful sensation. This poetry suited her dreamy imagination, which was always personifying nature. She felt that she would enjoy this book to the full. This last poem was just a description of that exquisite sunset last week. She was grateful for the gift of the book, and dimly felt the high, fine perceptions of the young man who had selected it for her. The music of these words and their coloring gave her pleasure clear to her finger tips.

And then in the mist of these thoughts appeared her answer from Heaven and her work ready laid out for her. It was a contrast, perhaps, but a well-tuned nature should always be ready to turn from the high to the low and feel none the worse for it, and sometimes even recognize that what is rated the low is in reality the highest of the high, while the high is merely a picture of what pleasure may be after all.

"Did your ma want any clams to-night?" It was the clear metallic voice of the singer from over the way who asked the question, and the voice was so sharp, and her coming had been so silent that Rachel, lost in her beautiful dreams, started. But the girl seemed not to notice this. Her eyes were intent upon Rachel's work-basket and the beautiful lace work on its pretty blue cambric background pattern.

"Oh, what a pretty thing that is!" exclaimed the girl. "Did you do that?" and as Rachel took up her basket to bring the work nearer for her inspection, "Ain't it awful hard work? You must be just dreadful clever. Does it take a long time? Now I'll just guess that stuff costs an awful lot. I see a woman over to the hotel the other day workin' at a thing like that. You don't say! That's the way you do it. Just sew that braid onto them lines! Why that looks easy! My, but I suppose it's all in knowin' how!" and the girl sighed wistfully. "My! but I would like to know how to do some of them pretty things! I never have no time in summer; but land! in winter, time just drags and drags. Seems like I was fifty years old every winter I go through in this place. I wish I could do something to shorten it."

And thus it was that Rachel's work came to her, and of all things! That it should come through a bit of renaissance lace work! She looked at the gray old cottage with its flapping, faded mosquito bar, after the girl had gone, and then down at her delicate blue and white work, and thought how incongruous the two were, and how little she would have dreamed of beginning to get an influence over a girl from that house through anything as fine as that. God knew best. It was really wonderful, when you left it all to him, how he made that to appear. Why had she never tried that before? It might not be that she would accomplish so very much, for after all she had only promised to teach an ignorant girl how to make lace and that might not lead to anything else, but she felt that she had been given a chance to try, and she thanked her Father for it.

Chapter 10

Howard Fairfield had not lingered in the heat of the city because it was his wish to do so. He had found an aged member of his church very ill and wishing to see him; and the man who was to have supplied his prayer meeting sent word that he could not come, so he stayed for that; then afterward he lingered by the old saint's bedside till he had gone where spiritual help was needed no more. Thus had come another funeral in that one short week, which yet had seemed to stretch itself out to such a length.

Saturday afternoon saw him free at last, for the pulpit was supplied for the morrow and the man on the ground. There was no need for him to linger longer. There was just time to catch the last train back to the quiet shore. He laid his head wearily against the cushion of the seat while the train whirled him on, and thought over all the experiences of the week. How he had been led! That girl with her dream, and the little girl's funeral, and his own experience in waiting for the hour to arrive! And then those hours by the bedside of the dying saint, where he had gained, more than given, spiritual help. He had a new feeling toward the old man who had just entered heaven, which he had never felt for any person who had died before. It was as if he had been given to know one of the apostles for a few short hours, and to talk with him, and have his eyes opened by him, and to grow to love him, and then the heavens had opened and he had seen the man carried up to Jesus.

Heaven had a new interest for him now. He felt nearer to it. He loved it more than he had ever before realized he could. He could not help wondering what sights and scenes that dear servant of God was passing through at that moment, while his friends were mourning his absence from the earth. To him the coffin which he had seen lowered into the earth but two hours before contained no thought of the grand sweet soul, who was not buried there, but was high in heaven with the angels. How he wished that he had known the old man better during the time he had been on earth. Oh, those wasted months, when such companionship and help might have been his. It reminded him of the days when the disciples had Jesus with them and had not half known how to value his daily companionship. To know intimately one who was like Jesus was, in a limited sense, like having known and walked with Jesus when he was in the body on the earth.

Perhaps there were others in his congregation who were like this man. Now that he could think over the list, there were several families whose simple, trustful Christian life had evidently strong faith behind it, and rich experience from which he might learn much. There were the Clarks! He had looked upon them as good souls, but had thought them ignorant. Ignorant, perhaps they were in some things, but they read their Bibles and they lived their Bibles, and now that he thought of it there were many ways in which he felt sure they could help him. How foolish he had been! How wise in his own conceit! He had felt that because he was fresh from the seminary he knew more than they all. Now he saw that he had not half learned the true heart-knowledge, which should have gone hand in hand with his head-knowledge.

Had he then wasted his preparations so far this summer? There was that series of sermons he had planned out and half developed on the mystery of the Trinity, and there was the other series which he had worked carefully over and had almost ready for use on "The Life and Works of the Prophets." They seemed empty and useless to him now. There were doubtless many good things in them. It might be that at some time they might even be useful to him for the especial purpose of helping certain minds over perplexing places, but in the light of his new experiences they seemed so wide of the mark, so almost unnecessary when one thought of the tremendous truths which needed to be presented, yes urged, yea, thundered from the pulpit day and night.

He had thought that a quiet summer by God's sea, with his own intellect and God's good teacher, nature, would be of vast assistance to him as a preacher: but perhaps he might have gone somewhere else, to one of those wonderful spiritual gatherings of which there were so many far and near, beginning with Northfield and Mr. Moody. He had always thought he might like to go to Northfield, but it had been in a lofty, condescending way, more out of curiosity than anything else. Now he longed for something of which he had heard, and which he knew by instinct might be found there. Perhaps he ought to give up his present plans and go there at once. It might be the best thing he could do. He closed his eyes restfully, and wondered what his Heavenly Father would have him do about it, and he prayed to be guided; for while he wanted to go, and felt it would be good, he yet had a longing for the quiet and rest of the still seashore place and the chance to talk with God alone. He would wait there at least till he was sure what God would have him do, or whither he would have him go in his great school, for he felt like a new pupil just entering a higher grade to be taught things he had not dreamed there were for him yet to learn.

As the train rushed on and drew nearer to his destination he began to open his eyes and look for landmarks. He had not realized how tired he was, nor how eager for a sight of the mighty ocean. He thought of the few friends he had met and wondered if they would be there; and if they would be helpful; and then, with a strange new feeling, if he could be helpful to them. There was that girl, there were those two girls in fact, whom he had met under such peculiar circumstances. He hardly knew where to place them, he had seen so little of them. The younger girl had asked some strange questions. And now there came back to him vividly his last walk and reverie by the sea. He would go back there and walk and think, but he felt with a grateful thrill in his heart that there would be answers to his questions now which he had not been able to give then. Now his eyes were open and he was beginning to see things differently. He thanked God for this. Meanwhile, if there was aught of good that he could get or do, he wanted to be ready for it. He watched eagerly in the deepening twilight, as the train drew near the station, for the few little cottages, bathed in the sunset glow of the bay, and sprang out on the platform, breathing in the salt air, glad that he was back again. After supper he took his way out beside the sea in the darkness of the starry night alone to think and be with God, and he came back from that walk to deep, dreamless sleep and awoke to the restfulness of the Sabbath.

Now the Saturday which had brought such brightness to the shore, and had blown such a life-giving breeze from across the bay had also brought the little mosquito. On the wings of that delicious breeze he came—not alone. He brought his entire family and all his relatives with him. They were small and sharp mosquitoes. They were harmless and unmusical mosquitoes, but they were wise. They knew those cottages of old with their wide cracks and roomy ceilings for daily hidings. They had been blown across the bay on just such breezes for years, at least if not they, then their ancestors, and they went as straight to their several stopping-places as if they had telegraphed ahead and had rooms reserved for them and meals ready. They arrived all at once and took possession. They swarmed through the piazzas and drove the helpless sitters there inside the screen doors; but they did not stop outside, they rushed in also, and those who failed of the door were not long in finding the other vulnerable points in the cottages. By night, when the lights had begun to appear, they had managed to make their presence almost unbearable.

Maria, like many other people of fair skin and highly strung nervous organization, was particularly susceptible to stings of any kind, whether of insects or tongue. She became irritable at once. Perhaps no one would have wondered who saw the enormous red and white swellings which immediately responded to the attack of the little insect. Mosquito bites poisoned Maria, and she really suffered intensely. Therefore it need not be wondered at that her temper was strung to its highest pitch. She actually sat down in the sitting room before the whole family and cried in vexation and despair over the torment of the little pests. She declared she could endure it no longer, that she would rather die, and a dozen other extravagant things which she did not mean, and then went to bed, sick and sore, to fight them there, and find little sleep to restore her calmness.

Sabbath morning found her aching in body and mind. The mosquitoes still continued. Maria refused to go to church, though the entire family condescended to urge her to do so, hoping that it would in some way soothe her troubled spirit. They had reason to be glad, however, that she had refused, when they arrived at the church door and entered, attended by thousands of the little insects, and found that they were thick on the white plastered walls, and that the assembled congregation looked more like a lot of dancing dervishes than a company of quiet and respectable church-goers, bent on the worship of God. Indeed, the mosquitoes kept up their part of the performance until people were nearly distracted, some going home in desperation. The speaker of the morning drew his remarks to a speedy close and the people hastened home remarking on the unusualness of the visitation of mosquitoes, and the wind, weather, and state of tempera-ture as causes of the plague. Those who had plastered houses hastened indoors and those who had not took refuge in penny royal oil and the smoke of various herbs, and then in despair betook themselves to the beach. There at least was a place of refuge. Even Maria was driven thither very soon after the noonday meal. She would not have gone if it had been tolerably comfortable at home, for she felt in that perverse mood in which she dreaded seeing any one or speaking pleasantly. She even felt a strong distaste to making herself look neat and pretty for the day.

Nevertheless, she finally consented to change her dress and smooth her hair and go to the sand with Rachel. Rachel, in her sisterly solicitude that the afternoon should be a time of comfort to Maria, loaded herself down with cushions, parasols, fans, and a beach chair. Then with her own little Bible and the new book, which had come to her the day before and which she had kept for this precious Sabbath afternoon's reading, she walked cheerfully through the sand and swarms of mosquitoes to find just the right spot on the beach where the breeze and the view were most pleasant, while Maria scolded with every step and declared she would go back, but nevertheless went on.

Rachel pitched her tent, as it were, arranged the beach chair comfor-tably, fixing cushions and sand for herself, declaring she preferred them, and pressed the chair upon her sister. Rachel opened her Bible first. Maria sat gloomily looking out on the smooth water which had calmed itself into one of those transparent blue-green sheens which look innocent of any possible boisterous to-morrow. Certainly the coloring of the ocean was worth watching to-day, and the sky and air seemed perfect. But Maria was in no mood to enjoy it. Presently she closed her eyes drearily on it all. She felt so weary, poor child. Her life seemed so empty. She was impatient of the day and of the summer, and even of the outlook of her whole life as she seemed to see it stretching before her.

Rachel felt her sister's gloom. It could not but be apparent, and Rachel was so impressionable that it made her quite unhappy. She knew there was nothing she could do to lighten her sister's heart, and yet she could not enjoy her own reading nor her own pleasure in the day. She read one of the short chapters in her new book, wondering over the helpfulness of every word, charmed with the plain, everyday language and tender sympathy expressed by the writer, but in spite of her interest in the book, her mind kept wandering to Maria and she was conscious of every movement her sister made. At last she thought she was asleep and instantly she gave thanks. Sleep would be the best thing for her in her present state of mind. Unconsciously Rachel relaxed her tension of muscles and resting back among her pillows enjoyed the day and her own happy thoughts for a little. She let her mind wander to the Higginses andthe promised lesson in lace-making, and wondered how she could get in a lesson on something else besides lace. By and by two little figures, which she had been watching for some time when they were but mere specks away down toward the lighthouse, came nearer, hand in hand, and now were near enough to be distinguished as the two younger members of the Higgins household, Katy and John, wandering along, bareheaded and barefooted, picking up a shell now and then and trotting on again.

Rachel watched them interestedly. How different the sea must seem to them, who lived there all the year and knew it at its wildest! It was evidently their friend and they loved it. Rachel could tell that from the way they looked out upon it, pointing now and then to a distant sail, or cloud of smoke from some steamer far-off against the horizon.

The girl, watching, wondered if the sea ever spoke to them of God, and what idea they had of its majesty and its Maker. Did they associate the two? Had they been taught enough for that, she would like to know; or did they perhaps have some natural instinct which would lead them to feel this without the teaching? She began to frame questions which she would like to ask them, and grew eager to know how they would answer.

And then her second opportunity came, as the children sat down on a great broken spar which had been washed ashore some time ago and been half buried in the sand. Katy dug her bare feet in the sand, making a soft cool hole for them, and the boy John sat quite still, looking out, perhaps the sailor instinct of his family stirring within him. They evidently meant to sit there some time. Rachel might go over and talk with them. They looked lonely too, perhaps they would like her to tell them a story. She missed her class of little girls at home in Sunday-school which met at about this hour. It would be a real pleasure to her to teach the lesson of the day, which for the sake of keeping in touch with her class during her absence she had been studying all the week. What if she should go over and talk to those two children and God should open a way for her to tell that beautiful Bible story to them? Might she? Would Maria miss her? She glanced at her sister, who seemed to be fast asleep, and then moving gently she laid her books by Maria's side and rose and slipped away. She would go for a few minutes, anyway, and see how she was received. And so with beating heart, for she was young and this seemed a grave and responsible mission to her, Rachel went to see what her first opportunity had for her of possibility in the way of soul winning.

Katy and John were startled when they found the pretty young lady sitting down beside them on their spar, and actually speaking to them, and they picked up their shells and prepared to flee, but Rachel's winning smile and her eagerness over the pretty shells they had gathered soon made them forget this intention, and before they knew what they were about they were sitting on the sand at her feet, listening with large, wondering eyes and wide-open mouths to a story she was telling them. She had found that the questions she wanted to ask would have to be deferred until she had won a place in their hearts and had been able to loosen their tongues, for they were shy of speaking any words at all but yes and no, and blushed deeply even at these. They evidently were not used to being talked with much by any one except their own family, and perhaps not much by them. And so Rachel's art of story-telling stood her in good stead. She made a shell lead up to the story, and she soon had them interested in it.

Then from that story she went on to tell of Jesus making a fire by the seaside and cooking the fishes for his disciples' supper. As they grew interested she forgot everything in her joy of teaching. She drew a bit of a diagram in the sand, using a razor fish's shell for a crayon, and the children, who had never seen anything of the kind before, bent eager heads over the picture and drank in her words as if they had been listening to music. Perhaps it was not the best lesson she might have selected for a first in religious instruction, but she presently succeeded in making those two young hearts beat with longing to have been of that weary boat load coming in to the supper and the dear and gracious Master.

And then, wonder of wonders! they heard from this beautiful young lady's lips that they also might be his children! his, cared for by him. That great, good Jesus, who was no more associated with their idea of God than they would have associated him with some of their own family, and whose name they never heard but in profanity, he might be theirs. If the young teacher could have looked into those darkened little hearts and known what they really did think and feel about God, and how very little they knew about him, her heart would have sunk at the impossibility of her task, and her words might have grown less eloquent in her hopelessness; but mercifully she did not know, as mercifully none of us know just what is before or about us, and the Father in heaven knew that they were filled with a great longing for the first time in their little lives to know Jesus Christ.

So Rachel talked on and on, and the children did not grow weary, and the sun was setting in the west before she realized how long she had kept her Sabbath-school, and how long she had been away from her sister, who would doubtless blame her for the neglect.

That night when Rachel opened her Bible in her own room she read these words, "Therefore, my beloved brethren, be ye steadfast, unmovable, always abounding in the work of the Lord, forasmuch as ye know that your labour is not in vain in the Lord." And she wondered wistfully just what those words meant, and if it were wrong for her to claim them and think her Father in heaven sent them as a message to cheer her heart in this new work.

Chapter 11

But Maria was not really asleep. She had closed her eyes because she did not wish to talk. She did not wish to see her sister bending over her Bible. It made her uncomfortable to think Rachel could enjoy the Bible. *She* could not. She told herself plainly that she never had; that she only read it from a sense of duty, as of course all church-members would do. It irritated her to think that Rachel pretended to enjoy it. In her heart she knew that there was no pretense about Rachel, and that she really did enjoy it, but it pleased her to say this to herself. It made her own unhappy, rebellious life seem less black in contrast. When Rachel laid down her books and slipped softly away Maria felt relieved. She wanted to be alone. She felt too utterly ugly in her heart to be near any one. Presently she wondered where her sister could have gone, and why she did not return, and raising herself and peeping under the parasol, she looked up and down the beach and saw Rachel with her young class gathered about her. Maria understood what it meant. She curled her lip a little. Rachel was always doing such queer things. What would the De Veres or some of the hotel people think if they came along now and saw her sitting in the sand with those two barefooted little heathen beside her. She half made up her mind to call her back and reprove her, and then sat back again, asking herself what was the use, and feeling a little relieved that she was likely to be by herself for some time, albeit there was growing in her heart a determination to charge her sister with neglecting her for two little vagrants when she did return.

She settled herself a little more comfortably with the help of some of Rachel's pillows, and seeing the red paper-covered book that had been left lying closed on the Bible beside her, she took it up. It surprised her a little that Rachel should bring a paper-covered novel out on Sunday along with her Bible, for Rachel was apt to be a little puritanical about such things; but she knew that Roland De Vere had sent some books over to Rachel yesterday; doubtless this was one of them. She reached for it, reflecting that Rachel's scruples would be easily overcome by that handsome young man, who seemed to have made up his mind to devote himself to her, even if she were nothing but a little girl.

She read the title, "A Castaway." It looked exciting—that is, the title seemed so. It was probably a story of the sea. She turned the pages and opened at the beginning, a look of satisfaction on her face that here was something to make her forget herself for a little while. But the look rapidly changed to disappointment as she read. A Bible verse at the beginning! It was nothing but a sermon after all, or worse still, one of those devotional books. She flung it carelessly down in her lap and leaned back again. How exasperating! Just when she thought she was going to have a little relief from the monotony and enjoy herself. She picked up the book once more and read half-way down the first page, but it was as if she were reading Hebrew. She knew not what manner of speech this was, and she did not take in the sense of the words. They meant nothing to her, and she closed it again and went on with her own thoughts, her fingers carelessly between the pages, but the look of settled discontent upon her face. It was well for her that the parasol was placed at such an angle as to thoroughly hide that expression on her face else she might have missed what had been sent her that afternoon.

Howard Fairfield had come out on the beach to walk and be alone. He had gone out at once after dinner, feeling that he wanted to get away from the gay chatter of the hotel guests, for the few guests that there were made much of themselves and of each other and chattered indiscriminately. He had walked up by the lonely lighthouse, and now had turned and was retracing his steps, thinking to go to his room to rest or read a little, perhaps. He had gained an uplifting in his walk by the sea. His thoughts had been with God, and there was a softened, sweet expression upon his face, an expression which in a man's face, seldom as it is seen, makes it the more noble and manly, as if he were growing more like the man God meant him to be.

He walked on slowly as he neared the part of the beach in front of the hotel and began to meet one and another of the guests there strolling and chatting in lazy fashion. He guided his own steps farther away, that he might not be drawn into conversation with any of them and break the solemn quiet which had stolen over him. Thus he passed just back of Rachel and her little group of listeners, and catching a word or two of her earnest lesson, walked more slowly and listened too. He recognized the tact and skill with which this mere girl was talking to these two ignorant little children, and wondered thereat. There were things he might learn from even a young girl's teaching, he said to himself, as he passed wistfully on, wishing he dared linger and hear more without danger of spoiling the lesson for the other two.

Then he turned his steps straight down to the sea and stood as close to the waves as might be, looking out and thinking. It seemed to him that his past life was rolling out there before him, wave after wave of it, too far away from him to ever come at and change it, rolling carelessly but certainly on to eternity to meet him again on the other shore. He numbered each wave with a year or period of his life, and saw its glaring mistakes, and wished he might ride over the waters and bring those farther ones back and live them again that they might be better lived. At last he turned with a sigh. It was no use looking back. He must go forward and see that the waves which followed these should be stronger and more resistless with endeavor for Christ. And so walking deep in thought up the sandy bank he came face to face with Maria Hammond, who had of course seen him, in fact, had been watching him for some minutes, and who while she was too proud to arrange her dress or alter her position as if she expected him to greet and talk with her, had nevertheless risen more to a sitting posture, and changed her expression from one of scornful discontent to one of quiet, dignified Sabbath thoughtfulness.

The young man, realizing suddenly that he was in danger of walking over a lady and sun umbrella, raised his head and recognized Maria. Of course there was nothing to do but pause a moment and speak to her, though in his present mood he would have avoided any one — especially a gay young girl, as he had imagined her to be — if he had had the choice beforehand.

But while pausing and exchanging the word of greeting, his eyes fell on the Bible and the little paper book. He looked up quickly, almost surprised, and yet glad, at the young girl's face. He had not somehow thought of her as one who would be likely to bring her Bible to the shore where others were. He must have been mistaken. She as after all a Christian, an earnest one, perhaps, like her sister over there who was doing her best to work for Jesus. He felt glad in his heart instantly that he had stopped, said to himself that perhaps he had been led to her for help, for he recognized in himself just then a great need for help. His face lighted up.

"May I sit down?" he asked, "or are you expecting some one else to occupy this luxurious chair in the sand? I'm a little tired from my long walk."

And Maria, all smiles and graciousness, though with not a shade too much earnestness for maidenly decorum, told him that he was welcome, and that the seat was Rachel's, but that Rachel had gone on a missionary trip to some little heathen, and there was no telling how late it would be before her return. If Maria had not seen a certain something which seemed new to her in this new acquaintance of hers, she might have put a shade of scorn for Rachel and her menial service into this sentence, but there had been that in the young man's face which had reminded her that he was a minister and that ministers were wont to respect and praise such acts as Rachel's present one, therefore her tone told nothing of the scorn she felt, and she spoke of Rachel's work as a natural, perfectly praiseworthy occurrence. She wondered afterward why she had done this and how she had been kept from saying several things which had been on the tip of her tongue and yet had not seemed quite to be what Mr. Fairfield would expect of her, as they would have seemed two weeks before, during their first few days of acquaintance.

"She is doing her work over there well," said the minister, his face growing grave again. "I could not help hearing a little of her lesson as I passed, and wishing I were a barefoot heathen too, for what I heard helped me. She must have remarkable talent as a teacher of little ones."

Maria was somewhat astonished, it is true, but accepted her sister's compliment with sisterly pride. Mr. Fairfield stretched out his hand while they were talking and took up the little paper volume. Maria's face flushed slightly, and she was about to disclaim any connection with the book, and to tell how miserably disappointed she had been a few minutes before over the contents, when again something held her back and she sat still while Mr. Fairfield turned the leaves.

"Ah! Mr. Meyer!" he said, as he opened the title-page. "You have been reading this?" He flashed his bright dark eyes up into hers again with that sudden pleasure and surprise that had confused her a moment before. "I never read it myself, and I was foolish enough to lose my opportunity of hearing the man when he was in this country, through listening to some adverse criticisms upon him, which I have since come to believe were utterly false and unfounded. I wish I could undo that loss and hear this address as it was delivered in my own city. A saint who has just gone to heaven told me of it."

Maria listened in respectful, surprised silence, glad that some intuition had kept her mouth closed a moment before. This certainly was not the same young man whom she had known, or thought she had known, two weeks before, and she prided herself on being a quick judge of character, and on being able to read faces readily. What had made the difference? She watched him while he turned the pages slowly.

"Have you been reading this?" he asked again suddenly. "Have you read it all? Perhaps you would not mind reading it aloud to me, if you have not. I never have any one to read aloud to me now that my sister is abroad. Are you fond of exercising yourself in that direction for other people's pleasure?"

"No, I have not read it all," Maria admitted, her face flushing slightly, and she wondered whether, if he knew the fact he would call that the strict truth to answer so, "but I am very fond of reading aloud and shall be delighted to read it if it will be any pleasure to you."

Now it happened that Maria was gifted in the art of reading aloud. It is true her family very seldom had the benefit of this gift, for there were few occasions when she thought it worth while to exercise it, and they seldom asked favors at her hand. But on occasions, when her audience was appreciative and worth while, she could charm a friend, or a whole room full of friends, as she read from story or poem, and bring their tears and their laughter at her will. Her voice was low and sweet and clear, and her expressive face helped to interpret whatever she read, by flashes of fun or earnestness. Everybody liked to hear Maria Hammond read, and in her younger days when she was a little child, guided by the wishes of her family, the father and mother and brother and sister had been exceedingly proud of her powers.

There was something exceedingly interesting, not to say romantic, to a girl who had been moping at a dull seaside with nothing to do but cook and be cross, in the situation of sitting by the lovely sea with a very handsome, evidently cultured, young man and being asked to read aloud something in which he was deeply interested, and which had to do with his own especial, personal lines of thought, all for his benefit. Even though the book was one which she had just now scorned, and the theme chosen was to her uninteresting, what mattered it? Religious writing was always easy to read and capable of much good expression in an elocutionary way. She took the book with alacrity, much pleased over the turn the afternoon had taken, and wondering why the sea looked so much more beautiful that it had done a half-hour before.

She read impressively the wonderful Bible text with which the address began, and then went on as naturally as if the writer of the simple, earnest sentences had himself been present delivering them. She was aware constantly of the pair of earnest eyes which watched her, listened intently to what she read, taking in every slightest turn brought out by her good rendering, appreciating to the full the homely, apt illustrations with which the short sermon was sprinkled, and unconsciously to herself, she was thinking most about what he thought of her reading, though as the reading went on, she could not fail to be interested too, for a good reader, like a good singer or a perfect actor, for the time being throws his whole soul into what he is voicing, and lives it and believes it with all his heart.

On to the end she read without interruption save an occasional half-articulate emphasis from the listener as some peculiarly good point was noted by him, and as she finished the impressive prayer with which the address closed, she raised her eyes to his and they were full of tears.

There seemed to be something almost dreadful about those tears to Maria, as she thought upon them afterward, as if she had given an impression she had no right to give, and she dropped her eyes quickly. There had been a strange, a kind of exalted, look upon his face too, as if he were pleading for forgiveness with his eyes from one unseen, and realizing something in his life which hurt him. He had hardly seemed conscious of the young girl by his side. But then he spoke slowly, quietly; he was very grave, with a strange light in his eyes, she saw, as she glanced shyly up again.

"Miss Hammond, I cannot thank you enough for the help you have been to me in reading that. It seems somehow to fit my life better than anything

I ever heard. Do you know, it touches me in a vital spot. I have been fearing within the last few days that I myself have been a castaway, even before I have ever been of any real use. I did not think an hour ago I could have spoken of this matter to any one, but perhaps it will do me good to tell it to some one, and you have been so kind and helpful. In fact I can see that you know just how to help some one in trouble." Here he looked up with a pleasant smile, not in the least the smile of the ordinary young man of society who is giving a young woman a compliment, but more a sweet, grave acknowledgment of her womanhood and its natural province of helper, comforter, sympathizer.

"I have had a strange experience since I left the beach so suddenly. I never thought to tell it to any one, but I believe I will tell you if you do not mind."

And then he went on and gave the astonished Maria an account of his hasty summons to the city, of his meeting with the dreamer, and of the strange fulfillment of the dream. He even told her of his own feelings as he waited for that summons to the funeral, and of his full surrender to God, and the following experiences by the bedside of the dying saint.

And when he had finished and they rose by tacit consent to walk slowly toward home, he gathering up the cushions and parasol and silently assisting her in getting her things together, she walked subdued and wondering beside him. Not that she was utterly silent. Oh, no; she was naturally too tactful for that. She knew how to sympathize with people in other things than religion, she knew how to put in the quiet, helpful word and to listen with rapt attention.

Moreover, she was wonderfully interested in this young man and his story. She had never listened to a real heart history like this before. No one had ever before given her his confidence to such an extent. She could not help but be sympathetic and to feel that there was something in all he said that was true for her as well as for him. She murmured, "It is all very wonderful," as they neared her home, and Mrs. Hammond, awakened by approaching voices from an uncomfortable nap in the mosquito-netted hammock on the piazza, looked up to see a strange new light on her elder daughter's face and to wonder over Maria once more.

They paused at the steps and the minister said earnestly, "You have helped me this afternoon. I should like to talk with you more about this matter. May I hope to have some more of that wonderful reading soon?" And then something was said about attending the evening service in the church. The mother, behind the porch screen did not hear nor heed. She was wondering how it was that Maria, the Maria whom they had known since their stay at the seashore, could possibly be of any help to anybody in her present state of mind.

Chapter 12

"That is a remarkable girl," said Mr. Fairfield to himself as he walked slowly back toward his hotel. "Her acquaintance will indeed be a help to me, I can see that at once. And what a fine reader she is! She seems utterly unconscious of the fact. She is as sweet and natural as a flower. She must be an unusual Christian!"

It is a good thing that people are blind sometimes, else much of the good of this world might be left undone because the workers would think it was hardly worth while. God in his mysterious kindness makes us see each other, now worse, now better than we really are, in order that we may help and be helped. It is doubtful whether the Hammond family, had they been permitted to know the young minister's conclusions about Maria, would not have thought it their duty to warn him how mistaken he was. And yet nothing that could have come to Maria would have been likely to do her so much good as this afternoon of being happily misunderstood and the consequent impression she made upon the minister. How, if this had not been, could she have ever spent those days which followed in reading and talk such as she had never dreamed of taking part in before, and of pleasant companionship of a higher character than any which had been permitted to fall to her lot before? God had just as surely sent Mr. Fairfield to be a missionary to Maria Hammond as he intended Maria Hammond to awaken and help the young man. And yet a weak human judgment would have kept these two utterly apart for the spiritual growth of each.

For the first time since her coming to the shore Maria entered the low door of the despised green cottage without a thought of the cottage or its shabbiness, or her own hatred of the surroundings. She went thoughtfully to her own room and laid down the two books she had been carrying on Rachel's little table, making a few slight changes in her toilet preparatory to getting supper, but her face did not wear its now usual expression of distaste and weariness. Instead, she really looked bright and happy.

It is true she was not thinking of the deep spiritual things she had read from the little book, nor yet entirely of the young minister's experiences which he had given her, though they had impressed her strongly. She was instead pleasing her own starved love for admiration with thinking that the young man had cared to confide in her, had thought her worthy of such confidences. She recognized that they were unusual confidences, and her own conscience, which was a well-educated one, soon began to trouble her that she had let him suppose her to be better than she was. She went back over the afternoon talk, and while she realized that she had not told any falsehoods, not indeed done anything or said anything out of keeping with actual truth, still she acknowledged to her own soul with crimsoning cheeks that she had remained silent several times, when, in order to have been perfectly honest, she ought to have spoken out and told him that she was not at all what he thought, that he must go to her sister, or others, whom she had half despised for their very eagerness about such things, if he wanted any help.

And yet, if she had done this, she would have lost the privilege of that talk, and she began to realize that it had been a privilege to her. Nor was it wholly on account of her desire for companionship and pleasure. There was something deeper in her heart, which had been so restless, which said to her, "Here, here is something you have been longing for. This man may show you a way to get it. He is different from what you thought him at first. and perhaps you are a little disappointed that he is, for you fear you cannot have quite so much of what you call 'fun' with him if that is the case; but underneath it all you know you like him better that he is of a higher type than you at first thought him."

What queer conversations people carry on with themselves, and how they analyze their own feelings and think they know themselves, and yet can only read a little piece of their own hearts and know not its follies, nor its goodness either, and then straightway forget what manner of men and women they are and go on committing the very same follies again.

But Maria's cheerfulness lasted while she prepared the evening meal. Rachel coming in and expecting a storm on account of her desertion, was astonished, almost uneasy, and finally felt called upon to explain to her sister how it was she had not come back sooner. But Maria answered pleasantly that she had been listening to an account of the delightful little lesson she had been teaching, and she hoped it was not all thrown away on those poor ignorant children. It was a pity Rachel had not some better material to work upon down here, but it was good of her to be willing to help those poor children, she supposed. Then Maria went out to the refrigerator actually humming a little tune under her breath while she took out the butter for supper.

And Rachel went to the piazza where sat her mother, and said: "Mamma, is Maria sick, do you think? She doesn't seem to act like herself. I wish I had not left her alone this afternoon, but I thought she was asleep."

The mother glanced up anxiously, always full of foreboding for her children, and then remembering, smiled and answered: "No, dear, I fancy she has been having a little glimpse of pleasure, and perhaps it is doing her good. She has had a hard time, poor child, though of course we could not help it."

"Well, mamma," said Rachel, a little careworn wrinkle coming in her smooth brow, "I think she is working too hard, and I wish you and papa would make her stop and go out on the beach and let me take my turn awhile. I know I can't do so well as she, but I will try my best. I don't feel happy having Maria work so hard."

"You dear child!" said the mother, drawing Rachel toward her and smoothing her hand. "I know just how much that means for you to say. You do not like kitchen work one bit, and you have been brave and good at it too, thus far. But it is not necessary for you to do any more than you have been doing. Your father and I have talked over the same thing, and have been worried about your sister's health. We decided last night to have that Higgins girl come over every day. She is not skilled, and will need help and watching, but she will learn; and she is willing to come for very little if I will teach her our ways, she says; so you need not think the expense will be too great. That will set both you and Maria free for most of the time, and I am much relieved."

Maria called her mother just then to ask some question about the supper, and Rachel was left standing in the dying twilight pondering. How wonderful was everything! God was actually going to send the girl whom she had planned to help a little, right into their daily life, and she would have endless opportunity. She closed her eyes and lifted her heart in prayer that she might be shown how to live so that her life would show forth God's glory, and that she might be given power to lead that ignorant girl to Jesus. It was sweet to her to remember the eager little faces that had listened to her lesson that afternoon, and now that she could not think of them without reproaching herself for having left her sister alone, she could not drive them from her mind, but went over and over again their questions and her answers and the way they had been received, her heart leaping within her at the thought of really telling the story of Jesus for the first time to two little human waifs for whom he had died.

Maria saw the minister only a few minutes more that night. The mosquitoes were too merciless for them to linger outside the house or to dare light up the cottage and invite people in, and the minister was not one who would propose a walk. He felt that both their hearts had received a benediction, and that the young woman would sympathize with him in wanting to be alone with God a little while after the Sabbath blessing.

But Maria's conscience had grown decidedly prickly. He had thanked her again as he bade her good-night for the help she had given him, and she felt guilty as she let him go away thinking of her in this way. She felt that her natural honesty would not long allow her to accept quietly this homage to her supposed goodness. She must explain soon, and then good-bye to all friendship with him, for he was evidently much in earnest. He would hardly waste time on such as she had been. Well, what did she care? She could go on as she had done and endure the summer to the end. The man was but a stranger, anyway, and not of her kind. Her restless spirit was returning. She knew nothing of the proposed domestic help. She remembered the morrow and all the petty miserable cares which she had of her own free will taken upon herself. The mosquitoes again began to be a terrible thorn in the flesh, and she saw in imagination the piles of greasy dishes which would have to be washed in the morning, and the struggle with the grocery boy to get him to send the yeast in time for the morrow's baking, with probably the necessity for buying some of the miserable baker's stuff offered under the name of bread which all the family cordially detested.

And then the brother came in with his never-ending flow of fun and capacity for teasing, and choosing the wrong time, proceeded to poke questions at her about Mr. Fairfield. Maria's replies were short and sharp; she said with freezing dignity that she cared nothing whatever for Mr. Fairfield and wished he would keep away; that she supposed he was some nobody, anyway, as no one else would come to such a place for the summer unless he had to. Then she went to her room with tears of vexation in her eyes and thought of the same man's earnest "thank you" spoken a few moments before, remembered her own gentle, subdued good-night, her assent to his words of Christian friendliness, how she had so evidently deceived him as to her character, and felt herself a very hypocrite indeed.

It is no wonder then that the morning found her unrested and unhappy as in the days that had passed. She was even disposed to resent the new arrival in the kitchen instead of being glad and relieved, and after repeated attempts to monopolize the entire work and so show that a girl was a superfluous addition to the family expense, she went grandly to her own room with a sweep of her head, declaring that if they would not let her work she supposed she could sit down and endure life in some way with folded hands. No, she would not go to the beach, and she would not go bathing, and she would not fix up her muslin dress to wear to Spray View that afternoon for she was not going to Spray View to call on those two stuck-up girls. She did not care to be patronized if Rachel did, and as for Roland De Vere, she thought she had been greatly mistaken in him. He did not seem nearly so intellectual as she had at first supposed. Then when Rachel in despair had left her, she had barred to door and burying her face in the pillow had cried as hard as her overwrought nerves demanded.

Fortunately for her, she had not cried long when Rachel's voice called to her again that there was some one in the parlor to see her. This stopped the tears suddenly, but not the stubbornness. She would not go to the parlor to see any one. Rachel might make any excuse she pleased, that she was too busy or sick, but she would not come out, and she would not unfasten the improvised door which the father and brother had contrived for more privacy than the cottage afforded. Nevertheless, she rose from beside the bed and went to the small disfiguring looking-glass. She knew by former experience that the few moment crying in which she had indulged must have left its marks already on her face. Yes, her eyes and nose were red and swollen. She could not go out if she wished to do so, without disgracing herself. She began to wonder who it could be who wished to see her; perhaps some of those De Veres, now become hateful, because she fancied they were looking down upon her and hers; perhaps, the minister. Well, if it was the minister, what did she care? she asked herself fiercely and she went nervously to the wash bowl and began to dash the cold water on her swollen eyes.

Then at the other door came the mother's voice, always low and sweet, but very low now lest the caller in the parlor of this very "open" house should hear. There was also a note of command in the voice which Mrs. Hammond seldom used toward her children, but which Maria did not dare disregard.

"My daughter, let me in at once. I have something to tell you."

Maria with the wet towel in her hand answered her mother's summons then, and quickly let her in, mopping her face violently the while:

"Are you ill, daughter?" asked the anxious mother as she saw the traces of excited tears on her elder daughter's face.

"No," answered Maria, choking suddenly at the tenderness in her mother's voice; she almost wished she were really ill and lying in bed to be petted and taken care of. It made the tears start again to her eyes.

The mother wound her arm about the daughter's waist.

"Well, then, dear, is there any reason why you do not care to see Mr. Fairfield? Tell me all about it. I must know the reason, you know, before I can excuse you."

"Is it Mr. Fairfield?" asked Maria, a little gleam of satisfaction showing in her voice in spite of herself. "But you see, mother, I can't go out. Look at my eyes. I am a perfect sight. It will be hours before I get over being a fright. You will have to tell him something." There was disappointment in Maria's voice, very evident to the mother, and she determined that she would make a strenuous effort to get Maria out of herself, and into the fresh air, where her overwrought nerves might have a little chance for rest.

"Nonsense! Your eyes will be all right in a few minutes, dear!" she answered quickly. "Bathe them and brush your hair. Here, slip on your pretty beach dress. You have not worn it since you came and the air is quite fresh this morning. I want you to get out and have the air and sunshine. You will be ill if you do not, and that we are not going to allow. Now hurry, dear, Mr. Fairfield is quite anxious to see you. I will excuse you for a few minutes, and Rachel shall take him down to the new clam beds while you are getting ready. Now hurry," and the mother hastened out to do what she had promised with more confidence in her manner than she felt in her heart that Maria would do her bidding.

But something seemed to have come over Maria. She desired suddenly above all things to go out with her pretty beach dress, walk beside Mr. Fairfield, have him think her good for a little while, and say she helped him. It would not do any harm just for once and she was tired of the hateful way things had been going. She washed her face feverishly and furiously and hastened her toilet as much as possible and between times took hurried trips to the disfiguring little glass to see if there was any hope of her eyes and nose soon assuming their proper color and shape, and the mother, coming back, was relieved to find that Maria was ready.

And so it came about the Maria and the young minister started out on a tramp to the life-saving station, two miles away, on that lovely summer morning, with a fresh breeze blowing in their faces, and Maria looking her very prettiest in her dark blue and white yachting suit, her cheeks becomingly pink from the recent tears, and her whole face as expressive of sudden happiness as could well be, for when Maria gave way after a fit of stubbornness she was often really lovely and subdued and humble, and somehow her mother's tones and wistfulness had conquered her that morning.

Moreover, she felt humiliated in her heart and the humility sat well upon her face, where there had been so much haughty pride of late. The minister, looking at her in the Monday morning light decided that she was very fair as well as good, and he was glad to walk with her and talk beside the sea, and before the morning was over they had found may points of interest in common. Maria coming back did not feel half so much a hypocrite that she had not confessed to him how unworthy she was of his praise, because the talk had not been on things in which she felt she was lacking. The Lord in his wisdom saw that this child of his needed a little of the brightness and joy of life and he had given it to her, weaving, as he gave it, about her the cords of his own love which were to draw her to himself. Let no skeptical one fancy all this beneath him. We barter away the whole comfort of life if we so think. For these things, and things like them, are among the "all these" the Master promised should be added to those seeking first the Father's kingdom.

Chapter 13

The afternoon was warm and lovely. It was several days since Maria and Mr. Fairfield had walked to the life-saving station together, and since then there had been several like expeditions. Maria lay in the screened and netted hammock on the porch with a book before her, but she was not reading. Instead, she was thinking. Her troubled conscience had pursued her day after day through all the pleasant walks and sails and rides and talks. She felt herself to be more and more a hypocrite. She had tried feebly, two or three times, to explain to the minister that she was not "good" as he seemed to think, in fact that she was very wicked and worldly and unlovely in her character; but her efforts had failed, for it had been so pleasant to have some one think well of her, and make her a part of his pleasure as his this man had done.

This afternoon her conscience had arraigned her most strongly.

Something ought to be done. She must not go on reading religious books and pretending to be devoted to them, though the fact was growing plain to her that the books themselves were not so wholly without interest as they had seemed to her last Sabbath. She had learned that there was much that was intensely interesting in them, and she liked to hear the minister talk of these things. Her own part in these conversations had been a meek assent to what he said, but still she had managed to assent in such a manner as to keep unchanged his first impression that she was heart and soul with him in what he said. She had even added a word or two now and then when he had seemed to expect her to say something, and when something quite original had occurred to her which seemed to fit into the discussion. He thought her an exceedingly bright young woman, and so she was; those little additions of hers to the religious conversations had been apt and striking ones. She knew that her bringing-up had been largely the cause of her ability to say such things well, and to know when to say them.

But she also knew that her life for some time had run counter to her words and she hated hypocrisy above all things. She had planned conversation after conversation in which she should tell her new friend exactly the truth about herself. In some of these imaginings she was humble and begged him to teach her to think as he did. But for that she was too proud. In others she withdrew from his acquaintance entirely, told him she was not of his kind and that he had been mistaken in her. And then it occurred to her, "Why not turn about and try to be what he thought she was?" She had reached that point this afternoon for the seventeenth time, and she had asked herself over and over again whether she could to it and how she should begin, and whether if she did, it would be exactly honest in her to do so? And then, why, after all, should she do it? Mr. Fairfield was a pleasant acquaintance, but in all probability he would go away in a few days and she might never see him again. Why did she care to try to appear well before him, and not only to appear well, but to really be what she appeared? She could not understand why he seemed to bring out the best and highest longings her soul contained.

Well, supposing she should set herself the task of being good, what should she do first? She might refrain from being cross, it is true, and saying sarcastic things; but that seemed rather a hopeless task, for her tongue was so used to bitter words that she scarcely knew when she spoke them. Then too, there was nothing interesting in that. Still of course that would come in as a necessary part of any such change in her life. She might take up some philanthropic work. But what could it be? Rachel seemed to always be able to find some work to do for others, but now that there was help in the kitchen. Maria felt that her life had been made too easy for her to show forth her good works by any great sacrifices such as she was seeking.

It was just at this point in her conversation with herself that her sister came upon the porch with low rocking-chair, work-basket, scissors, and thimble, and in the distance across the sandy dunes could be seen the lank, awkward form — arrayed in a neat blue calico and white apron — of their new serving-maid, bearing in her arms a bundle of old hats, apparently. Her work was done for the afternoon and Rachel's first lesson, instead of being in lace work, was to be in millinery, for it appeared that Annie Higgins' greatest desire in the line of worldly possessions was a nice hat to wear to an entertainment that evening over on the mainland, to which her cousin's wife's brother had asked her to accompany him in his sailing vessel, along with some other members of the family. Rachel, through tact and kindness, had discovered this need and desire of Annie's and had readily offered her assistance, sighing as she thought how much better hat Annie might have if only Maria were to make it instead of herself; but she quietly kept the matter to herself, as she supposed, dreading Maria's scornful looks and words which would be sure to come if she knew.

She had reckoned, however, without remembering the cracks in the kitchen wall. Maria had heard the entire arrangement that morning as she sat in her room mending a rent in her blue dress, and had thought to herself, how easy it seemed to be to Rachel to find out and do such things for other people. Had Rachel been there and known that she heard it, Maria would have felt called upon to show her scorn of such a proceeding, but away from sight Maria was able to appreciate something of her sister's kindness, although she wholly disapproved, and wished she would not do such queer things. Now as she saw Rachel come out and Annie also issue forth from the little unpainted house across the marsh she remembered, and half wished she were gifted with doing things for other people so that she might not feel so utterly unworthy of the friendship of a good and earnest Christian minister. She languidly watched Rachel as she put on her little white work apron and selected the needle with which she expected to work. She knew that to Rachel the task of making a hat was a great one. Rachel would much rather write a description of the hat, or draw a picture of it, than go through the necessary manipulations in order to produce one. It was not likely to be an artistic affair when done, either, as both the sisters well knew from former experience. However, Rachel would do her best, hoping for the best results.

Just at that moment around the corner by the little church came two beautiful horses drawing an elegant carriage in which sat Roland De Vere and his two sisters. The two sisters were on the back seat and the front seat beside the young man who was driving was evidently left vacant for some one they expected to pick up. The carriage drew up at the little green cottage doorsteps and its occupants greeted Rachel effusively. Maria was glad that she was well screened from their view, for somehow she felt as utterly out of sympathy with them as she did with herself or anybody else, though several months before her heart would have jumped with joy at their appearance and she would have done anything to be the fourth member of that riding party. Now she knew that they had come for Rachel, and she saw by the sudden rush of glad color to her little sister's cheek that Rachel knew and was glad, gladder perhaps than they had any idea of, for Rachel was always so quiet about her likes and dislikes that sometimes she was in danger of being allowed to lose much that she cared for in life through other people supposing that she did not care. Maria's eyes were opened a little by the look on her sister's face as she quietly laid aside her basket and went down the steps to greet her callers and ask them to come in. Maria was glad that they immediately declined, for she could not get away unobserved and she did not wish to be seen; but she could not well help listening to the conversation.

Roland De Vere, in his gallant and courtly way, invited Rachel to put on her hat and get into the carriage at once, as they were off for a long drive up the beach and must have her company else their pleasure would be spoiled. Maria saw, through the cracks in the porch screen, how the soft color stole again into Rachel's cheeks and then how her bright face clouded over with disappointment.

"Oh, I'm so sorry I can't go," she answered instantly; "I would love it so, and it is such a perfect day for a drive on the beach. I have often thought how delightful it would be to fly along on the edge of the waves with horses like those. But I can't, I really can't."

"Now we won't have any 'can't' at all. What is it in the way?" asked the young man earnestly; "because whatever stumbling-block there is, I shall remove it. Have you been a naughty girl and won't they let you get up out of your chair till you're good, or are you mending and can't leave your task till it's finished? If that's it, give me a needle, and I'll help and we'll have the work done in less than no time."

Amid the laugh which followed Rachel's perplexed face grew firm.

"No, it isn't anything like that," she answered, laughing, and yet sorry and troubled. "It's the Higgins girl."

"The Higgins girl! What has she to do with it, and who is she? Bring her along, that'll be all right; we can stow her in somewhere and make her comfortable, I guess. Fannie, can't you and Evelyn make room back there?"

But Rachel hastened to explain, with an irrepressible smile at the idea.

"No, no it's her hat. I promised to help her make a hat to wear to an entertainment to-night. She is the fisherman's daughter who lives over in that little house, and she wants to go to an entertainment with a friend to-night. I have promised her and she seems very happy over it, so I must not disappoint her."

Mr. De Vere emitted a prolonged whistle and the Misses Fannie and Evelyn looked curiously at Rachel, making Maria's blood boil within her.

"Dear me!" said Evelyn shrugging her shoulders, "can't you put her off?"

"Yes," put in Fannie seeing her brother's evident disappointment and Rachel's firmly-set red lips, "tell her it is a great deal more smart to go bareheaded to entertainments this time of year and wear a flower in her hair."

These girls were well-bred and liked Rachel very much, and moreover desired to please their brother, but they were not quite equal to giving up an afternoon's pleasure for the sake of making a hat for a fisherman's daughter, it was evident. Rachel felt this more than saw it. Meanwhile she also felt that she had the brother's sympathy in her perplexity.

Maria, listening, saw it all and suddenly resolved. This was her opportunity. Without her usual calm deliberation, she acted impulsively, almost as Rachel might have done. She called her sister's name.

"Rachel!"

Poor Rachel! No small part of her perplexity, embarrassment, and trouble had arisen from the fact that Maria was listening on the porch, unable to get away, and that she would let fall all sorts of sneering comments upon her, ruthlessly, as soon as the visitors should be out of sight. But she had not supposed that Maria would dare speak at the moment, bringing out the fact of her presence, for she knew Maria's hair was tumbled with lying in the hammock, and Maria's gown was not the one in which she would array herself to appear before the De Veres. With cheeks crimsoning and eyes burning with tears she was too proud to let be seen, she excused herself a moment and went to her sister, trembling as if she had been a little child lest Maria was about to reprimand her severely in the hearing of these friends, as she had once or twice threatened she would do if Rachel persisted in her puritanical notions.

But to her utter amazement, instead of the proud, scornful look she expected to see upon Maria's face there was one of interest, and Maria's tone was low and sisterly as she said: "Rachel, go! I will trim Annie's hat. Yes, go on at once; it's all right. You know I can do it as well as you. Get ready right away."

Rachel could hardly believe her ears. Maria offering to trim a servant girl's hat! Maria giving up her ease, without being urged, to do a work of kindliness for one she despised!

But the friends in the carriage were waiting and Maria was hastening her. She must go and explain. She hesitated but a moment. She saw her sister meant it, and would be displeased if she did not accept it, so she went back to the carriage with a happy face and explained that Maria would see to the hat and then ran in to make her hasty, simple preparations and soon drove away with a bright face. Roland De Vere as he touched his whip to his gay horses said to himself: "I must have been mistaken in Maria after all. I would not have expected her to do so kind a deed."

It seemed that Maria was fated to give false impressions of her goodness nowadays, in spite of herself and of her honest endeavor to right matters with her conscience. As soon as the carriage was out of sight she went in to the kitchen to the solemn-faced girl, who had slipped around to the back door with her pile of old hats and soiled ribbons and funny bright artificial flowers, watching the expected helper drive away in the beautiful carriage with growing dismay gripping her heart, the thought of her own expected pleasure dimmed by the shade of the old worn-out hat.

She was only a poor girl after all, and of course Miss Rachel wouldn't stop for her when she had pleasure of her own on hand! Then she sighed and told herself Miss Rachel was no better than other folks after all, if she did teach the children a whole lot of religion last Sunday. Christian folks were all alike. She had been almost tempted to believe Miss Rachel was different, but now she would never believe in anybody again who had pretty clothes and lots of friends and pleasures. Then she had sat down disconsolately in the back door and looked off at the sea, and felt gloomy, and thought of the long dull winter which would come so soon.

Maria explained how it was that Rachel had gone, and said pleasantly that she would do the work, inviting Annie at once to bring her materials that they might look them over; but Annie had not formed so charming an idea of Maria's character as yet that she did not feel a trifle afraid of her, so she only sat still and said she needn't bother, it didn't matter, anyhow. Maria found that her services, which she knew were so much better than her sister's in this particular line, and which she had expected would be accepted with overwhelming joy, had actually to be urged upon this poor fisherman's daughter. It made her indignant and she told herself that she wouldn't touch the hat if she had not promised Rachel, that the girl deserved no hat at all.

However a promise was a promise, and so she set herself to win Annie out of her glumness and soon had her interested in the hat. And while Annie heated irons, according to her direction, for steaming velvet, she hunted among her own ribbons and flowers for something suitable to help out the meagre array of trimming, and she pondered within herself why she had done this. Was it for Rachel, or for the minister, or for her own conscience' sake?

Chapter 14

The porch was the only comfortable place in which to work that warm afternoon, so after a brief struggle with her pride, Maria transported Annie and her trimmings to a place behind the screen. It was true there was a possibility of some neighbors passing, or of the return of the driving party, or that the minister might come by before she had completed her task. But for the neighbors she cared little, and her feeling toward those De Vere sisters was such that she would rather enjoy shocking them, and, as for the minister, well, she was not sure but she had done this for him, and if he did not understand, her work would have been in vain.

She settled down determined to make a pretty hat and be friendly with this uninteresting girl if she could. She was determined for once to try her hand at philanthropy. On the whole, after the first half-hour she found it not so uninteresting. Trimming hats was always pleasant work to her. She enjoyed thoroughly making "a whistle out of a pig's tail," figuratively speaking, and to make this old hat into something respectable, nay even into a work of art, was as good as playing a new game. She really liked it when once she got into it.

Annie was kept so busy steaming velvet for the first few minutes that she had not time to talk, for which she was thankful, for she felt half resentful at Maria for touching her hat. She had had no reason as yet to like Maria, and would almost rather have done without a hat than take a favor from her. She felt as though she were being patronized. But when she at last emerged from the kitchen with the carefully brushed and steamed velvet and saw the hat which had looked such a hopeless, shapeless mass to her but a few moments before, assuming under the skillful hands of the manipulator the shape of hats she had seen in the stores and on the heads of the ladies of fashion in the hotels, her heart gave a great bound of joy and her allegiance forthwith went out to Maria even more warmly than it had done to Rachel. Such is the vanity of all flesh. Shall we say feminine flesh? To watch those white fingers tastefully twist the renewed velvet folds about the now gracefully shaped straw, was a wonder. Annie sat and gazed in speechless delight, proving herself a sharp and foreseeing helper, because of the quick, alert way in which she always seemed to anticipate the needs of the milliner, handing her a pin or the spool of thread at just the right moment, and restoring the scissors when they slipped to the floor, as scissors have a habit of doing. Maria could but notice and appreciate this, and felt an impulse to speak a kind word, but could think of nothing except about the hat.

"I think it will look very well when it is done," she said at last, holding the hat off to survey it, and feeling that this admiring silence was becoming oppressive.

"It's jes' perfec'ly lovely!" exclaimed Annie effusively, her eyes shining with the delight of possessing anything so altogether satisfying. "I jes' don't see how you can do it so good! Don't you feel awful proud to be able to? How did you learn how? Did you ever work at a milliner's store?"

Maria's cheek flushed. She did not like this question. She felt inclined to be indignant and take the girl's words for an insult. The idea of her working in a milliner's shop! This came of their hiring such a ridiculously cheap cottage and making even the poor fisher folk think they were from the common walks of life. Then she glanced up and seeing the evident admiration in Annie's face, reflected that the girl had lived on the island much of her life and knew little of the different strata in society. Of course she had no intention of insulting her. Indeed, she perceived from the girl's face when she answered no, that she would have stood a trifle higher in her estimation as a skilled artisan if she could have boasted that advantage. So she let the little discomfiture pass, a fact which almost surprised herself and would have astounded her family beyond measure; she even smiled at the queer questions which followed, getting a little quiet amusement out of them.

"Your sister Rachel says you know how to do most everything," went on Annie, clasping her hands about one knee and rocking back and forth on the broad low step on which she was seated. "She said you could paint pictures. Say, did you ever do any of them crayon pictures of live folks? What they hang in best parlors, I mean, that look just like the folks, only all dressed up better than they gen'ally are when they're alive? They have two of them over to my friend's on the mainland. They've got red plush and gold frames, awful pretty, and they hang over the organ and the sofa. It's of her ma and pa when they was first married. I'd like awful well to get one of my oldest brother, that died when he was ten, for ma. She hasn't never forgot to mourn about him. Jes' seems if none o' us could take his place. Do you s'pose you could do one if I was to tell you how he looked? You see he never had no photograph taken, cause they didn't even have a tin-type place here when we come here to live, nor in Spray View either. Could you do one o' them kind o' pictures, do you think? If you could I'd work all summer jes' fer nothin' to get that picture, fer it would please ma and pa so; and I know where I could get a real pretty frame made cheap; a friend of mine is in a store where they make 'em."

Annie's eagerness quite overcame the milliner. She tried to repress the smile that would keep coming and to explain that no one would be able to make a likeness of a person who was dead, without some kind of a photograph to go by, especially one who had not known the person in life. Annie looked disappointed. She had gone from one extreme to the other and felt that a person capable of transforming her old hat could do anything. She was silent a few minutes watching the deft fingers at work, and then she began again.

"Your sister says you made them couches and pretty stuffings and curtains in your parlor. I think you must be awfully smart. You're sort of a 'Jack at all trades' as the sayin' is, aren't you?" She laughed heartily over this intended joke, and Maria could not refrain from joining in. Maria coupled with her powers of elocution a rare ability as a mimic of the tones and manners. She began to think she would have rich material in this girl for quite an amusing entertainment of her friends if she should choose to give it to them.

Annie, in a wistful sort of way, finally asked: "Say! if I was to get some caliker, would you kind o' pin it up fer me like that there green stuff hangin' in your dinin'-room door? I'd like awful well to fix up our front room a little. I hate it the way 'tis. I never knew how to do them kind of things, but I always knew it looked horrid. I tried once or twice. I sent all the way to New York for a motto I saw advertised in a paper I had. It was "Little Church around the Corner." That was just the year they built the chapel there and I thought it would look kind of nice to have that motto in the parlor. It said it had the directions how to make it, and the stuff an' all fer twenty-five cents, so I got it an' it took me a good part of the winter workin' evenin's to finish it. I done it in blue with green trimmin's and a brown steeple, them was the colors they sent, and it looked real pretty and I stuck some shells on pasteboard and made a frame for it, but I ain't never had anything else to go with it. I would jes' give anything if we had a organ. It would look so nice under where it hangs, an' Jim and the girls would all like the music so much. I guess they could play it too after tryin' a little, for Jim can play the accordion real good. He plays 'Swanee River,' and 'Home Sweet Home,' an' 'Sweet By an' By' every Sunday night when he don't have to go down the bay. Say! How did you get them cushions in that corner to stand out so pretty with them ruffles all around? Do you s'pose I could fix up our house a little like this if I tried real hard?"

Maria could not help being interested in the poor, forlorn little house and this girl's helpless, hopeless attempt to "fix it up." She began to suggest some simple things which seemed to Annie quite too simple to make any effect, but as Maria went on and grew interested herself in describing the changes she should make in a bare room if she had but limited means,

Annie's eyes began to sparkle and her cheeks to grow red with eagerness. She really saw ahead of her some chance that their home might have a few bright, cheerful things some day as well as others.

"Why, I could do that," she said, as Maria paused with a pin in her mouth to try the effect of the ribbon she was arranging on the hat.

"Jim, he could saw the boards. I know he wouldn't mind helping. He has lots o' time Sundays."

Maria's strict training as to the Sabbath as a day of rest made her feel a little doubtful of the good she might be doing if she were but starting a family to work on the Lord's Day, but Annie's eager tongue went on, leaving her little time for reflection.

"Say! would you mind coming over some day soon and jes' lookin' at that room an' tellin' me where you thought that shelf you said how to make, would look pretty, and how far down the side of the wall the seat had ought to reach? It ain't very far over there, you know, an' I could show you some cunnin' little chickens and ducks if you'd come."

Maria began to see that her philanthropy was expected to last beyond this afternoon, and she was doubtful whether she relished the idea. She had been willing enough to make a hat, but as for enduring much of this cross-questioning, and being taken on such a friendly social level, she did not have any such intentions. She already felt herself swelling in her own estimation until she almost came up to the minister's ideal. Surely she must be pretty good, after all, to smilingly undergo such a storm of talk as she had been sitting under for the last hour.

But worse was to follow. She did not like to refuse the girl's eager request, so she said perhaps she would come some time, in what she meant to be an indefinite time, but the eager Annie accepted it all in good faith and began to thank her in most intense terms. Suddenly she turned full upon her. "Say!" said she earnestly. "You're one of them church folks too, ain't you? I didn't think you was at first, because you didn't go so much to the chapel, nor seem to run around talking Bible like your sister, but I knew quick as I saw you at that hat so nice an good that you was. I never thought much of them church folks till lately. Pa he thinks they're all frauds, 'cause some of 'em have treated him mean; but then folks ain't all alike, an' I always used to say that folks that is mean will be mean even if they are church folks, an' the church can't make 'em any worse, only it looks worse, them pretendin' so much; but when that there minister come along and was so awful nice about our boat an' all, — I s'pose he told you how it was, — why I jus' made up my mind it wasn't the church that made 'em all so mean, 'cause he bein' a minister an' a kind o' head of it all, he would be meaner than the hull lot of 'em if 'twas the church made 'em so, an' I began to tell pa that he must uv made some mistake. Well, he did allow that if that young feller should run the chapel awhile he would go an' hear him preach himself. He's awful nice, ain't he? Say! ain't you an' he goin' to marry? Folks says you are. I heard it over to Spray View. It's awful nice you like the church an' are so good if you're a-goin' to marry a minister!"

Before Maria could lift her flaming face, or steady her voice to reply to this remarkable series of questions and remarks, she heard a step on the single board which formed a walk over the sand in front of their cottage, and looking up, annoyed beyond measure, to see who was coming and perhaps overheard the last remarks, she saw Mr. Fairfield standing before her. His face was a study, to say the least, perhaps a trifle too grave; but it was evident that the gravity was put on to hide a twinkle which Maria felt must be in his eye. It was impossible to tell how much he had overheard. He betrayed no sign whatever of anything having been over-heard at all, but the irrepressible Annie arose from her step in confusion, adding to Maria's consternation.

"Goodness gracious me! If here he ain't now! 'Talk of angels an' you hears their wings,' as the sayin' is." And she disappeared most unceremoniously into the cottage and began rattling the cook stove to hide her embarrassment.

Chapter 15

The minister sat down on the step vacated by Annie. His acquaintance in the Hammond cottage had progressed so far that he felt sufficiently at home to be seated without an invitation from the young hostess, who was evidently too perturbed to think of offering him any seat less lowly. He looked her over with a new and curious expression upon his face. She was appearing to him in a light in which he had not as yet considered her. Her blushes were certainly becoming. He rather enjoyed her embarrassment. He was quiet for a moment, not caring to interrupt his study of her face. She meanwhile was earnestly engaged in struggling with her thread, which had snarled in the most unaccountable way just as she was taking the final stitch in the completed hat. Her cheeks instead of cooling down grew fairly purple, and her horror and indignation over what that impertinent girl had dared to say to her grew with every minute, as she realized how much the man before her might, yes, must, have heard.

"What are you supposed to be doing?" at last questioned Mr. Fairfield, with an amused expression upon his face.

At the first sound of his voice the spell which had been cast upon Maria's tongue seemed to be broken. She ignored his question. Indeed, she did not know a word he had said:

"Mr. Fairfield," she burst out impetuously, "I do hope you will not believe from the last words that impertinent girl said that *I* have been discussing *you* and your affairs with *her!*" She emphasized each pronoun a little more till the final one was intense and well expressed the scorn she felt.

"And if you had, am I to understand that my humble self would have been a subject so far beneath your notice that you should speak of me in that tone?"

Howard Fairfield's tone was light and cheerful. It was more the tone in which he used to speak to his young associates ten years before when he was just entering college, and before the grave things of life had as yet reached him. Something in this afternoon's occurrence had seemed to put him back again for a little and make him feel young and full of mischief. Besides, he was one of those rare beings who possess wonderful tact, and he saw that Maria was extremely embarrassed and could only hope to regain her composure through being able to laugh it off. He proved himself correct in this conclusion, for his tone, so different from the grave, earnest one he had been accustomed to use in their intercourse, roused Maria from her painfully overwrought feelings to look up and wonder, and even laugh. She essayed to make him understand once more that she had not been discussing him, but had been treated to a catalogue of his virtues, — something connected with a boat, — and she suddenly remembered to her relief that Annie had suggested that he might have told her the story, therefore she at once asked an explanation. Although the young man was evidently annoyed that a mere act of kindness on his part should have been so brought out that he was obliged to tell of it himself, he saw that it would help Maria to regain her composure if he did, and so in a few words he told her how he had helped the father with a bit of advice and a trifle of a loan of money when their fishing boat, their largest source of revenue, had been in danger of being confiscated for a small debt. Had Maria been less upset in her mind she might have read much between the lines which was to the young man's credit, for she must have seen how little he made of the affair and how lightly he told of it. And then he launched into an account of a walk he had taken that afternoon and a most beautiful spot he had discovered, and made Maria forget her discomfiture entirely in the charming powers of description which he exerted for her benefit.

Suddenly he asked, "And what have you been doing all the afternoon? What is that creation you are holding? It looks as if it might be pretty, and certainly is marvelous in its construction. Are you preparing to leave this desert island, and fly back to civilization, and is that a part of your plumage?"

Maria had to laugh again, although the color mounted in her cheeks as she looked at the hat, now grown contemptible in her eyes, and wished she had never seen it nor ever might again — realizing that it had been the cause of her discomfort. It came to her at the same time that she had made an utter failure of trying to do good, and she made a resolve, to be honest with herself and him and everybody else and not let people think her better than she was. She would show everybody just how mean and contemptible she was. Then at least she would be no longer tormented by her conscience, whatever other unpleasantnesses she might have to endure.

"No," she answered half laughing, half troubled, "it represents a vain attempt on my part to right myself in the eyes of the world and be honest. I have been trying to be 'good' and do unto others — well — as they would have me do to them, at least, if I did not do as I would have them do to me. But I think I will give it up. I am not constructed on those lines, I see, and seem to have made a failure in every way. And, indeed, Mr. Fairfield, I have been rarely punished for my attempt to deceive others and myself."

"I don't understand," said the minister comically, puzzled and reaching out his hand for the hat. "It seems to be all right as far as I can judge, though I own I'm not a judge of millinery; but I was told that a hat to be all right must have so much straw, so much ribbon, so much velvet, and so many flowers or feathers, put together in the right proportions. You seem to have all those things. Isn't it becoming? Is that the matter?"

Now Mr. Fairfield had seen at once that there was behind Maria's half-laughing, troubled face something deeper, something which he felt he would like to know. Their intercourse together had been of the sort which draws human hearts to sympathize with one another. He saw she needed help, or thought she did, and as he felt she had helped him, he wished to help her. But he would find out what she meant from her own lips, he would not ask her questions, for he judged from his own nature that that method might only serve to shut the truth from him forever, so he continued his bantering tone.

But although Maria laughed, her face sobered suddenly.

"The hat isn't mine," she answered him quickly. "I am supposed to be doing it for the love of doing good to others. It is for Annie Higgins. It is some of my sister's philanthropy. I never originated any, not to carry it out, in my whole life. Ray had promised to trim this hat so that girl could go to some sort of a picnic to-night, and then her friends came for her to take a drive, and I acted on a sudden impulse and offered to do it for her. I think the real reason I offered to do it was to see if I could just for once be as good as you have persisted in telling me I am. But I'm not. I want to tell you the truth. I can't be miserable any longer at being thought to be good, and helpful, and all that, when I don't know nor care the first thing about it. I let you misunderstand me in the first place and then it went on, and I began to see it was all just as bad as if I had started out to act a lie. I have not had the usual experience of the rich reward of doing good that you find in the Sunday-school books. I may have succeeded in making a respectable looking hat, but I have had a most uncomfortable afternoon, in addition to having been almost insulted by questions and an intimacy which is exceedingly disagreeable thrust upon me, and which I can foresee will cause me endless embarrassments. Now you can see just how much of a fraud I have been. Of course it does not matter to you, for there are other people in the world who are really what you thought I was and can talk with you on these subjects you enjoy and be honest, but I cannot rest comfortably to have any one think me what I am not."

Maria had tumbled these words out one on top of another, scarcely realizing what she was saying, only being anxious to get the horrid explanation over and have the visitor go, so that she might escape to her room and cry as she had never cried before. The tears were already coming to her eyes, and as she raised her face to make her meaning more impressive Mr. Fairfield saw them. He became aware also at that moment of what neither of them had noticed before, that the carriage containing the De Veres and her sister Rachel was just driving up to the door. His heart went out to the overwrought girl before him with sympathy and something deeper—a longing to help which he could not understand. His ready tact stood him in good stead now. He arose with a graceful bow and came forward to the carriage and shaking hands with the young ladies and saying a bright word to his friend Mr. De Vere, thus gave Maria time for recovery before she came forward. He spoke of the charming day and how delightful the drive must have been, and said in a loud cheery tone that he had just dropped in to see if Miss Hammond would not like to walk to the pavilion and watch the double sunset on bay and ocean for a few minutes, that there was to be something rare that evening. Then he half turned toward Maria, and said in an aside:

"Are you nearly ready to go, Miss Hammond? I am afraid that we shall miss the best of it unless we hurry. Just get your hat and let us go without waiting longer, can't you?" and he turned again to the carriage to help Rachel out.

It was a venture almost doubtful in his mind, for he felt one could scarcely tell what Maria in such a mood might or might not do, but he was relieved to see that she took his words as a cover for a hasty retreat into the cottage, ostensibly to get her hat, and he hoped she would there get her equilibrium as well, at least enough to come out and meet and pass the De Veres and go with him to some secluded spot where they two could understand each other and where he might if possible help this young woman who had seemed before so strong in faith and without need of help.

When Maria reached her room and the tears came tumbling down with more prepared to follow, she was tempted, nay she was almost determined, not to go out of that room that night, but to give herself utterly over to misery. And yet, so queer a thing is human nature, she wanted to go out and walk with the minister to the beach and see what he would say to her—for she knew that he had some intention in his kind and strangely given invitation—more than she wanted anything in life. And so without the least delay she dashed the refreshing cold water over her flushed face, smoothed her hair, and seizing her hat made haste out to the piazza, relieved to find that the ordeal of speaking to the visitors was made a short one by the evident haste of her companion to get away and see the sunset.

And the walk to the beach was a brisk one in which the minister talked incessantly, letting Maria have no chance for even a word, pointing out a cloud over the bay, or the etching of a lonely deserted fisher's hut in the distance, against a sea of pink and gold off at the right. He even joked about the shape of some of the cottages, and indulged in a humorous remark or two on some of the inhabitants of the small town, not in any malicious way, only a little laugh, just to keep Maria from thinking of herself or what she had said, or what she meant to say. He was scarcely aware of what he was saying as he strode along. His one aim was to talk. And so he guided her to a quiet knoll a little way up the beach, too far to be disturbed by loiterers at this late hour. He even talked on while he arranged a seat for her in the sand, with two pillows, and shawl which he had not forgotten to take from the hammock on the porch, and he made her sit down in the purple and golden light which hung between the glittering bay and the opal-tinted sea. Then he stopped a moment and turning to her with a quiet smile, as a reminder that their friendship was deeper than the talk of the afternoon had been, said:

"And now, will you explain just what you wanted me to understand by what you said a few minutes ago? I think you are troubled in some way, and I couldn't get quite at it. You surely did not mind my hearing those foolish things that poor girl said. It was something deeper. May I understand?" His tone was gentleness itself, a tone Maria had never heard him use before except once; and that to a little frightened child they had passed one day running in terror from the incoming waves. She felt as if she were a little child adrift and now that he had found her, somehow she would be brought ashore. She dropped her eyes to the sand and tried to tell just what was in her heart.

"I mean that I am not 'good.' I am not like Rachel, or like you, or anybody that *loves* good things. When I first knew you, I did not feel that I was so different. You seemed to enjoy fun and I did not think you cared very much for grave, solemn things. But when you came back and were in some way changed, I was quite surprised. I understood the difference after you honored me by telling me of your strange experience. You were good before, I think, only I had not seen that side of your nature brought out yet. You took me for better than I was because, when we first met, I had my sister's Bible and a religious book which Mr. De Vere had sent her, lying beside me on the sand. I saw you thought more highly of me because they were there, and it pleases me always to please those with whom I am thrown. You asked me to read, and I like to read. I am afraid I am proud of my reading too, and it was mere selfish pride that made me read that book well, for I had scoffed at it a few minutes before, having taken it for a novel at first and thinking I would enjoy reading it. I let you think that I had been reading and enjoying it before you came. Then you told me all those wonderful things about yourself, and I felt ashamed to think I had let you do so, for I knew I was not worthy of so grave a confidence. Well, there isn't any more to say only that I have let you go on from day to day supposing that I was interested in religious things more than in anything else, just because I was lonely and it was pleasant to have an intellectual person to talk with who could make anything, even religion, interesting. I have been ashamed of it every day, but I did not know how to get out of it, and there seemed to be a sort of a spell upon me when I was with you which prevented my showing you my real character. I have tried once or twice to see how it would seem to really act out what you thought I was, but I don't succeed. I'm nothing but a frivolous creature who loves a good time and her own way. I feel very much relieved that at last I have mustered up courage to tell you the truth; but I would like to thank you for the very pleasant hours we have had together before we part, for I feel sure that they *have* helped me, and you have been very good to spend so much time in making it pleasant for me." All this in a torrent of words as though it had been one long sentence.

She started to rise, as if she were ready now to bid him farewell and go, but he detained her.

"Please sit still," he said quietly. "I want to ask you just a few things. In the first place, you surely do not suppose that because of what you have said that you and I are going to be any the less friends than before? Friendship cannot be cut in two by a few words and a farewell. You have come into my life, and have helped me, in spite of all you say, and if you have felt as you say you have there is all the more reason that I should try to help you if I can. Will you tell me one thing, Miss Hammond? Do you mean by all this that you do not love the Master?"

It is very strange how hard a simple little question is to answer sometimes. Maria had heard and read that question so many times, and in her childhood had answered it glibly and carelessly, taking it as a matter of course that she did. Now her eyelids and voice trembled and she hesitated long before the earnest question. At last she said:

"I'm afraid I don't," in a very low voice, almost inaudible above the sound of the waves.

"And do you mean you do not *want* to love him?" went on the quiet voice.

This time the hesitation was longer than before. Maria was questioning her own heart carefully, and shuddering at the thought of answering it in the affirmative. Very slowly came the words, by and by:

"No, I do not mean that."

"Thank God for that!" said the listener under his breath, and Maria looked up to see a light in the minister's face which awed her into silence and made her drop her eyes again and wait for him to speak.

One step further the minister dared to go as he breathed a prayer for guidance, so much concerned was he about this young friend, who suddenly seemed in his sight one very precious to his Master.

"Wouldn't you *like* to belong to him, to rest in him, just as we have talked about so many times? I cannot think that all we have said together has been utterly without interest to you. Do you not care in the very slightest to be his dear child?"

And Maria answered in an unsteady voice and humbly, "Yes, I _care_. I believe I care about that more than anything else on earth. I didn't know quite what it was before, but that is what I want. But, oh, I cannot get it. It doesn't belong to me," and the cry of her soul reached out to her Father in heaven, as she seemed to be groping in the darkness for his hand.

Chapter 16

The sunset flashed and faded unnoticed. The twilight crept softly over the ocean and stole up the sands; the young moon looked out and began to climb the sky; and still they sat and talked.

What they said is recorded above, and it meant much for both lives. The minister was going through his first real experience of leading an immortal soul to Christ, and the girl was face to face with the Master. Out of the gathering shadows on the waters it seemed to her that he came, as of old, and spoke peace to her troubled heart. Many days after, she found a poem among others in a book sent to her sister, which seemed so to fit into her memory of that evening and her experiences that she copied it on the margin of her Bible. These were the words:

> Out in the night on the wide, wild sea,
> When the wind was beating drearily
> And the waters were moaning wearily,
> I met with him who had died for me.

And there was a sense in which for a little space the existence of each to the other was blotted out as these two held converse concerning the things of the kingdom. The man felt that he was conveying a message of vital import from his Master, the first of the sort ever entrusted to him, perhaps, or at least the first whose importance had ever so impressed him. He must not think of himself, he must choose only the words, the Spirit spoke, he must not let his faith waver, he must pray as he breathed every instant, for he felt that Satan might set in at any moment and thwart the work. It was wonderful beyond any experience of his, this overpowering anxiety, this trembling joy, as she seemed to yield hers to her Saviour's will.

To the young woman who sat thus reviewing her life and her motives, the man beside her but carried a heavenly message. She forgot that he and she stood in mutual relations in the world which made it natural that she should desire to appear well in his eyes, and that she should admire his earnest, well-spoken words and be pleased that he cared to spend his effort upon her. Her heart-hunger for something better in her life than had ever been there before had at last spoken and she was recognizing its eternal right to be heard. She heard Jesus pleading through those words spoken without any excitement, and yet with such tremendous earnestness.

And yet each knew that there was a sense in which Maria was already a Christian, that is, before the world. She had taken Christ's vows upon her. She had been brought up to keep the commandments outwardly at least. She had even not been inactive in Christian work, to the extent of being zealous at certain times, when the work was particularly pleasant to her. And yet she sat and waited and hesitated, and knew that if she once gave over her will the decision would mean that her whole life hereafter must be changed.

They sat so long upon the sand that their figures, etched against the fading sky, became blurred by the mist of the evening, and when the great decision was finally made and the minister sealed it with a prayer whose few low-spoken words were from the deep new joy of his heart that God had blessed his message, the quiet night shut out their bowed heads from view.

Supper in the hotel was long over when they walked back along the sand and passed the gay piazza, filled with the merry talk of guests who watched the new moon travel its silver pathway over the waves, and laughed and made commonplace remarks, as though it were a common night and a common sight.

Supper in the green cottage was long over also, although it had been delayed for Maria's coming for some time. Rachel had gone over to the Parkers' with her brother, the father and mother had taken a stroll to the bay, and could be seen in the distance slowly walking up and down the little platform by the water, the sky, lit by the last memory of the dead sunset, making a clear background for their dark figures. The Higgins girl was seated on the front steps impatiently waiting to tell Maria, when she should come, that the hot biscuits were in the oven covered with a tin plate and the butter was in the top of the refrigerator, and the rest of the things were on the table for her supper, before going home to join in the merry evening attendant upon the arrival of several brothers-in-law and other relatives. Boisterous laughter issued across the marsh from the little house. Her errand accomplished, the Higgins girl hastened away. She felt embarrassed before the minister and Maria after what had happened in the afternoon.

Maria was relieved to find the house empty. She wanted to understand herself before she met any of the others. She paused at the top step to say good-night, and then bethought herself that the minister had missed his supper. She asked him to come in and have something to eat, and to her surprise instead of declining he hesitated and said: "May I?"

Maria scarcely knew whether she was glad or sorry he had accepted her invitation. It was rather an embarrassing position, this eating supper together, after foraging in the refrigerator and the oven, exposing the crudeness of their dwelling to this young man evidently used to luxury, and yet it was pleasant too. He entered into it like a boy and held the lamp for her while she got the butter, and stirred the fire to make the kettle boil for a cup of tea which he declared he should enjoy if she did not mind making it. It covered her shyness too, for after their long, serious talk, and the solemn words she had spoken, it had seemed to her she would scarcely dare to attempt common every-day living again at once lest she should do something to mar the wonder of the great peace which filled her soul. She did not take her change of heart as Rachel would have done, with a bubble of joy that entered into everything that touched her life. It was too new, and her nature did not so quickly accept and appropriate new situations. She felt that her experience was too sacred even to think about yet awhile. Indeed, it could hardly be called an experience. She felt no joy though she did feel at peace; she did not think that life was now to be all rose-colored. She was not perfectly sure but to-morrow she might fall from her high resolves. The only difference in her feelings from two hours ago was this deep peace, a peace which comes of decision, and a fixed purpose to surrender her will and to trust. Henceforth her life was to be different. Not because she could make it so, but because she had chosen another motive for its center. Now she only knew that her life was to be ordered for different ends, and whatever of joy or sorrow came, they were alike to be brought to Christ, the end to be his glory.

It was a novel experience to Maria, this free and easy getting supper together with the minister. Heretofore her intimate friends had not been of the sort who were admitted to the kitchen, and indeed the kitchen in their home had always until lately been under the rule of a regiment of good servants. There was a homelikeness, a comradeship, in their sitting down together. Maria felt embarrassed at first at the idea of it, fearing lest Rachel should come in, or her brother, and find what was going on and be surprised at her, for she had always looked down upon such proceedings as plebeian in the extreme and not to be encouraged — more like what the Parkers might be expected to do. And yet here she was actually enjoying it. She wondered why it was, and then forgot to wonder. Mr. Fairfield seemed boyishly happy, and Maria could but catch the infection of his spirits and be happy too. Each realized that there was deep feeling in the heart of the other, and the minister fully intended to go away at once as soon as they should have put away the remains of their impromptu repast, thinking that Maria needed the rest and quiet and a time alone with God after the long strain of the struggle of decision. They were just going to the piazza, the minister to say good-night and leave Maria with her own thoughts, when they heard steps and merry voices. Maria hastily set the lamp, now turned low, on the little shelf back in the kitchen, where its light would but dimly reach the front door, and so tell no tales of the tête-à-tête supper, and quietly, with all possible speed, followed her guest to the piazza. She did not wish her brother and sister to find room for teasing in anything that went on to-night, for it seemed to her she could not bear it. It was Rachel and Winthrop, with the Parkers and some others, come to sit on the veranda and sing.

In the little change that took place while the quartet grouped themselves on the steps and Rachel brought the lamp for them to see the penciled words of a recently written song, Mr. Fairfield drew nearer to Maria and said in a low tone; "You are tired."

He did not put it with the rising inflection of a question that demanded an answer, nor was there time for an answer before the singing began, but Maria felt that he was reading her thoughts and feelings with a fine sympathy, anxious to aid her. She smiled gratefully. Then the singing began. All at once Maria realized that these were the people to whom she had most clearly showed her dislike and disdain. With a sudden resolve, which seemed to her to be in response to a hidden, bidding voice, she determined to take the first step in a new direction at once. Throwing aside the distant manner which she had worn ever since coming to the shore, except then in the company of the minister or the De Veres, she forthwith joined in the talk and laughter, when the song was ended.

The Parkers were delighted with her bright words and ready assent to any plans they might propose. She was indeed a charming girl, and why had they been so deceived in her at first? Rachel and Winthrop sat silent through sheer amazement, and the minister wondered and divined the reason. It was strange how well he was beginning to understand this young girl who had been to him a stranger a few short weeks before. He sat looking at her in the dim lights and shadow thrown by the flickering lamp, as she talked, and he saw a gentle, softened look which was not wholly stirred by the pleasant things she was saying. He remembered now her face at different times as she had been pondering his questions down by the shore that evening, and the grave sweetness in her eyes, when she at last decided. To him she seemed all sweetness. He had not yet realized that she had indeed been hateful, as she told him. Isn't it blessed, sometimes, that there are people who cannot and who will not see our faults, even though we tell them they are there?

Maria was glad when they all rose to leave; not that she was not enjoying the talk. It was pleasant, and she was surprised to find herself interested in those Parkers; but she longed for the quiet of her own room.

Mr. Fairfield had been watching her during the last few minutes and now, as they rose to go, he took her hand for good-night and said in an undertone: "Are you any happier, Miss Hammond, than you were this afternoon?"

"I think so," she answered softly. "And oh, I want to thank you. I never should have found the right way if it had not been for you."

The young man bowed his head humbly. Said he:

"I think that is the most welcome thanks I ever received, for I never before to my knowledge was the means of leading any one to Christ. That seems a terrible admission for me, a minister of the gospel, to make, and perhaps, oh, I hope, it may not be true! But I never knew it at least and I have not been the sort of minister I should have been, you remember. You have helped me, you know, in spite of all you have said to the contrary, and so I am grateful beyond expression to be allowed to bring a little of the same blessed comfort to you."

Then Maria went in to the quiet moonlit window of her room and sat there in wonder, thinking of all that had passed since she left that room so hastily a few hours before; of the kindness of the minister, his earnest face and tender words, of the quiet lovely night about them, then of the walk home, and the pleasant little supper together. Somehow the fact of their eating alone together had made them better friends. There was something about the thought of that supper which she did not like to put into words yet, a strange, pleasant something, into which she dared not look for explanation. Perhaps sometime she would think it all out and see if there was any foundation for real pleasure in it, but now it was to be allowed to hover on the horizon of her mind, a pleasant memory connected with this wonderful night. Then she thought of the coming of the young people, and their songs. And there had been a new duty for her in their very fun. She must learn to join in it. She realized that perhaps this might be one of the hardest things for her to do, this letting down of her prejudices and being agreeable when her heart was not in what was going on. Would she be able to do it? She trembled at the mountain of difficulties which rose before her untried feet.

Of the great central event of that day, the decision that she had made to make Christ the center of her life, she almost feared to try to think as yet, it seemed so new and sacred. She could not begin to get used to it. She must wait till all the others were asleep before she could let her thoughts dwell much upon that.

Rachel came in soon and softly stealing up behind her, put her arms around her neck and kissed her, and she returned the caress lovingly and rose to prepare for rest. She felt she could not sleep soon, there was so much to think about, and when she knelt to pray, as was her habit, the act and the words meant so much more than they had ever meant before. Then, contrary to her expectations, she fell into a deep dreamless sleep, for her Father knew she was wearied and needed rest, more than to think of high resolves and to plan difficult paths. Now that she was willing to walk as he would have her, he would choose her paths and carry her over the hard places without the resolves which are sometimes merely signposts for Satan to read which way we are intending to go, that he may lie in wait for us there and intercept our progress. If she would but put her hand in Christ's all would be well.

> Trusting the one great Pilot of the deep
> To be for aye my tender, low voiced Guide,
> I look aloft and say—
> Though tossed upon life's ocean wide—
> "All's well! All's well! By day or night, all's well!"

Chapter 17

"She is a great friend of Maria Hammond's," said Fanny De Vere, as she skillfully opened an egg at the breakfast table. "I suppose that is the reason she chooses that place for the remainder of the summer."

"Well, I should imagine she would be just about Maria Hammond's stamp," said Evelyn; "they must have a good many interests in common. Nannette Davenport cares for nothing whatever but her own pretty self. She is the most self-centered person I know of. I suppose it's very unkind in me to say so, but positively, I don't believe her grief over her mother's death is more than skin deep. She never seemed to care for her in the least when she was alive."

"I am sorry she is coming," said Fanny. "Of course we shall not necessarily have much to do with her, but at the same time there will be a certain amount of civility which must be exchanged for decency's sake. It is a great pity she could not have gone somewhere else, but truly I suppose the real reason of her selecting Lone Point this summer is because she is in deep mourning and the society in which she moves would be scandalized if she were to appear anywhere else. Here she can do as she pleases. She is supposed to have retired from the vain world. If she chooses to indulge herself in a little amusement no one is a whit the wiser. I suppose Maria Hammond could not stand it any longer without some of her friends about her. Roland, I wonder why it is that girl is so different from her sister. You never would dream they were of the same family, would you?"

Thus appealed to the young man hesitated a minute before answering.

"I'm not sure," he said. "I've seen several things lately that led me to think she might be other than we at first thought. There must be something about her that's interesting or Fairfield would never waste his time on her. He isn't a lady's man, by any means. In college he would never have anything to do with shallow, insipid girls. There had to be some intellect before he would look at them, much less talk with them, unless he was absolutely compelled to do so."

"Oh, I suppose she is bright enough, as far as that goes," said Evelyn; "but for my part I think she is decidedly disagreeable, and I can imagine that she will be twice as much so when backed up by Nannette Davenport. I can't think how Nannette will endure the simplicity at the Lone Point Hotel. She never washed out her own bathing suit in her life, nor waded through deep sand to get to the beach. As for the rude cottages there, she will probably take the next train back home when she has seen them. Are you sure, Roland, that Miss Hastings said she was going to Lone Point?"

"Perfectly sure," answered the young man. "Miss Hastings had been up there yesterday afternoon to engage her room for her at her aunt's request. The young lady in question is coming unchaperoned, as her aunt considers that in so quiet a spot, so near Miss Davenport's intimate friends, a chaperon is hardly necessary."

Evelyn laughed.

"If she is the same Nannette who went to Boston a year ago, she will need a chaperon more in Lone Point than she does in a crowded city. She is kept somewhat in check there by custom and her position, but Lone Point she will consider good game. If you have the least friendliness in the world for your friend, the intellectual minister, you would better warn him to flee, for in spite of his intellect and his devotion at present to Miss Hammond, he will shortly be in the wiles of Miss Nannette. Why, consider, my dear brother. He is about the only eligible young man in the whole of that lonely Lone Point, unless perhaps Mr. Hammond and Mr. Parker might be counted in. But she counts it nothing to have three or four on hand at once."

"Well, if Fairfield can't take care of himself, I'm sure he deserves to suffer, that's all I have to say," said the young man with a laugh as he arose from the table and took up the morning paper.

It was by the morning mail Maria received a letter from her quondam friend, Miss Nannette Davenport. It was gushingly characteristic of her. She was always gushing when she had a point to gain. Just at present it suited her purpose to spend a few weeks in a quiet place, and Maria would be very useful to her in helping to pass the time. The letter expressed great delight over the thought of a quiet summer in which to hide the deep grief she professed. She said she wanted to get away from the world and had decided to come near to her friend. She had delayed to send Maria word until the day before her arrival that her coming might be a pleasant surprise, but her room was already engaged at the hotel and Maria might meet her at the Lone Point Station at three the next afternoon.

That this was a surprise to Maria need not be doubted; but it was anything but a pleasant surprise. Nannette Davenport had never been a deeply loved friend. She had a certain prestige because of her mother's wealth and standing in society which Maria had thought she could not well afford to ignore. Through Nannette she had gained entrance to several homes in a high social circle where she feared she would not have been able otherwise to go since her father's failure. Indeed it was through Nannette she had met the De Veres. The two girls had been thrown together not a little at the beginning of their friendship, if it could rightly be called a friendship where there was no real love nor even very strong liking, when they were both away at school. Maria knew just how much real friendship Nannette held for her. She knew what a shallow, heartless girl she was. And she did not rejoice at the thought of her coming to Lone Point.

Had the letter come three or four days before it did, she would have worried greatly that Nannette should come and see her in such humble surroundings, but somehow the events of the past few days had made surroundings seem of less importance; so that now, as she read the letter and pondered over it with a distressed little pucker between her eyes, it was not because of the little green cottage nor yet of their straitened circumstances that her first objection was raised. Her first thought was for her new life. How hard it would be to mix thought and feelings so utterly at variance! Her utter distaste for Nannette's pleasures was a sort of a revelation even to herself as she read. She had not known how much her own likings and longings were wrapt up in her desire to carry out her new aim in life.

She sat down and began to ponder what she should do. It would not do to be rude to Nannette. Christ would not wish that. Was her trouble that she was afraid to stand out against her and say decidedly that her motives in life were changed? Or was it that she feared her own self and dreaded lest she might lose this wonderful calm that had come into her life three nights ago? Did she think that it might be she would be tempted back to old ways, old thoughts, old bondages? There came to her suddenly with this thought a remembrance of a verse she had read that morning from Rachel's Bible. Rachel's Bible was always lying open somewhere about, and Rachel's Bible always had marked verses to catch her eye when she was in a hurry. She used to say she kept her Bible near at hand that she might snatch a thought now and then as she was going by, as it helped to keep her from temptation. Maria had not yet gained the courage to bring forth her Bible openly as Rachel did. She wanted to read it by herself first and get used to the thought of her new way of living, and so she had chosen a verse from her sister's Bible as she dressed. It was:

"God is faithful, who will not suffer you to be tempted above that ye are able; but will with the temptation also make a way to escape that ye may be able to bear it."

How strange that that verse should have come in her way that morning! How wonderful to think God was actually answering her thoughts in his own words! Surely, this girl's arrival was nothing she was responsible for, and therefore she was not to blame. He had allowed the temptation; could not she trust him to make a way of escape for her? She arose and fastened the door, and then knelt down to ask for faith. She knew it would seem very strange to Rachel to come in in the daytime and find her praying. She was still in bondage. Her fetters had been forged tight, and it was hard for her to drop them even now that they were broken.

She did not feel that she knew how to pray very well, but she knew that God would understand; and as she rose she began to wonder if perchance he would in some way turn the decision of Miss Davenport and send her somewhere else even at the last minute. Or had he other ways of working? Of course he might mean that this was a discipline through which she was to pass before she was fit to be his child. If so she would try to do what was right, but it seemed much harder even than to take in the Parkers. They had grown quite tolerable, even to pleasantness, and it was only three days since she had decided to become acquainted with them. With the remembrance of the Parkers came the question, "What would Nannette think of the Parkers? Would she make it very unpleasant?" Maria knew that Nannette possessed, among other uncomfortable qualities, that of sneering at people and things, and making one feel that one would rather do anything than confess to a friendship for the person or a liking for the thing which she had scorned. What was she to do with Nannette?

It must not be supposed that Maria had grown good all in a night. By no means. To all outward appearance she was the same Maria grown a little sweeter tempered, a little more willing to give up her wishes for those of others, and in one respect rather surprising, in that she freely mingled with the young people and notably with the Parkers, making them feel perfectly at their ease and happy in her company. She had lost her temper once or twice. She had forgotten to refrain from a scornful remark about the pump on one occasion, which, while she felt no peculiar animus at the time, had still grown to be such a habit with her that she scolded without realizing it. She had noticed the weary look about her mother's eyes at the time the words were spoken and she instantly knew the mother was sighing over her. There had come an impulse then to throw her arms around her mother and tell her how different she meant things should be, but something within restrained her and the next instant her mother had passed out to talk with the grocer's boy and her opportunity was gone. She reasoned also that it would be better for her first to show some "works meet for repentance" before announcing to the others what she was going to do. Moreover, she felt that her recent experience, if it could rightly be called an experience, was too sacred yet to be talked about, and that it was no question of witnessing for Christ in this case, as they already knew she was his professed follower. It would be much wiser for her to let them see that she was different. She forgot that to the mother and sister there would have been great relief in the fact that she was willing to try to be different: that they would have overlooked many things in her and helped her in numberless ways, if she had once taken them into her confidence. If people only understood each other in this world there would be much less of friction, less sighing, and less worry about one another. And so the mother was praying daily for her daughter, and wondering why it was her prayers were of no avail – whether because she was unworthy to be answered, or because of her lack of faith; while all the time the dear Lord had prepared a loving answer and put it down beside her and she was too taken up with worry to notice it. It would be well, in our praying, to sometimes lift the head and see whether the answer to our prayers is not shining in the heavens or standing joy-clothed beside us, or even lying at our feet waiting to be recognized.

Maria pondered deeply over what to tell her new friend the minister about her old friend Nannette, and finally decided to let him judge for himself. However, she had no opportunity to tell him anything, as it turned out, for Mr. Fairfield was all that day and the next away attending to some business on the mainland, and only arrived at Lone Point on the very train which carried Nannette in her black robes.

The three days which lay between Maria and her decision had been bright ones to her. Her friendship with the minister was growing to be an exceedingly pleasant thing to think about, not that the intimacy had as yet grown into its larger possibilities as personal; but there was growing in each of their hearts something warmer than a mere interest for the other, and occasionally little glimpses of alluring perhaps would flit across the mental horizon of each. It is just possible that underneath Maria's distaste for the arrival of Miss Davenport there was an undertone of uneasiness lest the pleasant friendship between herself and the minister might be broken in upon, but if this was so she did not even confess it to herself. She was never a girl who was quick to think a man wished to pay her special attention, nor to seem to appropriate one to herself. She rather erred in the other direction; and he on his part, while he admired her for this, was, in a certain sense, kept at a distance by her, even though they talked more intimately than most young people are apt to do about that most sacred emotion of life, one's personal love for his Saviour.

Chapter 18

Maria waited on the little platform the next afternoon for the incoming train. Her emotions were not pleasant. She seemed to see Nannette's curling lips as she first took in the situation and observed the rude cottage life. She seemed to hear her sarcastic comments, and strange to say they were, in her mind, much what her own had been on arriving here. Suddenly there flashed over her the thought that she had changed, in this respect at least, for she seemed to have in her heart some real love for the place, some desire to protect it from what scornful strangers might say. Why was it? Was it because she had found Christ here? Or was it, perhaps, on account of her new friendship with the strong true man who was becoming her friend? She looked up at the blue sky and smiled in answer to its heavenly look. She gazed over the yellow-green waves of the marsh grass, so bare to her once, and lo! they had taken on beauty, and she felt a sense of gladness in their smooth stretches of level green, and discovered that in a night they seemed to have burst into a million stars of meadow pinks dotted all over among the grass as far as eye could reach. She stooped and gathered a handful of them and placed them in her belt, adding a very pretty touch to her toilet. Nannette's influence had already begun to be felt in her careful arrange-ment of that afternoon's toilet. She had worried more about her dress and taken more time for it that day than she had done altogether since she had come to the island. Even now she looked down at herself doubtfully. She hardly cared to come in for sarcasm herself just at the outset. She had chosen, after much indecision of mind and careful scrutiny of her wardrobe, to wear for that day a white duck costume. It was plain, of course, and in a sense inexpensive. Its great beauty in her eyes was its exquisite cut and fit. She had committed her greatest extravagance of the summer by taking that duck dress to a notable tailor to be cut, and in her eyes and in the eyes of Nannette as well, she knew that fact would cover a multitude of sins in other directions. She half intended Nannette should soon discover that Melton had cut her dress. Nannette would then be sure to admire it. And yet, do her the credit to observe that she was annoyed over finding herself so deeply concerned about her dress, and descending so low as to actually think how she could tell where it had been cut. She sighed and wondered if this were a sign that Nannette was going to win her forever back to worldly things. Then before she went out she knelt and prayed. She had seen Rachel kneel often before going out, when she thought she was by herself, and she felt that now perhaps such a habit might be a good thing for her. Certainly she needed much help.

She did look fresh and pretty and thoroughly in keeping with her surroundings, all in white with black velvet belt and collar and band about her sailor hat. Even the most exacting taste could have found no fault with her. The fresh ocean breeze had blown loose a few soft strands of a waving lock about her forehead and flushed her cheeks, and the touch of pink blossoms in her belt made her look exquisitely pure and sweet. At least so thought Mr. Fairfield as he alighted, hot and dusty from his ride in the train, and his face lighted with a sudden joy that was pleasant to see. In spite of herself, the color would come into Maria's cheeks as she bowed to him. She was a trifle embarrassed too, for just a moment, since it must look to him, until Nannette appeared, as though she had come to the train to meet him.

But now the porter handed Nannette, with her bag, and her dress-suit case, and her bundle of golf sticks, and her tennis racquet, and several other accessories of the fashionable girl at a summer resort, down upon the platform, and the train moved on toward Spray View, and Maria found her hands full.

Nannette's greeting was effusive, a mingling, of kisses and adjectives, and a few stylish tears which necessitated the pushing up of the very becoming black veil in which her head was swathed in spite of the heat. This over, Miss Davenport turned her dark eyes upon the minister who stood by Maria as if he belonged there, and an introduction of necessity followed.

Maria felt annoyed beyond measure that she had not ere this told the minister of Nannette's expected arrival. Just why she should feel so much annoyance she did not then look into her heart to see. As a matter of course the minister rode with them in the surrey which had been sent down from the hotel to convey the new guest from the station, and though Maria also went with them and sat in the back seat with her friend, Nannette monopolized the conversation entirely and addressed it all to Mr. Fairfield. She spoke gushingly of her friendship with Maria, dating its origin much farther back than Maria had supposed it could be, showing reasons why Maria was her warmest friend, and therefore had been the one to whom she turned in her deep trouble. Here she punctuated her remarks with a few tears wiped carefully away with a correct handkerchief, deeply bordered with black.

She was a dashingly handsome girl; tall, slender, with black eyes and reddish brown hair. She wore her hair loose over her ears and coiled low at the nape of the neck which gave her an innocent, childlike appearance. She was an excellent actress when she chose to be. Mr. Fairfield was non-plussed and disappointed. He felt instinctively that this girl would have little sympathy for the quiet walks and talks in which he and Maria had been indulging of late. He feared that her presence at the shore would be anything but a good influence for the girl in whom he was becoming so deeply interested.

Maria, on her part, was greatly distressed. What would Mr. Fairfield think of her friends? What would he think of her past life? She must hasten to explain, at the first opportunity, how little of real friendship there ever had existed between them; and yet how could she, without deliberately making the other girl out a liar? It was all very unpleasant. She was glad when the surrey drew up to the hotel and they could get out. She was more glad than she dared say, even to herself, that no conversation concerning the place, and the various cottages they had passed during the short ride, had come up, for at least she was spared having the truth dawn upon Nannette while the minister was with them. She went upstairs with Nannette at her request, though she would have preferred going straight home to have a good cry, or wandering off on the sand and telling Mr. Fairfield all about it. She felt a childish desire to tell him her troubles and ask him what she should do, but she shut her lips tightly and walked up the stairs like a soldier, so that he thought she was only too happy to have one of her own sort with her again and he would have no more opportunities to see her.

Nannette's several trunks were at last deposited and unstrapped and she was at leisure to take off her hat and talk with her friend. She laid her hat on the bed and settled herself in a rocker by the window: "Now, 'Ri, tell me all about this hole," she said familiarly. "Is there anything going on to keep one alive? Isn't it dreadfully dull? But you see Aunt Mortimer is old-fashioned and terribly rigid, and she wouldn't at all consent to my appearing at any interesting place. She wanted me to stay at home with her all summer! Just fancy! She said I ought not to want to go anywhere when my mother was dead, but dear me!" — with a shrug of her shoulders — "what good would it do mother for me to mope? I told aunt I should die of grief among those associations of mother, and that seemed to touch the right spot, and she consented to my going away. She would have come with me if she could, but Cousin George is worse this summer and not able to be moved and she couldn't leave him. I think she would have liked me to stay and devote myself to him, read to him and make messes for him; but Cousin George is altogether too devoted to the memory of his dead wife to make it interesting to waste one's time on him. Besides I hate sick people and he isn't likely to get well, anyway. So I'm here. First of all, who is that very handsome Mr. Fairfield? A minister? Dear me! Is he very good? Because that would be dreadfully tiresome."

"I'm sure I don't know," said Maria; "you'll have to find that out for yourself." Her voice showed her disgust plainly, but Nannette was too much interested to notice. She went rattling on.

"Say, 'Ri, is he very devoted? I thought he looked at you as if he was. Are you engaged?"

"No, *indeed,*" answered Maria freezingly. It flashed over her then that there was something about Nannette's face that reminded her of Annie Higgins and she thought if the two were compared there would be a balance in favor of the Higgins girl.

"Not engaged? Then I give you fair warning, 'Ri dear, I shall do my best to have a good time. You don't mind, do you, dear?"

"Certainly not," said Maria again, in a voice which the minister never would have recognized.

Nannette seemed to feel that it would be just as well to change the subject. She leaned out of the open window nearest her, looking toward the cottages.

"And now do tell me where the town is, what there is of it. Of course I know it's small, but I've seen nothing but cow-sheds so far. What in the world do they need so many of them for? Or are they bath-houses? No, they are too far from the ocean."

The Maria of a few weeks ago would have blushed crimson and hesitated, tried to apologize and explain, or even have invented some way out of the truth, perhaps; but the Maria of today was too deeply stung and disgusted. She was shown herself and just how low she had fallen in being ready to bow down to a girl whose thoughts and feeling were as low as this one's. It was so great a contrast with the high and holy thoughts in which she had been dwelling with the minister lately that she was in great danger of going to the other extreme and despising this girl for motives really lower than belonged to her. For Nannette Davenport was only selfish, that was all. But that is perhaps enough.

Maria arose and with grave dignity walked to the window and pointed out.

"Those are cottages," she said, trying to control her voice steadily. "That white one nearest to you is where our friends the Parkers live. The green one trimmed with white next to it is ours. The others belong to very nice people. You will meet them all soon. There is no reason why one should not have a pleasant time here if one chooses."

Maria remembered her own actions of two weeks ago, and was amazed at herself. Nannette looked curiously at her, and then without further remark turned toward her trunks, saying with a sigh:

"You don't say so! Well, I suppose I've no choice but to make the best of it this year, with these horrid black things on, but I shall make up for it next year, you may be sure. And I warn you I'm going to be just as wicked as I please, so look out for your own interests. By the way, 'Ri, haven't you a brother? Is he nice looking? How old is he? One must have friends, you know, in such a desert as this. They say Roland De Vere is over at Spray View. He and I had a terrible quarrel a year ago, but I may be able to patch that up. He is so old-granny particular! Now what shall I put on for dinner, and what hour do they have that meal in this out-of-the-way place?"

"They have dinner at one o'clock. It is over four hours ago. Supper is at six," answered Maria severely. She somehow took a fierce pleasure in shocking this girl. She felt glad that this feeling possessed her instead of the fear which she had been afraid would tempt her to do things out of accord with her new views. She felt so little trust in her own self, poor child, and her trust was so recently given to her Saviour, that she did not realize that he would hold her and she would not need to worry lest she should not hold to him. She was anxious to get away now, and the many elaborate dresses which Nannette began to take out and spread upon bed and chairs for her admiration, wearied her. She felt as if she had always given an undue amount of time and thought to clothes. No doubt these things were pretty, yes, they certainly were. She could not help letting her eye dwell in pleased delight upon an elaborate waist of black taffeta. Nannette certainly had good taste, there was no denying that, and plenty of money with which to exercise it. It was hard, of course, this gay season when everybody was flaunting bright colors, to get up a beautiful and varied outfit with only black and white, with strict severity and much crêpe a necessity, but Nannette had succeeded, and Maria, in spite of dislikes and resolves, began to grow interested in the pretty clothes. Nannette insisted upon her remaining until she had arrayed herself in a severely plain white gown with black ribbons, and Maria was obliged to say, at the demand of the new-comer, that she was bewitchingly pretty even in the trying dead black and white.

"Now, you may go, dear, for I suppose you are awfully tired of me. But please tell me first," — holding Maria off at arm's length, — "do you think I shall captivate him? I mean that young minister, of course. I must have something to amuse me, and I should hate to fail at the very beginning."

"I'm sure I don't know," answered Maria in her most sober tone. She drew back, stung deeper than she realized.

"Ha, ha!" laughed Nannette, "he must be good and have infected you. Never mind. I shan't hurt him much, you know, and I'll let him go in the end. Don't blame me much, dear. It's all I have to live for now, you know." And she put her mourning handkerchief to her laughing eyes in the smart little pat which she affected.

Maria coldly promised to come back that evening and walked away. She could stand no more. All she had to live for! Flirting! How boldly she had confessed it.

Was it possible she had ever admired a girl like that? She bowed her head and was ashamed.

The minister, standing at the window of his room in the hotel, saw her, watched her down the street, wondered and sighed and turned away thoughtfully.

Chapter 19

When Maria reached the cottage her mother looked at her searchingly, expecting to find her face wreathed in smiles on account of the arrival of Nannette. Instead she saw a gray, weary look about her eyes, and felt the anxious tugging at her mother-heart again which had been there so often the last few weeks. Was Maria plunged again in gloom because of the talk and dress of her gay friend? Was she contrasting her own life with that of Miss Davenport?

When at supper her brother Winthrop asked some laughing question about Nannette, Maria looked up at him anxiously and answered him more shortly than she had spoken to him for at least three days. The family could not understand it. They had expected her to be pleased at the accession of a friend in this lonely place. She ate very little supper, and when Winthrop proposed going with her to the hotel to call upon the young lady, she promptly declined his escort, saying Nannette must be tired and would not want to see any one that evening. Her conscience gave her a sharp twinge as she said that, but she looked after her brother with a sigh as he whistled and left the table. Then she went quickly out to the piazza and stood alone in the purple and pink twilight with tears blurring her vision. There had suddenly stirred in her heart a new feeling of love for her brother. She saw a possible danger to him lurking in the future and she felt herself inadequate to ward it off. Oh, if she had but always been such a sister to him that a word from her would have been as a shield to him. But now she felt that if she should point out to him her fear he would walk straight up to it laughing, more perhaps to tease her than anything else. Things were becoming complicated. There was her brother, and there was the minister, and there was Nannette, and there was she, and where was the Lord? She thought it reverently. She stood looking up into the clear opal tints above and wished she might see him, if only for one little second of time, that her poor weak faith might have something to bind itself to forever. She felt a great longing for Christ to come and touch her. She wanted him more than anything else just then.

Her mother came softly out behind her and putting her arms about her daughter drew her head down to her shoulder.

"What is it, little 'Ri, tell mother," she said tenderly, just as she used to speak when Maria was but a baby and came in with bumped head or bruised knee from a fall.

Then Maria hid her face in her mother's neck and cried, and tried to tell her all her troubles, and of how she wanted to live a changed life.

The mother's heart grew glad and light suddenly. It seemed too good to be true. She drew her down to a chair beside her on the porch, stroking her hair, talking low and tenderly with her as they had not talked together for many a long day. Yet even as the mother talked and comforted and was glad, there came and stood beside her the shadow of a possibility of happenings for the future which held in them both sorrow and joy, and she put away what she heard to think of by and by. She was not a mother who often talked with her children about personal religion, therefore it would have been hard for Maria to tell her mother of her changed feelings on the subject if it had not been for this sudden letting down the bars of her nature and her mother's opportune coming. It was hard too for the mother to talk on religious subjects and therefore her words of comfort were not many, but to Maria who well knew her mother's nature, they meant much, and carried true solace with them. When she said, "Maria, I am glad," Maria knew that she meant more than if she had used a whole dictionary full of adjectives, and when she advised her daughter to "give over worrying and take her trouble to her Heavenly Father," then Maria felt that her mother spoke whereof she knew.

One load the mother carried on her heart when her daughter finally kissed her and went to the hotel, which she had not had before. Maria had dropped a hint as to possible danger for Winthrop in the coming of Miss Davenport, and the mother-heart grew anxious at once as soon as she had time to think, and she had need to take to herself the advice she had given her daughter.

Winthrop, her only boy, was very dear to her, and she knew him to be fond of bright company and very susceptible to its influence.

When Maria reached the hotel, she began to frame an excuse for being so late, but on ascending the steps of the long wide piazza which ran all around the building she saw in the distant corner, standing out against the background of moonlit ocean, the figures of Miss Davenport and Mr. Fairfield. The sudden chill which crept over her made her pause and draw about her shoulders the light shawl she had carried on her arm. She half turned to go away again, thinking Nannette was in no need of her presence and she would come again in the morning, but Nannette had seen her, and waved her handkerchief and called, so there was nothing for it but to go over and sit down in another large rocking-chair beside them.

"You dear naughty thing, you deserted me!" said Nannette in her most gushing voice. "Why in the world were you so long coming? If it had not been for Mr. Fairfield I should have been so lonely that I should have wished to take the morning train back to the city. But he had been so exceedingly kind that I actually forgot this place was called Lone Point."

It had been no part of Mr. Fairfield's intention to have any more to do with Miss Davenport than was absolutely necessary. The feeling of dislike he had experienced for her at first sight only deepened as they rode along to the hotel. But a gentleman cannot be actually rude to a lady, especially if that lady is a professed friend of one who has his deep friendship and respect. Therefore, when, by some skillful maneuver, the old lady who usually occupied the place at the right of Mr. Fairfield in the dining room, was placed across the room, and Miss Davenport was found seated beside him, he was obliged, in ordinary courtesy, to talk with her. It could not be said that he exerted himself to any great degree to make the conversation pleasant for her. Indeed, this was not necessary. Nannette was vivacity itself. She was an adept in small talk and almost made the studious young man feel ill at ease. His replies grew short. But the young woman perceiving her mistake at once subsided, grew meek and inquiring, and presently discovering that books were a delight amounting almost to a passion with the gentleman, molded her conversation accordingly. Before the meal was over she had professed an overpowering desire to read and have explained to her a certain book about which there was a great deal of talk in the literary world. To Mr. Fairfield's exceeding disgust he found that he had not only promised to lend her the book, but to give her at no late date an exhaustive explanation of the discussion in current magazines over certain passages in the book. How they had come to get quite so far as this he was not able to explain, but he awoke to the fact as Nannette was thanking him most sweetly for being so kind as to be willing to help her.

As they rose from the table she said innocently enough, "What in the world do you do here in the evenings? Won't you show me where to go? I don't know a soul but you, you know." She flashed her fine eyes up at him confidingly and he felt in duty bound to take her to the piazza. He went there rather than to the parlor, in a vain hope that Maria might soon come and redeem the situation. But time passed, the sunlight faded from the sky, the moonlight came over the water, and still the young woman by his side gave him no opportunity to leave, without absolute rudeness on his part. He was growing more and more uneasy, when Maria at last arrived, and if she had not been so engrossed with her own feelings at the sight of him and Nannette sitting together in such evident good fellowship, she must surely have noted the joy that broke over his face at sight of her, and the warm welcome he gave her. Be assured Miss Davenport saw it, and ground her pretty white teeth, that in spite of all the charms she had exerted she had not once been able to bring to his face that true pleasure which was there now. She resolved that before many days should have passed this should be different, and thenceforth Lone Point was no longer a desert island to her, for there was a man there who must be conquered, and added to the long line of conquered admirers in the past.

Maria, however, in spite of her mother's comforting words, was ill at ease again the moment she came into Nannette's atmosphere. If she roused herself to reply to Nannette it at once threw her back into a past which she did not like to feel had ever been hers, and with which she did not wish Mr. Fairfield to know she was familiar. If she should speak to Mr. Fairfield, what should it be about? Not Mr. Meyer's book! Not the Bible verse about which they had been talking so freely but yesterday, for what would Nannette think, and how could she drag sacred things into a conversation so filled with the froth of that young woman's remarks?

Mr. Fairfield finally settled back to wait till Maria should go home, thinking he would walk with her and they could have a little quiet word together after all, and he found his mind wandering out of the talk so that he was often silent. He was thinking what he should say to Maria.

Did Nannette read what was passing in his thoughts? Certainly she acted as though she did. When Maria rose to say good-night, she followed her to the steps and then, as if the thought had just occurred to her, she put her hand lovingly on Maria's arm and said: "Why, I guess I'll walk over with you, 'Ri, if Mr. Fairfield doesn't mind bringing me home. I should get lost, you know, if you didn't," she said, turning laughingly to him, and she looked him straight in the eyes in the full moonlight and saw that he was disappointed.

When Maria reached her room that night it was late, for Mr. Fairfield had determined that he would take his revenge upon the new arrival and therefore he proposed a walk. He knew that Maria was used to the sand, and could stand it well, and that to the young woman from the city streets it would be harder work. He hoped perhaps to tire her out and take her back to the hotel before Maria had been taken home, and still have his quiet half-hour with her.

He had reckoned without his host, however, Nannette possibly perceived his intention, or it may be that she was stronger than he had judged possible. She bravely waded through the sand wherever he led the way, exclaiming in delight over scenes which only half pierced to her mental retina at all, and still saying she was not tired. On he took them, this way and that, now nearer the by now nearer the ocean. Not to the walks which he and Maria had taken together; they were full of pleasant thoughts and should not be marred by the memory of this walk. He grew quite gay in his effort to gain his point, and Maria wondered at him and grew more silent herself. And now he perceived that she was growing very weary, for there was a white droop about her mouth he had not seen there before, and for her sake he proposed that they go straight home.

There was triumph in Miss Davenport's eyes as she faced herself in the mirror of her room at a late hour, and her lips had a firm set. It had been a hard race, for she was very tired, but she had not given up, and she had gained her point. She would win him yet even if she had to be "good," as she phrased it, to get him.

Maria in her room, with only the moon to light her to her couch, threw herself on her knees beside her sleeping sister she was tired out, soul and body. She was too weary to pray and too weary to cry. She felt as if it would be so good of the dear Christ could just come to her gently, as her mother had done, and tell her what all this meant and why she was so very unhappy. She did not want to try to think and reason it all out. She supposed there was an ugly feeling of jealousy in her heart. It must be that her trouble was because she wanted that young minister to admire her and be with her all the time. It was all very humiliating. She had not known before that she was so selfish. He had helped her to a better life, why did she not want Nannette to have the same opportunity? Was it possible that she had made that great decision just because she admired the man who asked her to do it? Had she fallen so low that her motive was only self-pleasure, after all, and that she did not give up to Christ but to a man whom she admired? Did she not love Christ? With this question came a surge of feeling. Yes, she did love Christ. She felt now as if her all depended upon him. She would give up everything for him. She only wanted his rest, his peace. He had promised it, she had accepted it. It was hers. No one could any more take it from her. Nannette could not touch it. The minister might turn his entire attention to Miss Davenport and forget her. It would be as well if he did, for evidently she was beginning to think too much of him. He might help to bring Nannette to Christ, and then perhaps have a deeper feeling for her, marry her, perhaps. It ought to be nothing to her. She was Christ's. Henceforth she would do as he bade, go where he sent her, live as he would live in her. What a glorious, what a precious thought that was! Would it last till morning? Could she trust it still to be there when she awoke, and could she go to sleep saying, "I am Christ's, I am Christ's. He is mine?"

Strangely, wonderfully, it seemed to her, came an answer from her inmost soul, "I can," and she fell asleep.

If the minister could have know her thoughts as he stood disappointedly beside his window, looking out on the now dark night with only a glimmer of light her and there of a belated cottager, for the moon had set, he might have prayed for her a prayer whose words he knew and loved, instead of wondering gloomily why everything seemed to have gone wrong:

Rest her, dear Master!. . . draw very near
In all thy tenderness and all thy power.
O speak to her. Thou knowest how to speak
A word in season to thy weary ones,
And she is weary now. Thou lovest her —
Let thy disciple lean upon thy breast,
And, leaning, gain new strength to "rise and shine."

Chapter 20

Mr. Fairfield, as he looked out over the sparkling waves the next morning, felt new life and joy come into his soul. What was the use in being downcast when the world was so lovely? He was a child of the living God. He would be given all that was needful for his good and happiness in life. Why should he begin to doubt and grow gloomy because he feared the Lord would take some pleasure from him? Surely it was not worth while to begin to fear anything until he saw it plainly before his eyes? What was it he feared, any way? Was his anxiety wholly unselfish? He recognized clearly that there was a danger menacing Maria's new-found joy in Christ, but could not he and she both trust the One to whose keeping she had committed herself? He remembered the words, "He is able to keep you from falling and to present you faultless," and knew that he was wrong to fear for her.

No, that was not all, though there had been a quick recognition of Maria's danger. What was this other feeling which came and went, a warm, rich, new current in his heart? Miss Hammond had grown to be more than a mere acquaintance; more than one to whom he was trying to bring a message from God, though that relation is a very precious one. There had grown up a personal tie. He told himself that she was the first really intimate friend he had had since his chum in college died, and tried to be satisfied with that way of putting it, but somehow he knew there was something not altogether sincere about that statement either. He decided to go for a quiet stroll along the beach in the early sparkling morning and think it out. There he would be quite alone with God. There was something serious here which ought to be settled at once, he felt sure. Strange he had not thought of it before! Was it possible that this girl, an acquaintance of but a few weeks' standing, was growing indispensable to him? Before he had walked very far, or turned that thought over many times in his mind, he knew that it was so, and that he loved Maria. He sat down on the sand and looked off at the ocean without seeing a single wave of it, to take in the wonder and the beauty of this thought. It fairly overwhelmed him. It was another day and another experience something like the one when first he had realized that he loved his Saviour. He remembered now to have heard Henry Drummond once say that an earthly love was the highest and best example of, and the only thing really approaching at all, the soul's relation with Christ. "Get acquainted with Jesus just as you would with an earthly friend," the great simple man had said, and the young theologue had been rather inclined to call him irreverent then. But now he saw it in all its beauty, the earthly love, so real and warm and dear, a type of the heavenly, just as close and warm and dear and real, only infinitely more in every way than the human heart could comprehend. Was this what God had made earthly love for, that he might the better show us what his love for us must be?

The thoughts rolled past him, rather than were thought by him. He felt, as he sat there in the midst of the lovely morning, as if God spoke to him out of his grandeur and beauty, and was very gracious to him. Most gracious of all because of this wonderful gift of love which he found in his heart for another of his children. He felt that he loved his Heavenly Father more intensely, more intelligently than he had ever done before, because of the sudden blessed realization of another love.

He arose from his hour's meditation feeling that whatever came after, he should always be a better man for that sacred experience, and that he would be able better to preach of the love of God now that he could understand a human love, like the love of a man for a woman; aye, he would be a better man for having harbored this love in his heart, even though he might fail to win her — though, please God, he would *not* fail if he could help it.

As he walked back toward the hotel he suddenly remembered Miss Davenport and her proximity to him at the table. He wished that he had remembered sooner. It must be late. He would like to get his breakfast and get away before she came. He did not care for a tête-à-tête with her just now. He felt that her rattling conversation would be a desecration to his joy-filled mood. How hard it was to have to come down from the heights to every-day living, and every-day disappointments and perplexities! And yet, that was the discipline of life and must be cheerfully borne. He hastened his steps, hoping that she would be late to breakfast, as indeed she was, and he hastened his breakfast, to get out before she came. He did succeed, but little good it did him.

Miss Davenport awoke with a feeling that she had slept later than she intended, for she had business of moment on hand that day and must not let the enemy get any small advantage at the beginning. She found to her dismay that her watch had run down, and she had no means of telling the hour. Glancing from the window, she saw Mr. Fairfield, watch in hand, hurrying toward the hotel, and rightly concluded that breakfast must be ready. With unusual alacrity for a girl of her ordinary lassitude she hurried through a charming toilet prepared with much forethought and intended to deepen the interesting pallor of her supposedly grief-stricken face. Then she hastened to the dining room.

She found to her chagrin that the prize had already escaped her, and the maid was clearing the dishes away from Mr. Fairfield's place at the table. He must have breakfasted hurriedly, or else she had been longer than she thought. As she sat biting her red lips in vexation, she saw him through the opposite window at the other end of the long room, going with determined steps down the sandy path. One comprehensive glance at the landscape told her that he was going in the direction of the green cottage. She watched him a moment and saw that her guess had been correct, for he ascended the steps, knocked at the door, and then sat down in one of the big rockers standing on the piazza. Her purpose was taken in a moment. Taking a few swallows of coffee from the cup just set down beside her, she slipped up to her room for her parasol and hat and followed the path he had just taken.

Mr. Fairfield had felt during his brief breakfast that the thing he wanted most in life just then was to look upon the face of the one whom he had just discovered he loved. Not that he intended to tell of his love just now; no indeed! He saw instantly that it was too soon for that. She had not known him long enough. She might not love him — how could she? — and he would not startle her by telling her of it abruptly. No, he would teach her daily to love him. He would wait and see if there was any chance for him, before he told her. But whatever came of the telling, the fact, the precious fact, remained that he loved her, and he wished to see her in the light of the knowledge of that fact. He had hastened his morning meal that he might go to her home and ask for a walk, before Miss Davenport could be around to claim her time, and thus he had gone happily down the path, whistling a few notes of a popular song, then humming a line of a hymn, and so, joyously, scarcely knowing what his thoughts might be. Rachel answered the door and told him her sister had run in next door on an errand for her mother but would be back almost immediately. He sat down to wait while Rachel went on with the work she was doing, which she could not leave just then. The acquaintance between the Hammonds and Mr. Fairfield had grown sufficiently intimate for Rachel to feel privileged to go on working and occasionally come to the door to make some pleasant remark or answer something Mr. Fairfield called in to her.

Maria coming in the back door with the basket in which she had just carried some fish to Mrs. Parker, a present from her mother, who had purchased more than she needed, heard the minister's voice and answering Rachel's motion slipped into her room to change her dark working calico for her beach dress. Rachel, buzzing about in the kitchen finishing Maria's morning work that she might not be kept from her friend any longer, did not see the tall black-robed young woman who presently came up the steps, on the veranda, and greeted its occupant with such effusiveness, seating herself in the next rocker and entering into an immediate discussion of the morning and its charms.

It seemed to Mr. Fairfield as if some black cloud had suddenly been cast across his sky, but he tried to remember that this was Maria's friend, and while she was not in the least like Maria, she might have a great many delightful qualities if one could only get at them. At least she had a soul, and if he could not be interested in her in any other way, he would try to remember that, and let his courteous treatment of her reflect his Master's example. If he had but known her heart he might have felt more tempted to assume a scourge of small cords with which to drive her out from the temple of that day, into which she had set tables for her barter in hearts. If good was to reach her soul, at least he was not intended to bring it, not in the way in which he brought it to Maria. This one was not capable of receiving the good word, not yet at least, for the ground was stony and shallow and barren.

Maria, coming with a bright face to meet her friend, found the two seated side by side. Nannette was bending over the other's chair to inspect a tiny gold ring which he carried on his watch chain, and which she had herself asked about. That this action on Nannette's part was greatly to the annoyance of Mr. Fairfield Maria could not possibly be expected to know. She would never have been willing to ask about a gentleman's personal adornments, nor to reach out and handle them of her own accord, and she naturally judged that no other girl would so far forget herself, especially with an acquaintance of barely one evening. The natural inference was that he was telling her the story of the charm, and had invited her to examine it. Of course it was evident that they had come together from the hotel to see her, anybody would know that. She half wished in her heart that they had gone off together, and not brought her in at all, then her life and her troublesome feelings would not perplex her so. Nevertheless they had come, and her part was to be pleasant and polite. She hastily drew to her the memory of the night before, as a child will reach out its hand to its father when in fear and remind him of his promise to protect. She understood the swift upward look of her soul to the Saviour, asking him to help her to forget all but that she was his, and her heart thrilled with the answering strength that came to her need.

Nannette instantly saw her advantage. Indeed she had hastened her steps and given up her breakfast, scarcely hoping she might succeed in gaining the porch before Maria came out, but wishing, if possible, to give her the impression that she had come with Mr. Fairfield. If Maria would draw off and leave the minister to her, her task would be more than half done. It was Maria's presence which hindered her own charm from working. It piqued her to think that Maria could be supposed to be more charming than she, but then Maria had been there first, and there was no telling what a man might not take a fancy to if he had nothing else at hand. Nannette's idea of a man was that he must always have a woman to amuse him, as her idea of a woman was that she could never be happy without an adoring man or two about.

"You were so long coming last evening, dear, that we thought we would run right over after breakfast and stir you up," said Nannette gayly.

It occurred to the minister that Nannette must have eaten her breakfast long before he had, or else had gone without. He gave her a searching look and decided for the latter theory. Then he wondered what was her object. He was not a conceited man, and therefore her real object had not yet dawned upon him. He took her merely for a disagreeably bold, worldly girl, and decided to keep away from her as much as possible. He did not know yet how much control this skillful coquette had over the possible when she chose.

Maria sat down clothed in her new strength. She tried to look at Mr. Fairfield merely in the light of a chance acquaintance in whom she had no interest at all, and to heartily enter into Nannette's talk, at least in so far as she conscientiously could. She did not talk to Mr. Fairfield this morning. It was easier for her not to do so.

Mr. Fairfield was disappointed at the way things had turned out, and solaced himself by retiring from the conversation, as he had done the evening before, except when absolutely pressed into it by Miss Davenport. He was studying the fair lines of Maria's face, and thinking how lovely she was, and wondering why he had never noticed her beauty as being so unusual before. He thought there was a new touch of gravity and earnestness about her too, which sat well on her countenance. As he watched her and noted her replies, he made up his mind that she was in no present danger from Miss Davenport's influence.

But Nannette perceived that the conversation, of which she had the monopoly, was becoming strained, and casting about for something to change the situation she discovered in the distance along the Spray View road a carriage containing the De Veres. She immediately began to dilate on the excellencies of that family, and remembering that quality in man, jealousy, which had often served her a good turn, she professed especial delight in the coming of Roland De Vere.

"We always were such good friends," she said, turning her eyes sweetly upon the minister; "we used to play together by the hour as children, and as we grew older our friendship was really something lovely till he went away to college. Don't you think he has a very remarkable mind, Mr. Fairfield?"

Maria, remembering Nannette's account of her quarrel with Roland De Vere, listened in wonderment. Nannette had omitted to state that her intercourse with Roland De Vere from their earliest childhood had been strictly upon a war footing. He had never been afraid to tell her of the shams and falsehoods he saw in her, and this had made her almost hate him.

Nevertheless, it was sometimes expedient to seem to love your enemies, at least for a time. This was one of the unwritten commandments in Miss Davenport's code.

Maria felt greatly relieved at the appearance of the De Veres. So did Mr. Fairfield, and so did Nannette, but each for a different reason.

A sailing party was the order of the day, and the De Veres had driven over to secure their Lone Point friends to join them. The yacht was to be at the Lone Point wharf in an hour to wait for them, and they were to send the carriage back by the driver, and go out across the bar and fish in the open sea, returning by moonlight. It was a thoroughly delightful plan. Maria could not help but be happy, and forget all her troubles. Somehow they seemed to melt away in the light of the genial company. She hastened in to call Rachel, and consult with her mother about some additions to the ample lunch which the De Veres had brought with them.

"We'll go in and tell the Parkers," said Fannie De Vere, catching Rachel's hand in quite a girlish fashion, and starting off through the sand.

"The Pahkahs! And who are the Pahkahs?" asked Nannete, amid the pleasant hurry that prevailed. Nannette always used the Southern drawl when she wished to be interesting.

"They're nobodies, Nannette; just nice, pleasant people, not at all like you and me. You won't care for them in the least," answered Roland De Vere with a touch of the old rudeness which had characterized his conversation with her always.

Chapter 21

Mr. Fairfield, during the preparation for the excursion, had been diligently studying how he might secure Maria's company on the way to the boat, and for as much of the day as possible. But although he made himself variously useful, offering assistance to Maria and Rachel in numberless little ways, and gladly taking upon himself all the burdens of wraps and lunch baskets that he could find belonging to the green cottage, he did not seem to succeed. Maria was busy and dignified. If he essayed to walk beside her she suddenly discovered an errand with another member of the party, or rushed back for her forgotten parasol. Laden as he was he could scarcely follow her, and when he waited behind the rest he was at once pounced upon by Nannette, who called him a "poor, lone man," and sweetly insisted upon holding her parasol over him and carrying Maria's blue jacket, in the possession of which he had taken especial delight. He could do nothing but submit, for he was helpless. There was nothing for it but to walk grimly on to the wharf as fast as possible and hope for better fortune. Maria did not seem to see all this. In fact she was remembering just then that Mr. Fairfield had never told her the story of the dainty little gold ring he wore, nor even spoken of it. He took her for a girl who did not care for such things. Well, it was as well. He had helped her, he was a minister, a — no, it would not do to call him her friend. There must be a more dignified name for their relation than that. The Catholics had a good name for it: "Spiritual adviser," that was what he was. As such she could enjoy his conversation, and feel that she did right to take pleasure in his company; but not when Nannette was about. Maria, therefore, walked forward and began to talk eagerly with the first unoccupied one of the group. This happened to be Marvie Parker, and Maria silently blessed her for her bright, girlish conversation, which in spite of her, cheered her thoughts and turned them in another direction from the one which they were constantly tempted to take.

George Parker at the last moment joined the group on the wharf. Nannette had given his sister a comprehensive sweep of her big, brown eyes, and ignored her beyond the slightest possible inclination of the head. When the brother arrived, tall, grave, somewhat diffident in his manner toward strangers, and with a rather homely face and figure, by some mischance she was not introduced. It was as well, perhaps, for she stood in the shadow of a sail, and curled her lip as she looked at him. Of the happy little party standing about and warmly greeting the new-comers only Marvie saw that glance. Instantly her warm, loving heart resented if for her dear brother, and her anger flamed up till she was ready to blaze out in a well-deserved reproval, for Marvie Parker was a girl of tremendous impulses. But fortunately her impulses were under the control of One wiser than herself. A moment more, a hasty prayer, and she was ready to look again at the silly, conceited miss, and forgive her, and say, "Poor thing." Then she set herself to see if she could not in some way do a kindness to the one who had smitten her so hard upon the one cheek. She knew her brother far too well to carry revenge in her heart for his sake.

Maria took care to place herself between Fannie De Vere and Marvie Parker when they seated themselves in the boat, and when Mr. Fairfield cast about to get near her he found no opportunity. Miss Davenport had not been so discreet. She took good care that there should be a vacant place beside her, but the disappointed young man for once got the better of her. If he could not sit beside Maria, at least he would not subject himself for an entire morning to the chatter of her disagreeable friend. He went to the bow of the boat and seated himself among the coils of rope. Here he could be quiet and think and watch Maria without being observed.

Roland De Vere swung himself aboard at the last minute and took his seat, without noticing, beside Nannette, and when he discovered her proximity he was fully as dissatisfied as she with the arrangement. He began to wonder what he had done to deserve such punishment, but as Rachel was at his other side, with George Parker next, he devoted himself as much as possible to them.

Like some beautiful, intelligent creature, the boat spread her white wings, and turning glided from the bank. There seemed something almost unearthly in the beauty of the day and the flying of the boat along the shimmering bay, swiftly, swiftly to the place where the soft, benignant blue of the sky came down to meet the water. Perhaps Mr. Fairfield was the only one who thoroughly enjoyed it all. He was by himself and with pleasant thoughts for company. The others were arranging themselves comfortably and answering one another, as bright shafts of sarcasm and bubbling mirth went from one to another. Nannette was cross. She had missed her aim. True, she had managed to separate Maria and Mr. Fairfield, though she felt pretty sure that Maria had done the herself, and she could not even claim the credit of it. But she had not gained his company. She had felt certain that a whole day by her side amid such lovely surroundings would surely fix her in Mr. Fairfield's good graces by night. Now she had no one but that hateful Roland De Vere, and she saw instantly that he was not disposed to be forgetful or friendly. She decided to show her pique by making fun of those ungainly Parkers. If the young man had been just the least bit better looking, or seemed at all to glance at her with admiration, she might have been driven to flirt with him, but with such a man as Mr. Fairfield by, unwon, she felt she could not stoop so low. She decided, however, that Mr. Fairfield must not see her making fun of that solemn looking Parker boy, for as he was a minister she supposed he would be obliged to disapprove. She had a theory that young ministers always disapproved of wrong things because their churches obliged them to do so, and not at all because they felt any strong convictions on the subject.

Her opportunity to practice on young Parker came soon, and for want of better material she fell to work at once. Roland De Vere as early as possible during the morning made an excuse to change seats with George Parker. He felt sorry for George when he did it, but George Parker was one of those people who always have the disagreeable people and places thrust upon them in this world, and who seem to be given the grace to accept them pleasantly. His sister watched him as he sat down and turned his keen, gray eyes upon Miss Davenport, with a remark about the beauty of the day. Nannette had fancied him shy, and was astonished to find that he had a fine voice and spoke with perfect ease and unusual grace of manner. She plunged into a conversation with him, her most disagreeable expression upon her face, determining to put him to embarrassment as soon as possible. She had found from the talk of the others that he was something of a musician, and fancying him wise in his own conceit as a superficial amateur, she thought this would be as good an opportunity as any to "take a rise out of him." Summoning all her slight knowledge of the truly musical world, which amounted in all to the names of a few leading performers, with perhaps the titles of a number of brilliant productions, though it is doubtful if she knew which piece was being played without her programme, she began.

"Did you say you lived in the city?" she asked him, turning toward him with one of the cold stares which was usually so disconcerting to the poor victim whom she chose to transfix with it. "Then I suppose if you are so fond of music you heard Josef Hoffman last month."

Her expectation was that he would hardly know to whom she was referring, but to her amazement his plain face lit up with joy, thinking he had discovered a kindred spirit. "Yes, I did," he answered at once. "I heard him both times. It was a treat I would not have missed for the world. I was unable to get a seat, to be sure, as I had to rush there just at the hour, and there was scarcely standing room left. However, I might have been standing on my head for all I knew about myself while he was playing. Wasn't it fine? What did you think of his rendering of Beethoven's E-flat major sonata? Wasn't that first movement absolutely perfect? Didn't he bring out the orchestral effects most marvelously in Liszt's transcription of the overture to 'Tannhäuser.' "

It was Nannette's turn to be embarrassed. She had not heard Josef Hoffman, and would not have understood him if she had, for she was not a musician. Worse than that she had not one atom of delicate appreciation of good music; it was a bore to her and nothing more, unless it was the accompaniment for dancing. Then, and then only did it find an answering chord in her soul.

She flushed slightly, paused, but rallied and tried again. Her malice was stirred. She never quite forgave any one who made her feel uncomfortable. She flew to a subject in which she felt more at home.

"Were you at the opera house last month? Did you see 'The Wife's Revenge'?" she asked, a wicked look flashing across her face.

The young man looked at her with instant comprehension of the mistake he had made at first.

"Yes," said he, "I was at the opera house last month: but I did not go to see a play. I was with Mr. Moody."

Now Miss Davenport was so utterly out of the religious world that she did not at first know who Moody was.

"Moody," said she puzzled; "who is Moody?"

"Moody, the evangelist. Surely you heard of the two weeks' series of meetings held in the opera house."

"What! Moody and Sankey Sunday-school songs?" she exclaimed with a disagreeable laugh. "Oh, you're good, are you?" The sneer on her face was decided this time; but to her disappointment it did not seem to have any effect whatever upon her listener.

He turned his grave, gray eyes full upon her. "Just what is your definition of goodness, Miss Davenport?" he asked quietly.

Nannette was nonplussed. She had not expected to be answered like that. She had looked for a wave of color over his face, and immediate disclaiming of any right to the adjective she had applied, in the midst of which she would laugh scornfully and make him to feel that to be "good" was above all things else a thing for one to laugh at and disclaim.

"Oh, I never deal in definitions," she answered uneasily. "I leave that to the dictionary."

"The dictionary gives some ten or twelve different meanings to that word, if I am not mistaken," said he; "but the one I like the best was given years ago by Paul: 'For scarcely for a righteous man will one die; yet peradventure for a good man some would even dare to die.' If I might claim that sort of goodness, Miss Davenport, I would count it the highest honor."

After that, conversation between these two languished. Nannette had really nothing to say. She felt that she had been worsted from the first, and with weapons which were new to her. She took refuge in teasing the fish which they presently began to catch. Strange to say, she was among the successful catchers that day. The line she held was often taken by some poor unwary fish, and she would jerk him out of the water and let him down again, only to give the line a stronger jerk and keep the poor creature in agony. The girls protested once or twice, and at last Roland De Vere turned with sudden vehemence upon her;

"Nannette, stop torturing that poor creature. It will rise in judgment against you at the last day." He perhaps did not mean his words literally, but he was angry at the cruelty of her action.

Nannette laughed scornfully and gave the fish another jerk. "Your theology is all wrong. They don't have fishes in heaven," she responded saucily. "Mr. Fairfield," she called laughingly, "do set Mr. De Vere straight. He thinks we shall have fishes in heaven. Do tell him they haven't any souls."

"I leave it to you, Fairfield," said the young man, turning toward the minister, "if some animals haven't more soul than some human beings."

Thus appealed to, the minister recalled his thoughts from their pleasant wanderings and answered: "Certainly, De Vere, I fancy animals will have some part in the future life. Whether they have anything answering to souls or not, I cannot say; but I surely do think they will have their part, with all of God's creation, in the heaven that is being prepared."

This statement aroused much discussion and many exclamations from the rest of the party, and Nannette and her fishes were left to themselves while the others contemplated the new thought. Maria, who was charmed with the idea, which was a new one to her, found herself looking at Mr. Fairfield with her old admiration and thinking what a delightful talker and deep thinker he was. She wished he would go on and tell more about this; but he was not inclined to say much. He seemed to be changed somehow from the genial friend she had known so well for a few weeks. She wondered what had made the difference, and if Nannette had been the cause. How pleasant it would be if she could have him by herself just for a little while, so that she might ask him some questions about her new life which were perplexing her; but she supposed that must not be, for it was better for her not to see too much of him. What if he had seen how much she had enjoyed his company and had drawn off from her on that account, to save her from the shame of showing him her heart. Her face burned at the very thought. How dreadful that would be! Surely she could not have seemed to care for him! How could she when she did not know it? Of course she did not really care for him, she only feared she might. But she would not, now that she saw her danger. That would be terribly unwomanly. It was bad enough to have to realize her own danger. If she had been more careful she would not have had to endure the humiliation of that thought. But then, she might have missed this blessed joy of finding Christ. And her heart was really happy with the feeling of the perfect peace she had with God. She could be willing to endure even to have him think humiliatingly of her for the sake of that sweet peace. But she would take care to show him in the future that she had no interest in him apart from the spiritual help he had given her.

What a happy day this would have been if these two could have looked into one another's hearts! But God knew best, and he had some wise end in view through this discipline.

I cannot say, beneath the pressure of life's cares to-day, I joy in these
But I can say that I had rather walk this rugged way, if Him it please;
I cannot feel that all is well when darkening clouds conceal the sun;
But then I know God lives and loves; and say, since it is so, "Thy will be done."
I cannot speak in happy tones; the teardrops on my cheek show I am sad;
But I can speak of grace to suffer with submission meek, until made glad.
I do not see why God should e'en permit some things to be, when he is love;
But I can see, though often dimly, through the mystery, his hand above!

Chapter 22

Altogether Nannette felt very much discontented and dissatisfied with her first week at Lone Point. The weather had been perfect, but what is weather when there is a storm within? The party had been a merry one, but somehow she felt utterly out of harmony with it. Perhaps they felt this inharmoniousness more that she did.

The fishing had been abundant and successful. What fishing party could ask more? The sea had been calm. The sunset was one of the most magnificent ever seen at Lone Point and the moonrise was equally resplendent. They had floated slowly home, drawn by zephyrs that seemed willingly to obey the hand that held the helm. But one thing had been lacking in it all for Nannette, the only thing that made fishing parties and moonlight trips home again filled with pleasure, and that was an adoring man at her side who would chatter nothings and feed her vanity by likening her eyes to the sparkles on the wave and her complexion to the dazzling whiteness of the moonbeams. Mr. Fairfield had persisted in keeping a dignified distance, at least as far as was permitted by the length of the boat. Once, during a change of places she had gotten beside him as they came back from supper at the hotel on the mainland and were re-embarking for their homeward ride, but he had after a few words abruptly excused himself and gone to the aid of one of the sailors, who she felt sure needed him not at all. It was all very humiliating to her pride.

Any one, even George Parker, would have been better than no one at all. She was absolutely tied down to the companionship of the girls, and to her that was as low as she could fall. She had never taken pains to make any true friends among the girls, and felt, what was true, that she was only tolerated out of politeness. This she cared not one straw for when she had plenty of men at hand. She looked over at George Parker and wished she had been less disagreeable to him in the morning. It would at least have amused her to subjugate him, she felt it would have been an easy task, and to have enjoyed the dismay of that pious little sister of his. Altogether, Nannette was as thoroughly unhappy and disagreeable as she ever had been in her life. All the way home there had been singing. She had asked for one or two songs, but no one seemed to know the airs she called for, most of them society sentimentalities, or if they did, they did not care to break the harmony of the evening by bringing them in. The songs they sang were old ballads mostly; soft, low, sweet strains which seemed to be in tune with the murmur of the waters. By and by some one started a hymn, and they sang

on from one to another favorite. It was wonderful how much more the words
seemed to mean when sung on the water.

> "Far, far away like bells at evening pealing,
> The voice of Jesus sounds o'er land and sea."

Nannette had an uncomfortable feeling that there might be a supernatural voice going to speak to them pretty soon. The songs chosen seemed
all to follow one thought:

> "Jesus, Saviour, pilot me,
> Over life's tempestuous sea,"

and as the last words died away Rachel's voice took up the words of
another:

> "Jesus, Jesus, visit me,
> How my soul longs after thee.
> When, my best, my dearest friend,
> Shall our separation end?"

Then Roland De Vere started with

> "My Jesus, as thou wilt."

and his sister took it up at the close with the lovely tune of "Dorrnance"
in the words,

> "Jesus calls us, o'er the tumult
> Of our life's wild, restless sea;
> Day by day his sweet voice soundeth,
> Saying, Christian, follow me."

Maria sang the words, feeling every one in her heart. She was enjoying
this service of song more almost than she was able to endure, for tears of
deep, unspeakable gladness would come to her eyes now and then, as she
said over to herself: "He is my Jesus. I can feel it. I know it. I love him." And
she realized at that moment that all her Christian life she had been dissatisfied with herself and longing for just this thing to come to her, only she had
not been willing nor known how to take the necessary steps to bring it about.

As they neared the shore and the lights of Lone Point began to shine out over the water, Rachel and Marvie, sitting together, started the sweet strain:

"One sweetly solemn thought, comes to me o'er and o'er,
I'm nearer my home in heaven to-day, than ever I've been before."

Nannette felt the hush that hung over the little company as the boat silently slipped up to the dock when the last words were ended, and she was reminded so strongly of her mother's funeral that she felt tempted to jump overboard in order to create some kind of an excitement. Just as the boat touched the wharf, Mr. Fairfield repeated in the clear rich voice which had hushed a congregation to instant attention so often:

"And I pray that every venture
The port of peace may enter,
That safe from snag and fall,
And siren haunted islet,
And rock, the unseen Pilot
May guide us one and all."

It seemed like a benediction at the close of a beautiful meeting.

They landed in silence and went toward their homes with a hushed reverence upon them.

Nannette, seated before her mirror — she always made a practice of sitting before her mirror after she had been anywhere, that she might see just how she had looked and what sort of an impression she had made — curled her lip in intense scorn.

"I feel exactly as if I had attended a revival meeting and been sitting on the mourner's bench all the evening. I declare this is worse than reading to Cousin George. I have half a mind to go home. If it were not for making that stuck-up minister come down a peg I believe I would, but he must be conquered! If I could only catch Maria at a disadvantage when he was along! I must see if I can't work something up along that line. I see plainly, however, I shall have to try the pious dodge before I can do very effective work. Ah me! What a bore! I shall make up for this next summer!"

Then she went to her bed, but not to sleep. She lay there planning a campaign which meant victory and the downfall of the ministry in Lone Point at least.

The days passed by with much the same relation between the three, Maria, Mr. Fairfield, and Nannette, that there had been the first day of Miss Davenport's arrival. Nannette annoyed Mr. Fairfield not a little, asked services of him, and accepted them in a gracious manner, as if it were a favor to him to be allowed to run her errands. She circumvented his plans to meet Maria in the most ingenious ways, often making it appear perfectly natural that it should be so, so that he had not even yet begun to suspect how deeply laid was her plan.

Nannette had not forgotten her wish to show Maria off to disadvantage before him, and constantly her mind was trying to discover some means of doing this. She went about her work with an ingenuity which was worthy of a better cause. One day at the table she began a conversation with a view to ascertaining his views on certain questions.

"Mr. Fairfield, what do you think of cards? Aren't they awfully wicked? Don't you find they do a great amount of harm?"

She asked the question one morning at breakfast. Mr. Fairfield turned in amazement from the contemplation of his plate. This was not a subject in which he would have supposed Miss Davenport interested. As for discussing the right and wrong of card-playing, he did not deem that it would be at all profitable. He supposed, of course, she must be a card-player, as indeed she was, though she chose this morning to pose as one greatly disapproving the folly of it.

"I find that card-playing among Christians, as a rule, leads to worldliness," he answered stiffly. He judged Miss Davenport's object in asking the question to be to force him into an argument, and he did not care to discuss worldly amusements with a person who professed to belong wholly to the world. He was a little surprised that she did not further pursue the subject, but thought no more about it. He had more important things to think of. There was to be a concert by a fine orchestra on the veranda of one of the Spray View hotels. The Lone Point young people were invited over to spend the evening and attend it with the De Veres. Mr. Fairfield was hoping that the evening would give him an opportunity for at least a few minutes with Maria, so that he might ask her to walk with him the next day. He had a new address by Mr. Meyer which he was sure she would like to see, and he wanted the pleasure of reading it with her for the first time. It must—it surely could be planned. It was absurd that he actually could not get a chance to speak to her alone any more. He would have to resort to writing pretty soon if things went on as they were going, though he feared that for him to write would appear strange in her eyes, and precipitate matters before the time was ripe. He wondered, with a sigh, how long Maria's friend would stay in Lone Point. Perhaps he could ask her and find out the limit to this, to him, most distasteful state of things.

The fact was, if it had not been that Maria was resolved that Mr. Fairfield should not imagine her anxious for his company, Nannette would not have been able to contrive so many separations as she did; but with them both at work to keep him from his object it was a difficult thing for him to gain his point.

It was about this time that Winthrop Hammond had remained in town continuously for some days, taking care of a friend who was alone in the city and was ill with typhoid fever. The young man's parents had at last arrived and Winthrop felt at liberty to leave him, and so had come to the shore for a few days to stay, without going up to the city, as he felt he needed rest after his many nights of nursing and wakefulness.

It so happened that this concert at Spray View was the first one of the gatherings of the young people at which Winthrop had been present, and therefore was the first time Nannette had met him.

Strange to say they had never happened to meet in town.

Maria prayed earnestly before going out that evening. She asked Winthrop anxiously several times if he would not rather remain at home and rest, saying she would gladly stay with him; but as he seemed to be really anxious to go, she ceased talking about it.

Perhaps Nannette was so interested in Mr. Fairfield that she would not set any snares for Winthrop. At any rate she had put the dear brother into God's keeping, and nothing more could be done. She hovered about Winthrop and tried to be as cheerful and interesting as possible. Indeed, Winthrop noticed how she had changed and wondered what it meant. It was pleasant to have her seem to care to be with him, though it was unlike her too, for she was one who always had plenty of admirers of her own.

Nannette's plans were not thoroughly made, though she knew she meant to make some decisive move that evening. She had a shadowed outline of a plan which should depend upon circumstances, and upon this occasion circumstances favored her. Early in the evening, she met a company of young people with whom she was well acquainted. Among them was a particularly fast young fellow, whose face showed plainly what his life must be. Nannette took pains to introduce them to Maria. This young man in particular seemed to be greatly taken with her, and whispered in an aside to Nannette:

"I say, Nan, she's a 'beaut'! Where'd you pick her up? I like her style. She's not so slow as a 'looker,' is she? Say, give a fellow a chance to talk with her for a while."

"All right, I will," she agreed readily enough, "if you'll do something for me in return. Promise me to get up a set for whist or euchre with her in it in the small card-room to the left of the office, the one with the wide windows on the piazza, you know. I have a special reason. I'm setting up a little joke on some one, that's all. I think she knows how, all right, but anyway, if she doesn't, you offer to teach her."

"You're a jewel, Nan," he responded eagerly, glad of the chance to teach so pretty girl as Maria anything; "just command me and I'll obey."

"Well, you be in there with the girls in five minutes and I'll manage to send her in," and Nannette went airily on her way. She was by no means so sure of Maria, as she pretended, but she would do her best. Fortune favored her a second time as she walked back to the end of the piazza, where the De Vere party was seated. Winthrop Hammond met her near the parlor door. He stopped her and begged that she would send the others to him as he had secured better seats for the music, but could not leave them lest some one else would pre-empt them. Here was one more aid for her scheme. A few minutes' delay one way or another would make no difference about the seats, and Winthrop Hammond would never find out. Yes, she would try it.

"Maria dear," she said in a low tone as she came up to the party, who had not noticed her absence, for she had only walked away with her old friends for a few moments, "Maria, I just met your brother and he wished me to ask you to come to him. You will find him over there in that small room to the right of the office."

Maria rose at once and went in the direction she had pointed, wondering what in the world her brother wanted, and feeling a glad little thrill of joy that he did want her instead of some one else. As she walked away, Mr. Fairfield broke off in the midst of a sentence to Marvie Parker and rose to go with her, but Nannette quickly stepped to his side and, in a tone which all could hear, said sweetly: "Oh, Mr. Fairfield, would you be so good as to help me find my friends again? I have lost them and I am very anxious to see them once more before the music begins."

Of course there was nothing else to do as a gentleman but to offer her his arm and march away down the wide piazza, inwardly fuming at his trying position and, let us admit it, at its pretty cause.

Now Nannette could not, for her own purposes, have better timed their coming to the part of the piazza where the little card-room window opened out upon it, if she had been gifted with supernatural powers.

"I think I heard them say they would be near here. Would you just look in that window, please, and see if you catch a glimpse of them?" With her quick eye she had already seen the forming tableaus within and knew that time and scene were ready for the intended auditors. A table stood in the center of the room, around which sat the company of young people whom Nannette had recently introduced to the Lone Pointers. One seat was vacant and the fast young man was just bowing and holding it ready for Maria to be seated as Mr. Fairfield looked in. From where they stood in the darkness, gazing into the brilliantly lighted room, he could plainly see the cards on the table and in the hands of those about it, and then a soft little hand stole quickly over his eyes and Nannette, in the gayest of shocked laughs, said; "Oh, please come away. I'm so sorry. I wouldn't have done it for the world if I had known. She wouldn't have you see her in there, I know; but you won't think hardly of her for it, will you? She has been having such a hard time keeping up, you know, and one can't be good always. One must have a little fun occasionally. Besides, Maria has done bravely. She isn't used to such a straight-laced life, you must remember. She has been telling me how hard it was for her. But she would be terribly broken up if you saw her. She had been telling me about your — well, perhaps, I would better not say any more, for she might not like it, you know," Nannette broke off hesitatingly. They had been walking on toward a secluded end of the piazza, entirely deserted now, for the guests were gathering for the music. Nannette determined to strike while the iron was hot, for she thought she saw that Mr. Fairfield was greatly taken aback at what he had seen. Here were seats and the loud dashing of the waves. No place could be better for confidences and a pleasant little flirtation. What if the music did go on and pass, no matter if she fought for and won this trophy.

"Let us sit down just a minute, please," she said as if out of breath, putting her hand to her heart; "I feel so upset by this; I am afraid she would blame me for it, and I should feel so sorry. She has been telling me all about it, you know, and well — excuse me, but I have these little turns with my heart ever since mother's death. It will soon pass away. There — oh, please sit down just a minute." She leaned her head back against the wall and let it incline till it almost rested against her escort. Only just an instant did she let it remain, and then she seemed to come to herself and gain strength to sit up, and to beg his pardon. She had hoped, that he might feel impelled to do as other young men had done before when she had been attacked in a like manner, but as she saw no sign of any such movement on his part, she concluded to discreetly withdraw.

Mr. Fairfield, on his part, was startled almost out of his accustomed composure. He would not have thought it so great a thing to see Maria playing cards, for she had told him herself that she had lived a worldly life, and she would not be expected to have thought over all these questions and to have decided them, in so short a space of time. But to be told that she had thought about it, and had deliberately gone in there to play, planning that he should not know about it — that she was actually trying to deceive him and appear better in his eyes than she was, was another matter. Worst of all, was it to know that the sacred words which had passed between Miss Hammond and himself about a better, nobler life, had been recited in detail to this worldly, unsympathetic listener. This was what cut him to the quick. He sat dumb for a few minutes with the pain of it.

Chapter 23

One might have supposed that Howard Fairfield, a minister of the gospel for three years, had lived long enough in the world, and had experienced enough of it, not to believe all that such a girl as Miss Davenport told him. Indeed he had never put much faith in anything she did or said from the first, but somehow the little that he had seen with his own eyes to-night had suddenly broken down his good common sense, and he began to doubt Maria. This was what Nannette had hoped for. She had thought that with his first doubts of Maria he might turn to her, and then she would have gained an influence over him which she well knew how to use. But Nannette showed in this that she was not a good judge of human nature. She did not understand the pure, high nobility of such a man's heart or she would never have thought to thus turn him to herself.

Miss Davenport, when she saw that the minister was sitting by her side and waiting, got out her little black-edged handkerchief and began to sob softly.

"It frightens me terribly when I get one of those heart attacks," she said in a soft, childish voice. She was a very good actor when the occasion demanded private theatricals. "I feel as if I were not good enough to die."

She paused. She thought if there was a spark of the true minister in him he would turn now and try to preach to her, but instead he sat quite silent beside her.

After a moment in which nothing could be heard but the beating of the waves, he spoke in a stern, controlled voice:

"Are you quite able to return to your friends now, Miss Davenport?" It was all that he could bring himself to say. He had detected the false note in her voice instantly. He could not try to talk to her of spiritual things. He felt instinctively that it would be casting pearls before swine. "If you do not feel able to go back, I will go in search of assistance for you," he added.

Nannette rose hastily from her chair, stung by anger and defeat, and during the long walk down that piazza neither of them spoke a word.

It was a pity that Mr. Fairfield could not have lingered just an instant longer before that brightly lighted window and have seen Maria coldly decline the seat at the card table, and after a glance about the room as if she were searching for some one, and a dignified word or two of inquiry about her brother, leave the room again. He might have been spared the pain which continually surged back and filled his heart, for then he would have seen that the whole thing was manufactured in the fertile brain of Miss

Davenport. Perhaps too, it might have dawned upon him sooner that the young woman in question had an end of her own to gain, namely himself. But the man's nobleness of character cannot better be described than by saying that such an idea did not even occur to him. It was not until he was in the quiet of his own room, and remembered that head almost laid upon his shoulder, that he began to see what sort of girl Miss Davenport really was, and a blush of shame mantled his brow for her sake, and for the sake of the womanhood which in his thought she, even in that slight act, had dishonored.

Meantime Nannette, humiliated and resentful, directed the party to where Winthrop Hammond was waiting for them, and disappeared for a while from the room as she saw Maria approaching.

Mr. Fairfield slipped away as the music began. His excuse was that he had promised to preach the next day, and needed the time for preparation. No one thought it strange, though all were sorry to lose his companionship. As he walked down the long piazza, intending to walk home by the beach instead of the road, he espied two people ahead of him. They were some distance away, and he could not see them distinctly. In the mingled, uncertain light of moon and dashing spray, he scarcely noticed them at first, except to know that the dark figure was a man, and the white draperies belonged to a woman. But as they turned out into the brighter moonlight to walk on the silver sand close beside the waves, his rapid steps gaining upon their lagging, lover-like ones, the man's dark arm stole out and encircled the waist of the white dress beside him; then in the settling, confiding, unresisting attitude of the woman he suddenly realized a familiar memory, and as suddenly became aware of two long, black sash ends, with fluffy little black chiffon ruffles about them, which he recalled noticing on Miss Davenport's dress as she walked before him on the way from the De Vere home over to the hotel. It had occurred to him as he first set eyes upon them that he had felt morally certain if her bereavement had not positively forbidden it, that sash would have been a bright red.

He was drawing nearer, and could see their faces now. Nannette was looking sweetly up into the man's eyes so close above hers, and he saw that the man was the same one who had but a few moments before placed Maria's chair at the card table. At least it was a relief to know that Maria was not playing with that man. He half wished he had remained to see what became of Maria, but he would not go back now. Moreover he had witnessed all the flirtations he cared for in one evening, and he turned abruptly off over the sand and struck straight across the country to the carriage drive, regardless of hillocks or wire fences, or even quicksands.

It was not a pleasant walk, and he felt as if perhaps he had lost rather than gained strength for his work on the morrow. He went straight to his knees, and in communion with his Heavenly Father he by and by lost the heavy strain that the events of the evening had put upon him, and was able to think of what he intended to say on the morrow.

He had chosen for his text, "For me to live is Christ"; that verse had been deeply impressed upon his mind since the first evening when he had visited the Hammond cottage, and Rachel had asked her innocent, earnest question.

By the hour of church service, the rest of the night, the beauty of the morning, and above all the peace which Jesus Christ had given him, had lifted him above his troubled thoughts of the evening before, and he felt "in the Spirit on the Lord's Day" as he went forth to speak in Christ's name.

For just a moment after he was seated in the pulpit, while the congregation were gathering, he felt a disagreeable sensation as Miss Davenport came in and seated herself before him in her elegant black robes. Perhaps he was hard upon her, but he was a noble man with high ideals of womanhood, and his very soul shrank from the thought of what he had seen of that young woman the night before. He caught however a glimpse of Maria's face, on which unconscious loveliness sat so sweetly, and of Rachel's calm brow, and he remembered that there were women in the world who would not stoop to what was beneath them. He wondered, as he looked at the sisters, why he had never noticed before how much alike they were. Happily for him he forgot for the moment the trouble about Maria that had come to him the night previous, for the sight of her face in its Sabbath peace seemed so foreign to anything deceitful that it was not until his work for the morning was over that the occurrence suddenly came back to his memory. There is no time when God's servants need so earnestly to watch and pray as when they have just finished some special work for him which required attention, and nerves on the alert. The tension is over, and they feel no more need for the watching and prayer immediately, and Satan steals up unaware when they are all unprepared for attack and takes them in their weakest place, sometimes undoing or rendering useless all the work of the time of action.

So after the hour of exaltation, when Mr. Fairfield almost stood upon the mount with his Saviour, and face to face with him gave forth the message of life, when as he spoke he felt in his heart that though to live for Christ was glorious, yet to die for him would be better than all, and that he would welcome death at once if Christ should send it; after all this Satan stole upon him on his way home and told him his preaching was of no effect, that his dearest hopes were vain; that the woman whom he felt was the one of all the earth for him was vain and deceitful, and possessed a number of other qualities he could not bear to think of.

However, as Satan was busy with the preacher, he had not time just then to go about picking up the seeds of good that had fallen upon the open mellow ground, and when he did get back to that work he found that much of the seed had already taken root and was growing. It was only that which had fallen upon the rocks that he could pick up and destroy.

Maria felt the uplifting of the morning sermon. It had helped her beyond anything she had ever heard before. It may have been because the preacher had written his sermon just for her. He had in mind her heart experience and he seemed to have anticipated all her doubts and perplexities and answered them. He had been much with God during the days when he had not been able to talk with her as he had done before and perhaps this separation had been good for them both for this very reason. They were learning each to first find help in God and only after that in one another. She thanked God over and over again that day for that sermon. She was not unaware that the preacher's face, in its high intellectual refinement, had worn a look of spiritual illumination which in her eyes made it more beautiful in a manly way than any face she had ever looked upon. It troubled her that the realization of the speaker's personality came so often to her mind, but after several vain attempts to put it away she decided to enjoy the day and the sermon and not trouble herself about this part of it, which apparently could not be helped.

There was just one speck of trouble on the bright surface of the day to her. Her brother Winthrop had walked beside Miss Davenport back to the hotel from church, and after dinner had declined Rachel's earnest request that he should attend her to the Sabbath-school and gone directly back to the hotel. From the piazza of the green cottage she had soon thereafter seen him emerge from the hotel carrying Miss Davenport's shawl and parasol, and with her by his side they had sauntered down the beach. She had evidently made up her mind that so spiritual a preacher would hardly be good material for a jolly Sunday afternoon and looked about for other prey.

As Maria had watched her during the past week or two, she had become more and more convinced of the shallowness and perhaps wickedness of her heart. She felt assured that she was an utterly unprincipled girl, and she could not bear to see her brother Winthrop walk into the net spread for him. In this fear she was evidently joined by Rachel, although neither said nothing to the other; but Rachel stood by her side on the piazza, her calm brow for once clouded with trouble and the ready tears gathering as she watched their brother. Maria had turned and looked at her and as their eyes met she obeyed the warm impulse of her heart and kissing Rachel gently, said "Come with me." Almost in amazement, Rachel had understood, though up to this time there had no word of any change in Maria passed between the two. Rachel followed her sister to their room and together, hand in hand, they knelt down beside their bed. They spoke no word aloud then, nor after they rose, but Rachel kissed Maria this time and then slipped softly away to the Sabbath-school. Because of this little incident, Maria felt that the day had been a wonderful one, and so did Rachel. It had touched Rachel's heart beyond anything that had even happened between them, to have Maria tell her in this way of her new deep feelings. She was a remarkable little sister or she might not have understood.

It may be that some little seed of the morning's word dropped on Miss Davenport's heart. She felt troubled. She was reminded unpleasantly again of her mother's death. She always avoided solemn things if she could, but that had been the one solemn incident of her life thus far that she had been unable to avoid. She did not wish to think about it, because while in her life that mother had not been so strong and faithful as she ought to have been, yet in her death she had aroused to the sense of her responsibility and had spoken a few dreadful words to her daughter, which by night and by day pursued her, unless she could keep her mind occupied with worldly things. However, her mind was shallow and she easily turned the tide of her thoughts to light things.

She had not been without some recognition of the illumination of the minister's face as he preached that morning, though in her words he was judged "decidedly handsome and distingué." She remembered his severity of the evening before, and a blush of actual shame crept over her face, unused to such blushes as it was. Then to drive out this unusual feeling she began to wonder if after all there was not yet hope that she might conquer this man. He had held out so long that it would really be quite interesting if she could bring him to her feet now. She might even fall in love with him. She really felt nearer to falling in love than she had for four or five years. And if he had a good church and large salary it might not be so bad a "catch" after all. She began to speculate upon just what the position of a minister's wife was, and how much would absolutely be required of her, for propriety's sake. The only drawback she could think of would be that she might be occasionally called upon to attend funerals, and *that* she *would not* do. She would never do it to please any one! Horrid places! She shuddered involuntarily and took up her fan, deciding that she would put her foot down upon that at once and declare she would not go. After all, as she had plenty of money, and probably would have more than he, there would be no danger but that she might have her own way about everything. Thereupon she looked up to the minister's face to see how it would seem to look at him in the light of a possible husband, and perceived that he had hushed the audience into tears by a simple story of pain and loss and love and loyalty to Christ which he was telling. She took up her handkerchief and tried to listen with the others as he recited impressively the words:

"When his steps
Were on the mighty waters —
When we went with trembling hearts through nights of pain and loss,
His smile was sweeter and his love more dear;
And only heaven is better than to walk
With Christ at midnight over moonless seas."

During the prayer that followed the sermon's close she formulated the plan which she carried out that evening, her final plan for his capture. Then with the benediction, she rose, satisfied with her morning's worship, and turned to Winthrop Hammond with her sweetest smile. If the plan should fail, there was this one left, and he was handsome and of a good family, and not very hard to subdue as she could easily see.

As Mr. Fairfield passed down the aisle, his exaltation yet upon his face, his thoughts hardly called back to earth from the message he had delivered, she stretched out her daintily gloved hand and just touched his coat sleeve with the tips of her fingers:

"Oh, Mr. Fairfield," said she with a sweet and reminding quiver in her voice, "thank you for that sweet sermon. It was just perfectly lovely. I did enjoy it so much."

And the minister suddenly remembered that he dwelt yet upon the earth.

Chapter 24

Mr. Fairfield received two letters of note in the Monday morning's mail. One had no postmark. The other was from his city home, telling of the severe illness of a woman who belonged to his church. He read this first, naturally anxious to know the home news, and sat with it in his hand pondering whether his duty did not call him home, at least for a day or two. Then he suddenly remembered the other letter. It was written in high, angular hand on a thick cream, violet-scented paper, and as the handwriting was very "high" indeed, and the letter long, it was consequently bulky. It read as follows:

My Dear Mr. Fairfield: My heart is filled with conflicting emotions as I sit down to write you this note. I feel as if I had come to a crisis in my life. The moment that I met you I realized that you were one who was to wield a great influence over me, and have something unusual to do with my life. This morning when I sat entranced listening to your words of eloquence I realized this still more. More than any one I have ever met, I believe you have influenced me. I was deeply affected. I have been thinking the matter over, and have decided to ask your help and spiritual advice. My dear mother used to tell me that some day I would meet with some one who would have the power to reach my stony heart religiously, and I now see that she was right. Oh, I am very wretched and miserable! If you can bring me any consolation from the religion which you so beautifully preach, I shall be forever grateful to you. I know you will not leave a poor girl who has no one else to whom to turn, comfortless. You will come to me and let me tell you the story of my life, and you shall teach me how to be good like yourself. I cannot endure yet to have any of my friends know that I have taken this step. It is too new and too sacred a thing to me. Therefore I ask you to meet me by the inlet, up toward the lighthouse, where the old mast is buried in the sand. There we can sit and talk to our heart's content without being observed. I shall be there at half-past ten in the morning, and I know you will not fail me. Until then farewell. Yours penitently,

Nannette M. Davenport.

The minister felt a cold chill creeping over him as he read this letter. He was more and more convinced of the insincerity of the writer as he thought over the matter, and read and re-read the letter. There was not in his heart one particle of response to that summons for help. He tried to examine himself and see whether it was his prejudice which made him feel so; but no, he could not think of any one else, no matter how humble, whom he would not gladly have gone to meet and help. He could not feel that the Spirit of God was sending him to this one. Saturday night's experience stood out too plainly in his mind, and the horror that he felt, grew as he thought about it. If there had been no one to talk with her, the case would have been different. He would have risked all on the mere chance that she was in earnest. Or if she had not worded her letter so strangely, and chosen so secluded a spot for their talk, he would not have been half so suspicious. What should he do? He felt strongly that this letter was written in much the same spirit as one a tramp had brought to him some months before, poorly spelled and ungrammatical in wording, purporting to be from a scholarly member of his church. It was to the effect that if he, the minister, would give the man some help from the church funds, this church-member felt sure that they might win the man to Christ. He was disposed to beware of this letter in the same way that he had been of that, for in the former case his suspicion that the man was an arrant fraud and the letter a forgery had proven entirely correct.

He felt now that for the sake of the love he bore Maria he ought not to meet this strange young woman. What if Maria should be walking upon the sand, and come upon them? Perhaps Miss Davenport meant to plan just such a *rencontre*. Now that his eyes were open there were no depths to which he felt she might not descend to gain her end, whatever it was. Then the letter had no genuine ring. There was too much talk about himself and his influence on her. There was no confession of having sinned. Why had she seen it necessary to write at all? Why had she not boldly asked him to talk with her upon the porch or anywhere? There were plenty of opportunities. Why, if she wanted religious help, had she not gone to Maria who, according to her own statement, had talked with her on these topics? He went to his room and asked his Heavenly Father's advice. This was a matter too important for his own inclination to decide. He could not easily refuse a call for help, even though he did doubt it. He prayed, trusting that an answer would come, and it did.

As he rose from his knees the other letter, the one about the sick woman, fluttered from his hand upon the floor, and on the back of the sheet where he had not noticed it before he saw a short postscript, asking him, if possible, to come home, as the woman had wished for him and seemed to have something on her mind to tell him.

Quick as a flash he felt that this was his heaven-sent answer, and he must obey. A glance at his watch told him that the next train was due at the station in one hour, just ten minutes before the time set by Miss Davenport in her letter for him to meet her at the inlet. He would go home. He certainly ought to go home, for his church was his first duty, and this woman was dying. Hastily he gathered together his belongings, and settled up the few matters which had to be attended to before he left, trying all the while to think what to do about Miss Davenport's request. He might ask some one else to meet her. He thought of a dear old Christian woman at home and wished she were here, but she was not. He thought of Maria, but disliked to ask her to go on such an errand to her own friend, lest she might suppose he had formed an intimate friendship with Miss Davenport, the circumstances of the past week well bearing out such a supposition. Nevertheless, he at last made up his mind that Maria was the only one to whom he could turn now. He went at once to the green cottage, leaving his orders about baggage at the hotel, so that he would not have to return.

Nannette was far up the beach practicing pretty little maneuvers with her deepest bordered handkerchief, and thus failed to see him go. But when Mr. Fairfield reached the green cottage he found to his dismay that Maria, with her mother, had been driven over to Spray View in Mr. Higgins' green wagon to do some Monday morning marketing, and would not be likely to return before the city train left. His heart was filled with a great regret when he thought of leaving her so abruptly, so that for a few minutes the thought of Nannette in her self-appointed trysting-place did not come to him.

Rachel was at home and had given him writing materials, and he was trying to construct a note of farewell to Maria. Perhaps he ought to write a note to Miss Davenport. It was only courteous to do so, but when he started he found that in him inmost soul he shrank from addressing a word to her. He glanced up at the earnest face of Rachel as she sat shelling peas on the upper step of the piazza. Her far-away, dreamy expression told that her thoughts were upon high and lovely things.

Suddenly a new idea came to him. It would be late when Maria returned, too late for her to reach Miss Davenport at the inlet before she had left there. Here was Rachel. She would know how to help that girl. There passed through his mind the verse about how the Lord had kept some things from the wise and prudent and revealed them unto babes, and while Rachel was no babe, still she was a child at heart. He remembered how well she had taught the little boys upon the sand. She had the root of the matter in her, and could surely bring the message of salvation to another soul. He would send her.

In a few words he explained the situation to Rachel, telling her only what was absolutely necessary, that Miss Davenport had been affected by the services of yesterday, and had written him a note, in his capacity as a minister, asking his help spiritually. He was called suddenly to the city by sickness in his congregation, and might be detained he knew not how long. Would she go and meet Miss Davenport, and help her to find Christ?

Rachel's face beamed with a holy light to think she was to be sent on an errand of mercy. She was genuinely glad that Nannette wanted to be a Christian. She had been secretly praying for her ever since her arrival, she seemed to Rachel to be so much in need of a Saviour. She promised eagerly to go at the appointed time, and immediately went away to get ready, such a joy upon her face at thought of the work before her that the minister was put to shame and felt he ought not to have shrunk from it. However, he reflected that as Rachel had no such doubts of the would-be inquirer as he held, she might be able to do much more good, for she was going trusting that her mission would be blest, and perhaps it would. He pledged himself to pray for this.

Then he found to his dismay that he had very little time left and could only write a line to tell Maria he was sorry to leave without seeing her. He left the Meyer book for her, asking that she would read it with him on his return, if he was able to return that summer. Then he heard the train whistling at Spray View, and hastily bidding Rachel good-bye went to the station, feeling that he was leaving behind him all that was precious in this world. It certainly was very hard for him to go. If only he could have had a little word with Maria and one of her lovely smiles to light him on his way!

Rachel, with exalted expression and her little Bible in her pocket, walked swiftly up the beach. She was praying as she went that she might be led to say the right words.

Nannette was seated on the sunken mast, her back turned toward the entrance of the secluded amphitheatre-shaped place she had selected for her morning's confessional. Her idea was to be deep in meditation of an affecting character when the young man should arrive, and thus make a good impression at first. She reasoned that if any one else came by and saw her sitting thus they would think she wished to be alone and pass on.

Rachel came with eager steps almost up to Nannette before she realized that any one was near, and then hearing the rustle of a dress, Nannette turned quickly to see who was there.

"Oh, Nannette! I am so glad!" exclaimed Rachel, stooping down and kissing the astonished girl on her forehead. "I am so glad for you, but I wish there was some one better than I to help you."

"What do you mean?" said Nannette coldly, pushing her back and looking at her strangely. It had been so long since any girl had cared to kiss her that it made her feel queer.

"There! I have done just as I always do, and plunged into the middle of things without any beginning," said Rachel distressed. "Why, Mr. Fairfield had to go away to the city this morning. He was called suddenly to a woman who is sick, and he stopped at the cottage and told me you were troubled, and you wanted to know how to be a Christian; and he asked me if I would come and tell you the best I could about it. I am sorry it is only I. If Maria or mamma had been at home one of them would have come; but he was anxious some one should come to explain at the hour, why he was not here, so I have come and I'll do my best, dear. I do love Jesus, and I think I can tell you a little about him," she said sweetly; "and oh, I am so glad you are going to belong to him too."

Nannette looked at Rachel blankly.

"And so he is gone!" she exclaimed, and broke into a harsh laugh. "Well, I have taken a lot of pains for nothing. It was awfully good of you, Ray, to travel way out here in the sand and sun, and you are doubtless just as good a talker as any one else, so don't worry your righteous little soul about that; but indeed you needn't trouble yourself to talk religion to me. I'm not in the mood for it, and it really wouldn't pay you. You'd better keep it for the fisherman's children. I hear you are quite converting them." Nannette arose to go back, a disagreeable look on her face. She felt that she was foiled again, and this time pretty badly. There was no longer any hope of reducing the minister to admiration of her charms; he was gone. He had evidently run away. She laughed aloud again. "Rachel, I have driven him from the ground. He didn't dare to stay and fight. It is a sort of victory, after all."

Rachel, who had been watching her in puzzled silence, was now completely mystified, and began to wonder if Nannette was losing her mind. "What do you mean, Nannette?" she asked.

"Oh, you dear little goose," laughed Nannette. She had not the energy to keep up her "pious dodge," as she called it for the benefit of a girl; what would be the use? She told herself it would make her no end of trouble, so she frankly admitted the part she had been playing.

"Did you really suppose I was anxious about my soul? Well, you must have known very little, indeed, about me. Don't look so worried, I was doing no harm. Your nice little words that you had all fixed up, will come in quite handy for some one else. If you were not such a blessed little goose, I would be very angry that he had dared to send some one else in his place."

"But, Nannette, he couldn't come, and I was the only one at hand he could send," said Rachel, with her troubled eyes looking earnestly at the other girl. "Perhaps he had not time to explain it all out to me. What was it you did want of him? I don't understand."

Nannette was very much amused, indeed. She laughed and laughed, using the black-bordered handkerchief to wipe away tears, genuine for once, even if they were born of mirth instead of grief.

"Well, I would have been a fool indeed if I had lured the minister out here just for the sake of talking religion at me, my little innocent," she said when she could control her laughter sufficiently to speak. "My dear, I wanted to bring him out here for a nice, little, harmless flirtation, that's all. Don't be so shocked. I wouldn't have hurt the poor man for anything."

"Oh, Nannette!" exclaimed Rachel in a horrified voice, "don't say that; you surely don't mean it, that you would plan such a flirtation with a minister?"

Nannette fairly shrieked with laughter now. "And did you suppose, my dear, that because he was a minister he had no heart?" she said between her peals of laughter.

Rachel was silent for a moment, taking in the meaning of what had been told her. "But, Nannette—" she hesitated as a new thought came to her. "Aren't you engaged to that other man? The one we met last night? Excuse me, but I couldn't help seeing. I stood on the piazza with Fannie De Vere as you went down the beach and I saw—him—put—his—arm—" She stopped. She could not bring herself to say more, and the tears were coming to the surface now with the effort she was making to do her duty.

A blush of as much shame as this girl could feel stole suddenly upon her cheek as she saw her own act, which had seemed to her an every-day affair, standing out in the light of this sweet, pure soul's ideals. It was perhaps the first time that Nannette had ever felt any real shame in allowing such familiarity with comparative strangers.

"Oh, little Ray! You are good fun!" she tried to say carelessly. "Why that was nothing. Any nice man would do that and think nothing of it. Just wait till Roland De Vere tries it with you and you'll understand."

And then Miss Davenport was treated to a touch of such righteous wrath as made her see that the gentle-hearted Rachel Hammond had more spirit in her than she had thought.

"Mr. De Vere would never do such a thing!" said Rachel, her bosom heaving and her face flaming, and then, her eyes flashing, she added, "But if he *did*, he would never try it again." She turned and walked a few steps with dignity. But Nannette rebuked, and not wishing to show it, sprang up.

"Oh come, now, Ray, don't be too hard on people who haven't risen to your heights. We can't all think alike, you know. I guess you're right about Roland. He's too much of an old granny to do anything of that sort. Come, let's be friends and go home, this sun is broiling. Don't tell your good mamma about this escapade of mine, I beg of you, or else she might write to my prim old auntie and have me sent home in disgrace."

Rachel walked along in silence. Of her in her every-day life it might be said:

"Other hope had she none, nor wish in life, but to follow meekly, with reverent steps, the sacred feet of her Saviour." It was not often that anything stirred her soul to the depths as this experience of the morning had done. And yet, as she grew calmer she realized that the girl beside her did not know Jesus, and that she had started out on a mission to help her to find him. She remembered how she had committed her cause to her Master before starting, and that she had confidently trusted in him to bless what she should do. And now she was going home without even having said one word that could make this other girl think more of Jesus Christ. Was the fault in her? Would it be casting pearls away to speak now, after what had passed between them? And yet could she in conscience leave her without having at least tried to fulfill her trust? All the way along the beach she was silent, letting Nannette talk as rapidly and vapidly as she would. Suddenly, as they came in sight of the hotel, Rachel paused beside a little side path that turned off from the beach and went down toward the green cottage, a shorter cut than going around by the hotel.

"Nannette," she said, putting out her hand gently to detain her companion, "I came out this morning to bring you a message from Jesus. I thought you were waiting for it, and would be glad to get it. I found you were not. I am very sorry. But I believe that Jesus sent that message to you all the same, even if you did not want it, and I must give it to you. Nannette, Jesus loves you, and he wants you to love him." The tears were in Rachel's eyes, and she felt that she could not trust herself to say another word, so she turned and sped swiftly down the sandy path toward home, and Nannette stood still looking after her, a strange smile upon her face, half of wistfulness and half of ridicule. As Rachel disappeared from sight behind the sand dunes she turned toward the hotel again, murmuring to herself, "She's a good little thing."

And who shall say but that Rachel's words were as the seed that often lies long in the cold, black earth before it gives sign of life? But at last it bursts and grows and brings forth fruit.

Chapter 25

After that Nannette plunged into a mad flirtation with Winthrop Hammond. She kept him by her side morning, noon, and evening. He was certainly devoted enough to make up for all the chagrin she had felt in the lack of admiration she had found in Mr. Fairfield. He bought her candy, and flowers whenever such were procurable in Spray View, regardless of the fact which he had heretofore kept before him that money was an article not to be carelessly spent by any member of the Hammond household just now. Nannette discovered a company of friends at Spray View who were altogether gay enough to suit her. There were little private gatherings for card playing and dancing, and Nannette, unrestrained by onlookers, took her part now and again, and began to feel that the summer was not such a bitter failure after all.

Having reduced Winthrop Hammond to subjection she set herself to make him drink wine. The young people with whom she went always drank it at their gatherings. She took him among them on all possible occasions where it was forthcoming. She ridiculed him when he declined it, and when he allowed his glass to be filled she dared him to drink with her. He had been brought up with a strong feeling against the use of wine, and he did not readily overcome it. Once or twice he drank to please her, because she made such a point of it. He was out very late at night these times, and his mother was troubled about him. His father even went so far as to suggest that it might be as well for him to return to his business, if he was going to use his rest hours to so poor an advantage. But he answered them all laughingly, and went on.

It was evident to the family that he had fallen in love with Nannette Davenport, and each wondered at it. They did not know how very charming she could be when she chose, and they could not know that she was choosing just now to very good purpose. Having been foiled in her first attempt she was angry, and determined to take her revenge out of the next victim. She appeared to think a great deal of her admirer, but in truth Mr. Fairfield's intellectual face and severe eyes turned full upon her, often rankled in her soul, and she felt deeply ashamed of herself and her whole life.

Things had been going on in this way for about two weeks. No word had come from Mr. Fairfield save an occasional paper or book addressed to Maria, and once a large box of beautiful flowers, which came by express and contained no card. Maria treasured all these things, but of course said no word to Nannette concerning them.

Maria's life just now was a little hard. She worried daily about her brother, and prayed often. She tried to make a friend of Nannette, that she might, if possible, prevent the intimacy between her and her brother. Nannette apparently had grown quite discreet. She asked one day as they were walking together: "Say, 'Ri, you wouldn't write to that minister, would you, if you were I? I should hate to hurt his feelings, but really I don't like letter writing, and when a man's gone, why he's out of it, you know. If he should come back, of course I'd be nice to him, I suppose, but I hardly like to go so far as to correspond, it seems to mean so much, you know. A man always means a good deal by asking for the privilege, especially a man like that. I haven't written him but once, and I don't believe I shall again, would you?"

And Maria answered, "I should do as I thought best," and turned the conversation to other topics, but she could not help thinking that Mr. Fairfield had never asked her to correspond with him. And she never knew that Nannette had been prompted to these remarks by a chance sight of the box of flowers at the express office addressed to Maria in a handwriting she recognized.

Winthrop Hammond was to return to the city to his business the next morning. He was out, and it was very late. Both his sisters had silently kept the watch, which was also being kept by the anxious mother in the next room, for his footsteps Rachel, as she lay quiet, lest she should rouse her sister from what she supposed was a happy sleep, wondered if her brother could ever fall so low as to treat Nannette in the way that other young men had done. She shuddered at the possibility, and yet she had seen enough in the face of that daring girl on the day when she met her at the inlet, to feel that her influence over any man would be a tremendous power should she choose to exercise it.

She and Maria had both spent much time in praying, during the past few days, for their brother. Rachel felt that an answer would surely come soon.

Winthrop came at last, but his steps were slow and lagging, and did not sound like him. He came into the sitting room and instead of going directly to bed sat down heavily in a chair. Once Rachel thought she heard a groan, and then, as all was still, she waited. Presently her brother threw himself upon the couch and groaned again, this time quite audibly. Rachel sprang to her feet, and, throwing a shawl about her, hurried out to the sitting room, but she found that her mother was there before, and Maria not far behind her. There was no mistaking the fact that their brother was ill. He was suffering too much pain to talk or give them any idea of what was the matter, but he had a high fever, they could tell that for themselves. The father started almost immediately for the doctor, while the mother and sisters got him to bed, heated water, and gave various simple home remedies. They then waited anxiously the coming of the physician.

It was as they feared—typhoid fever. The evenings of pleasure following the nights of nursing had told upon him. The doctor warned them that it was likely to be a severe case. Then the household settled down into that forced quiet where there is the dread anxiety of critical illness. Maria insisted upon staying with her brother night and day, and, strange to say, though Rachel had always been his favorite, he seemed best satisfied with Maria in the room. During the nights and days of waiting and watching and breathless anxiety, Maria had no time to think of herself. Whenever she had a moment to herself she spent it in prayer. Her life now was one long prayer.

She sometimes looked back on the days when all was bright and happy and she had been unhappy and unreasonable, and wondered at herself.

Then she thought gratefully of Mr. Fairfield and the change he had been the instrument, in God's hands, of making in her. She wondered how she could have gone through this long, tedious trial without Jesus as her friend. She seemed literally to be living in his presence now; to be bearing all she bore with his strength, not her own; to be watching his face to see if her brother was to be spared to live more years with them, or to be taken away. She felt an assurance that if God took him he would at least first give him time in which to take Jesus as his Saviour. He was delirious now for days, did not know one of them, and then lay in a sort of stupor. The time of the crisis had come. Maria was sitting by his side, while her mother rested near at hand, to be called should there come a change. She scarcely dared to breathe lest she should disturb the one so dear, who lay hovering between life and death. Her every breath was a prayer for him. Suddenly he opened his eyes, and in a feeble voice that was scarcely audible, whispered, " 'Ri, can you pray?"

Maria thought he must be dying, but without daring to wait, so momentous seemed that instant, she dropped upon her knees, and in low, controlled tones, prayed that Jesus might stand by her brother, and loving him, might take his hand and hold him in that moment, for life or death, for time or for eternity. She scarcely knew what she said, as with upturned face and eyes that seemed as though they saw the Lord, she prayed on. The burning, unnaturally bright eyes upon the pillow watched her, drinking in every word eagerly, as though thirsty, while Maria, praying, pleaded promise after promise from God's word. By and by the restless look faded from his eyes and there came a calm like a shadow of peace, and at last the eyelids fell, and Maria knew by the soft, natural breathing that he was asleep. By and by she dared to rise and call the others, and the doctor coming in told them that the crisis was past and the young man would live. Then the sister went away and thanked God.

But her work was not yet done. As the invalid grew able to talk he wanted Maria, and long converse he held with her about the things of life. Maria felt that she was having her reward for the days and nights of watching, and her soul rejoiced in God her Saviour.

All this experience had been so hard that it seemed to put the summer, with its pleasure and brightness, and its disappointments too, far behind her. She looked back to those days when she and Mr. Fairfield had walked and talked together beside the sea, with a wistfulness sometimes, but still with all the sting gone from heart.

Nannette, as soon as she learned the nature of the malady that had now befallen her devoted admirer, in dire dread and haste, picked up her belongings, tumbled them into her trunks, and fled. She had a horror of sickness at all times, and a superstitious fear that she would take typhoid fever if she were exposed to it. Besides her conscience troubled her. She knew that it had been her fault that the young man had spent so many evenings out late and had been drinking wine, a thing to which he was unaccustomed; and she began to fear that this had been partly the cause of his illness. Rachel was grateful that she was gone, yet indignant to think that the girl to whom her brother had devoted his entire attention for three weeks should depart at once without so much as a good-bye or an inquiry for him when she heard of his serious illness. The rest of the family felt nothing but relief.

The De Veres came daily to inquire and to offer aid, and in many ways showed their true friendship. Rachel often wondered that no word came from Mr. Fairfield, and felt sorry on Maria's account, for she recognized that he had been the means of making a change in Maria, and she was disappointed that he had left so suddenly, for she had liked him. She laid it all at Nannette's door, however, and tried to forget it.

One day in September, when Lone Point was almost deserted and only one guest left at the hotel, Maria was sitting on the piazza reading aloud to Winthrop, who was convalescent. The city train stole softly up the length of the island, its line of smoke, black against the sky, the only warning of its coming till the whistle blew near-by, for the sand seemed to dull all sound of rushing engine and whirling wheels. The two on the piazza were so deep in their reading that they did not stop to glance at the train, though they could easily have seen from the piazza who arrived or departed. It was the morning train too, and few ever came at that hour so late in the season.

Presently a step was heard upon the walk, and looking up they saw Mr. Fairfield standing before them. The pink rose to Maria's cheek, and the instant flutter of her heart told her that she had not forgotten, as she had hoped. Her embarrassment was heightened by his steady, earnest gaze, which seemed to be searching her face for some answer to an unspoken question. He took his eyes from her long enough to shake hands with her brother, who welcomed him most heartily, and then he looked back at Maria once more, with a glad, hungry look. Something, perhaps it was her downcast eyelids and the color in her cheeks, brought a half-satisfied expression to his face.

Explanations followed. Mr. Fairfield had suddenly gone to Europe, as much, perhaps, to his own surprise as to theirs. When he reached the city he had received word by cable that his sister was to be married at once in Berlin, and earnestly beseeching him to come over, if only for a few days. It was a sudden change of plans, for she was not to have been married for another year, but her intended husband was about starting on a trip through Palestine, Egypt, and the Mediterranean, and she and her mother were to accompany him. He had decided hastily, having very little time for choice as the only steamer which could possibly bring him to the other side in time for the ceremony sailed the next day, therefore he had had no time to send them a message telling them where and why he was going and for how long.

It occurred to Winthrop Hammond that it would have been rather an unnecessary proceeding to send them word, and he did not understand why Mr. Fairfield thought he should have done so. Then, as he looked at the young man, and beyond him at his sister's pink cheeks, a new idea began to dawn upon him. He whistled softly under his breath and drew his brows down. He did not want to lose this sister now that he had just found out what a sister she could be, but then — here he looked up at the minister — if she must marry, Fairfield was a fine fellow. He could remember some things in that sermon he preached just before he left. They had come to his mind during those awful days of fever and he had wished then that he had taken heed to them before. His face brightened with the thought that Mr. Fairfield would be one who would help him in that way now, and he was glad in his heart that he had come, whether he meant to take away Maria or not.

Then it was Maria's turn to explain how things had gone in Lone Point. She told in a few words the story of her brother's illness, and he, with a voice full of tenderness, added words in praise of her which brought a still richer color to her cheeks and made Mr. Fairfield look steadily at her once more, till she invented an excuse to slip into the house and bath her burning face.

By and by Mr. Fairfield went to the hotel, and when he returned he asked Maria to walk with him. All the long afternoon Winthrop was left to the tender mercies of his mother and Rachel, who did their best to fill her place.

Maria had taken out with her the much-read and treasured copy of Meyer which Mr. Fairfield had left with her when he went away, thinking to grant his request and read it to him, but though they walked or sat upon the sand the whole afternoon, they did not read Meyer. They had something even better and brighter and more delightful than that to read — and they read it in each other's eyes.

As once before, they lingered long upon the sands, till the sun went down and the moon came up, and when they rose and started toward the green cottage they understood one another.

> There comes a day when Love, that lies asleep,
> The fairest island in the mighty deep,
> Wakes on our sight;
> There do we stay awhile; but so on again
> We trim our sails to seek the open main;
> And now, whatever winds and waves betide,
> Two friendly ships are sailing side by side.
> In port of Love 'twas happy to abide,
> But, oh! Love's sea is very deep and wide.

Maria thought something like this as she stood that night, somewhat later, out on the piazza alone, and looked up into the quiet starlit night. She did not put it into these words, but her heart felt it all and more. She was very happy. Her whole soul went out to God in thanksgiving for the wonderful beauty he had suddenly put into her life. It occurred to her, as it had done before, only more forcefully, to thank God that he had not permitted her to have her way and go somewhere else for the summer, but had set her just here. How otherwise could she have been brought to know Jesus Christ as a dear personal friend? And, oh, suppose she had never met the minister — her minister!

Chapter 26

Rachel Hammond sat in her room by the open window with her Bible on her knee once more. It was summer again, and they were in their own home yet. Maria's door was open and a light breeze stirred the muslin curtain just a little and blew the breath of honeysuckles in, but Maria was not seated in the other room, for Maria was gone. It was just yesterday that she stood in that open doorway in her white robes and bridal veil and kissed Rachel. Upon her bed lay the identical white sailor, whose wings and ribbons had been such a trouble a year ago. By some mischance in the packing it had been left lying there, for Maria did not want to take it with her. Rachel looked up, saw it, and remembered their talk of a year ago.

Perhaps it was because she was used to opening her Bible at that place that the leaves that morning had fallen open of themselves to the very verse she had been reading when Maria began to grumble about the summer arrangements and she had left her reading to try and brighten her up. "For me to live is Christ." How strange it seemed to Rachel as she mused. She remembered just how she had longed, as she laid by her Bible with a sigh that morning, that Maria might feel that verse in all the depth and beauty of its meaning. Now, it seemed to Rachel, that in all the list of her acquaintances there was not one who could so nearly truthfully say that verse as her sister Maria, unless it might be her brother-in-law, Howard. How strange it seemed to call him Howard! A real minister in the family! She remembered how she had wished she might know one well enough some time to ask him some questions and now she had not only a minister but a minister's wife, to whom she could go with all her little perplexities and doubts.

A tear stole out and down her cheek as she remembered that Maria's room was empty and Maria would not occupy it any more, nor be nearby as of old as her companion, but she laughed and brushed it away.

God had been very good. She must not weep. She had tried to claim that promise, "Delight thyself also in the Lord and he shall give thee the desires of thine heart," and surely he had kept it and given her more even than she had asked or desired. She was glad and thankful, even though Maria was gone.

Then too, there was something in the fact that Maria lived down-town, only a half-hour's ride away. And was she not going down in a few minutes with Roland De Vere behind his beautiful span of horses to the new parsonage that the church had built for their pastor, to put in place several articles and hang a wonderful picture, the gift of Roland De Vere to the bride? And was there not something about this even more personal and more wonderful still for her? Oh, life was not shadowed much after all!

Rachel rose and went about her room singing, and knew not how appropriate to her life the words were, and were yet to be:

> Judge not the Lord by feeble sense,
> But trust him for his grace;
> Behind a frowning providence
> He hides a smiling face.
>
> Blind unbelief is sure to err,
> And scan his work in vain;
> God is his own interpreter,
> And he will make it plain.